A WHOLE LOT OF TROUBLE WITH A LITTLE BIT OF HELL

Rea Rahaman

WORKBOOK PRESS LLC
187 E Warm Springs Rd
Suite B285 Las Vegas NV 89119 USA

Website:	https://workbookpress.com/
Hotline:	1-888-818-4856
Email:	admin@workbookpress.com

Ordering Information:
Quantity sales. Special discounts are available on quantity purchases by corporations, associations, and others. For details, contact the publisher at the address above.

ISBN-13:	978-1-963718-40-9 Paperback Version
	978-1-963718-41-6 Digital Version

PUB.DATE: 05/06/2024

A WHOLE LOT OF TROUBLE WITH A LITTLE BIT OF HELL

Rea Rahaman

By Rea Rahaman
Education-Non Fiction
Anger Control Management-The Human Crisis
Anger Control Management-The Human Dilemma
Anger Control Management-Substance Use Disorder & Addiction
Anger Control Management-Making Love
Anger Control Management-Juvenile Delinquency
Anger Control Management-Emotional Inquisition

Novels Fiction
Calypso George
Marine Moon
Tradewinds

For my girlfriends

Rae Jean Bueschel – Florida, USA
Mati Leo, Queens, New York, USA
Melissa Rapp-Storath,New York, USA
Sandra Goodwin, New Jersey, USA

In memory of
Joseph Phillip Stanwood (1928-2012), Florida, USA

From the heart of Rea

This novel contained some reality mixed with some invention of characters, mostly truth about the lives of people in a retirement community. This novel is bound to spark controversy due to its blunt honesty.

The topics of discussion were basic on real people's discussions and various opinions. The pain and pleasure of lives mixed with love and true love is a reality of people who lived in pain and are vindictive trying to inflict pain to receive pleasure. They seek opportunities to inflict personal pain and anger upon others who are internally stronger than they would ever be in life.

In other words, people's pain turned them on. Yes, crazy as it sounds they are arousal by others' pain. My intention was written for pure entertainment. Hope you have a long hearty laugh. I did.

Contact: rizefromanger@yahoo.com

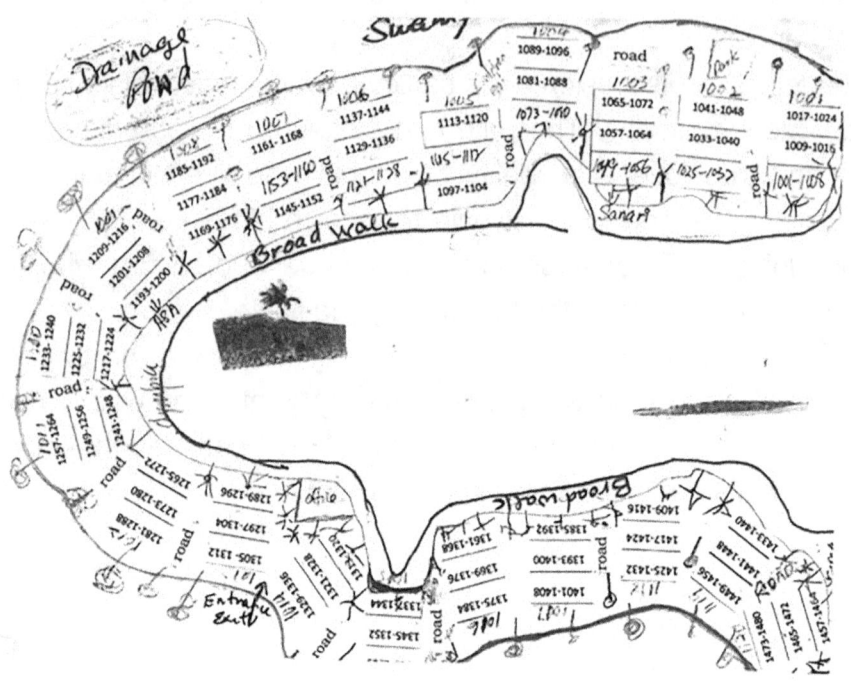

Helen Ville

Sussex Place

1

"Is he really, really dead?" The dark-haired girl asked.

"Oh, he's dead, all right?" The musty rusty brownish reddish short hair girl with a rise on her questionable brow replied.

"Does that mean we've to quit talking about him?" The dark shoulder-length hair girl wanted to know with much emphasis on the dead man lying in his deluxe solid copper casket.

"People said that you're not supposed to talk bad about the dead," answered the musty rusty brow hair girl, emotionless as usual and couldn't care less who heard her.

"Ah, why not? You mean people can do evil to others and then after they die you can't talk about them?" asked the dark-haired girl with a puzzled expression on her strawberry-looking shaped face.

"Since you put it that way." The musty rusty brown hair girl with an opal face looked at the strawberry-looking shaped face trying to comprehend the questions coming to her.

"Is there another way?"

"Hush you two. Take the conversation elsewhere." The boy-cut blond hair girl told the dark and musty rusty brown hair girl with a dead-set serious face.

The dark hair girl pushed her weight onto her feet and was leaving the funeral home when the blonde hair girl demanded from her. "And where do you think you are going?"

"I am taking the conversation elsewhere."

"Oh, no you don't." The blonde hair girl showed surprise and disgust at the same time, speaking with emphasis she said, "I don't mean now."

"Well, I am going to the bar and have a drink. I had enough," was the reply from the dark hair girl with strawberry shape face.

"Drinks you say, I am coming." The musty rusty brown hair girl answered as she rose onto her feet. "I do want to go and say goodbye to Gray over there." She finished as an afterthought.

"What now?" The dark hair girl asked in a whispering voice.

"Yes, right this minute. You have a problem with that?" The blond hair girl asked.

"Yes, I do. Oh God damn it! I guess I better go and say goodbye." She signed and walked towards the open casket.

The dark hair and musty rusty brown hair girls followed. Somehow along the short walk, the dark hair girl was first followed by the red hair one and the blond hair was last in the line by the side of the casket of Mr. Gray. They stood looking at the open casket watching the dead Mr. Gray lying there all made up and looking so sparkling beautiful before his burial.

Mr. John Gray was a heavy-set man of... well a man that is fat with a spreading waistline, more ridiculously overweight for his eighty years of Irish and Jewish heritage with fingers that walked uninvitingly on the bodies of females. His wide thick lips always with a wicked smile and on his head sat jet black hair, a wig no less.

Everyone knew that Mr. Gray cheated on Mrs. Gray except for Mrs. Gray who was overweight herself and was of German and some unknown heritage with thin lips, straight oversized nose, and pitiful blue eyes to match the hate for life and those who live in it. She also despised those who are happy and full of laughter and love.

Mr. and Mrs. Gray were living together as husband and wife, however, very distant they are in reality. Mrs. Gray is forever gossiping with Asa about someone and complaining about everything. She does the dutiful thing with her four grandchildren, however, neither she nor they appreciated the visit which is becoming less as they grew older.

Mrs. Gray cooks and cleans and shops while Mr. Gray pretended to go play golf and heads off in the direction of the strip club to fuck whoever he can get for twenty dollars. He is a dirty sleazy man with a thin mustache. He has those flirty dirty looking eyes that smell of rape. If he had a secret Asa knew because he stayed away from her as rain on oil.

"Did he pinch your bottom?" Sanari, the dark-haired girl asked the other two girls. She squeaked as the memory surfaced each time she felt two firm fingers pinch her softly rounded backside. He seemed to show up where ever she was and to avoid him, she changed her times and turned the other way whenever she spotted Mr. Gray headed in the same direction. Before they could reply, a woman of some eighty-five years of age with snow-white hair and a heavily wrinkled face replied or rather verbally attacked Sanari.

"How dare you? How dare you come here and accused my Carl of things he didn't do? My Carl was an honest man. He provided for me and my children. He was a kind, decent man. Get out! Get out of here and let me mourn my dead husband in peace." She was yelling trying to embarrass the girls into leaving.

A voice that began as a soft whisper now escalated to include almost everyone in the old wooden church. Voices rippled across the small grey room sailing above heads and picking up more voices on their way before reaching the girls. Bodies shifted in their chairs as ears were bent to hear. Those who didn't hear what was being aired, stopped to listen as they tried to understand the chaos that was being created at such a time in front of an open casket of a dead man.

Sanari turned to the old wrinkled face woman. "Mrs. Gray, no one ever said that your Carl was not any of those things. What was asked was did he pitched bottoms? And that indeed he did. You know it and everyone who came in contact with him also knew it. Why are you calling him Carl? His name is John." A questionable frown appeared over her forehead.

"Get out! Get out of here and leave me alone! You are a bunch of trouble. Leave now!" Old wrinkled face Mrs. Gray started to manufacture false tears as another old woman, Mrs. Scott tried to comfort her by putting her left arm a little below Mrs. Gray's shoulders.

"Now, now dear," She said in a squeaking voice that was barely a whisper. "You mustn't get upset when people speak the truth. Come, come rest. Take your weight off your feet. You have a long day ahead of you." Fragile Mrs. Scott winked at the girls and moved her head in the direction of the exit. She was small, skinny, and grey with a smooth soft voice tone.

Whenever Mrs. Scott spoke it was calming, nonetheless her words even though she speaks the truth rarely came across as the truth. Then again, her lies always seemed to be the truth and more easily believed by everyone. How she does it is everyone's best guess; it worked every time.

The three girls were out the door of the old wooden church with shoulders straight and a smile tucked under their lips. They kept their eyes in front of them and didn't look at anyone or each other for the fear that they would laugh creating more discomfort. They stepped out into the afternoon air noting the distant smell of rain to come.

With the slow return of breath, charging their energy into a high the girls came into an awareness of past situations that had viewed into something of a threat from an old man who lay dead about three hundred feet from them. A seriousness flashed over Sanari's olive skin faced missed by Asa, however, not by Fiona.

No one was in the parking lot except for the three girls. It was a hot afternoon as the sun pelted its heat of some ninety degrees upon the citizens of the small retirement community. They walked in silence, laugher tucked away, each in their thought of remembrance of what life was when Mr. Grey was alive, none regretting his death. The minute the girls reached the short distance to their car, laughter tumbled out of them again this time harder and louder.

The blond hair girl, Fiona verbalized to the two others who were rolling with laughter. "I can't take you anywhere. I can't believe you got us kicked out from the church."

The musty rusty brown hair Asa replied. "It was not me. She started it." She pointed to Sanari who was laughing extremely loud.

In the distance sky, the rumble of thunder can be heard. There was a moody grey sky overhead reaching out and joining with others forming an electric storm. Black thunder clouds moved in from the south bringing the sky so low to the lake that it sat behind the old wooden church.

Birds of various species and sizes coasted through the clouds looking for a place to hide out from the forthcoming storm. Fiona laughing proceeded to unlock the doors of her car and climbed into the driver's seat. She started the engine and turned the air conditioning on to cool the overheated interior of the silver four-door Honda Accord.

A bolt of lightning shot through the now darkened sky going beyond the old wooden church, on its heels thunder rocked the foundation. The old wooden church stood questioning the concrete structure. A light rain merged from the blackened clouds threatening to be a heavy downpour.

Sanari sat in front while Asa was in the back seat behind her. They were still belting out laughter upon laughter as they sat there in remembrance of the incidents they had shared with Mr. and Mrs. Gray. Eventually, about ten minutes later, Fiona began to revere the car, driving in direction, a short distance to their favorite bar, The Twixt Peach.

Behind them left a heavy downpour of rain trapping the people in the old wooden church upholding the charade of mourning for Mr. Gray. After all, everyone from the small retirement community knew him well, many more than just "well" while others including Sanari hated the sight of him. They all had reasons for their anger and all with good motives for wanting to kill him except that Mr. Gray died of old age and natural causes.

Fiona maneuvered the car quickly from the parking to the main road hoping to reach their destination before the rain caught up with them. The pounding rain lashed against the trees, soaked the road, and mixed the oil from old vehicles traveling over the years creating a slipping and sliding path for the Honda Accord. The rain caught up with them. This rainbow streak of oil and water mixture made Fiona grip the steering wheel of the Honda as the wipers swished and swathed across the windshield rapidly.

From across the sky, lightning threw a blinding steak of illumination into the path of the car. The crash of thunder with its deafening rumble rattled the pane of glass in the window of the Honda. In the burst of darkness, lightning cracked into a spray of neon brightness and for a split second the girls saw the ghost of Mr. Gray laughing at them from outside the front of the car. Lightning splintered again and he was gone.

The three girls sat with their mouths opened, in shock, none inhaling and blinking as each hoped the other would not mention the vision witnessed a moment ago. A release of breath can be heard from the back seat from Asa, then from Fiona, and finally from Sanari. They sat in silence as Fiona maneuvered the car to a halt at the side of the road with her hazard lights on.

Fiona looked at Sanari demanding silence from her and upon receiving it she looked through the rare view mirror at Asa. She couldn't see her, she turned in her seat only to see her looking at the pouring rain out the side window behind her. They sat in silence until the rain slowed its pace and die out eventually.

Fiona was about to start the car when a voice roared from the back of her apparently without realizing that the rain had stopped.

Asa blurred out louder with anxiety pitched tone. "He raped Mrs. Gray's young sister the night before the wedding." She was not aware that she didn't have to raise the volume of her voice to be heard, therefore anyone standing a foot away from the car with windows up could hear her.

Asa felt it safe to say that since Mr. Gray is dead. Fiona and Sanari wouldn't tell anyone. They don't give in to gossip.

Silence followed them to the bar, an uncomfortable silence that is, however, not to Asa, who was lost in thoughts of what to do with the new information she just acquired from someone about someone else. As they pulled up in front of the bar, Fiona began to laugh as the memory of Mr. Gray pinching Sanari's backside entered her thoughts.

Sanari seeing and understanding the laughter joined in. Asa becoming aware and seeing them began to laugh as if she knew what the laughter was about. She didn't nor did she care; she was part of their group and to her, that's what counts.

This is how the girls entered the bar of the restaurant and ordered their drinks, in roaring laughter. The bartender shocked his head and smiled at them. He knew them well enough as well as what they drank. They were regulars always laughing at or about something. It was always the blond and dark hair for the first nine years than in the last two years, the red hair joined in. They never included anyone else and when the men tried to join them or pick them up they received a courteous hello and a friendly conversation. They never collected nor gave their telephone numbers. They left after two drinks with dinner, always laughing. They were excellent tippers and it was always a pleasure to serve them.

2

"Is she really, really dead?" The dark-haired girl asked.

"Oh, she's dead, all right? The blond hair girl replied.

"I don't believe it, yet I can't help it. She deserved it."

"You are not supposed to talk bad about the dead," Fiona warned Sanari.

"Ahhh, why not? How are we supposed to get over what they have done? We've to talk about the experience when it hurts. She was a trip and a liar and a mischief-maker and....."

"Alright, we'll talk about her. Not here. We've to and you're right she deserved the bullet in her head." Fiona signed in somewhat of an agreement and Sanari's mood lifted.

They were silent for a few minutes and together without communicating they walked to the foot of the blue Star Legacy Dome casket with blue tapestry lining the inside and watched the red hair woman lying dead as a doornail, all made up as peacefully as ever. The musty rusty brownish reddish color was replaced by bright red and word had it she had left the beauty salon prior to being shot.

Contrary to popular belief Asa was nothing or anything peaceful, more of a rightful boldface riot.....a BITCH. As the ladies stood there watching her, trying to feel something for Asa the thunder roared and rolled across the old wooden church that had Mr. Gray's service a week ago.

Two deaths of two sinful people in two weeks; who's next? Death came in three so Sanari looked around the old wooden church and wondered who would it be, Mrs. Gray, Fiona, or her? The blistering streak of lightning spitted from the dark sky with a crack of bright light touching the face of Asa and for a split second, the two girls thought they saw her smile.

The crash of thunder followed, shaking the walls and floor of the old wooden church as if it was a sonic boom from a returning space shuttle, so loud that the girls jumped from the silence of private thoughts remembering life with Asa.

Sanari was the first to move away from the very dead Asa. Fiona followed a few minutes later nodding to others on her way out the door. Sanari was running into the parking lot towards her car when Fiona reached the door and stop to look around at the weather. The rain began to pelt down heavy in big fat drops that would sure to soak Fiona.

Sanari had reached her car when it started to rain and upon seeing this she opened the door and gunned the engine. She kicked the Jaguar sports car into reverse and then into drive. She directed the car towards the steps of the old wooded church as Fiona ran down the remaining few steps into the car.

A few cold drops of rain soaked her enough for her to tremble. Sanari booted the car into drive and skidded on the gravel of rocks that paved the road. She let the car skid for a second and wound the wheel in the direction of the exit onto the road heading towards the pub.

Not a word was spoken as silence was the main event. Each girl is absorbed with personal thoughts on living with and without Asa in their life. What life prevailed in the past? What life would unravel in the near future on Asa? Who's going to die next? Sanari directed the car towards The Twixt Peach, however, they never made it in, the very first time they missed their weekly drinks! Upon arriving, the thunderstorms worsened to the point that leaving the warmth of the car meant being soaked before entering the pub; the girls sat in the Jag for a good thirty minutes in silence continuing their private thoughts on Asa.

The lightning struck several times, as the thunder rolled and roared so loudly that the girls both jumped at each roar. The rain washed the car clean of grime. They sat as quietly as ever in uttered silence even when the thunder bellowed loudly. They were used to sitting in absolute silence.

Fiona's thoughts drifted to the moment of meeting Asa some

eighteen years ago while she was visiting the elderly couple next door, Fred and Gina Razzista in apartment 1070. She was checking on Fred who was a chain smoker and had lung cancer.

Asa had walked in and talked none stop. Yep, she inhaled deeply, a total run-on sentence she was and hell on wheels. Mischief maker, trouble maker, and name it, she was right in the middle of it all. Did she deserve to die as a common criminal, like that? Yes, she did.

Fiona exhaled and watched the lightning strike again. Yes, her very presence in the retirement community brought havoc on civilians. Never mind how much she had helped her work through her dilemma. Asa was in trouble and she loved the gossip and meddling in people's life.

In the driver's seat, Sanari heard her friend exhale and followed with one of her own. Oh, what a day! What a witch? She took a deep breath and exhaled again, taking her thoughts down to the memory of the first meeting with the wicked witch of the west, Asa! It happened with Asa's crazy ass driving and bumping into her car. She was pulling out from the parking by the office of the retirement community after dropping off her maintenance check when she heard the brakes of cars squeaking.

Sanari was about to start her car when she was pushed forward a little due to someone slamming into her. The shock of being hit had her at a standstill for a few dizzy moments. She climbed out of her automobile and looked for the suspecting vehicle and its driver. There was none; sheer hit and run.

She was clueless as to who hit her. Anger now beseeched her face with red. Questions hammered at her thoughts, too angry to think as confusion slipped in simultaneously as pain strike the back of her neck. She rubbed her neck where the pain had surfaced momentarily, now gone. She stood by her car looking for dent; a jerk of denial mixed with fear of thinking that she was imagining things entered her domain.

Whispering softly to herself for fear that someone would pass and think her mad, "tell me what happened before this fear I am feeling spread through, spread to the rest of my body. I was so emotionally depleted, my muscles ached." Self-doubt fastened itself on Sanari's emotions for a good five minutes before she shook it off and decided that it was not her imagination running wild; that someone had hit her car. Due to this, some muscles were causing her pain in the neck.

Upon seeing and hearing nothing, Sanari looked around again and again at her car; there was no evidence. She walked the short distance to the office and report the hit and run. She was on "thank you for listening," when she heard the squeaking with a bump. She ran the short distance out of the office through the door only to see a little red car with its driver pulling away from her car.

She ran as fast as she could, however, the driver had disappeared round the bend of the road out of the retirement community leading into the public road. Why would the driver return and deliberately hit her car for the second time? By the time she reached her car to follow the hit-and-run driver, the red car with its driver had disappeared, leaving a cloud of dust behind.

She checked out the damage instead of her car contemplating what to do next when another red car pulled up. She turned to acknowledge the driver only to be told that the woman who hit her lived in 1009. Before Sanari could say "thank you" and asked whether he saw what happened, the man with an awful electric tan zoomed his red car into drive, took off through the gate, following the first red car that carried the hit and run driver out the retirement compound and out of sight.

Is this really happening to me? Why can't people be responsible adults and fess up to their actions? What does that man have to do with the other car.......what do the two red cars have to do with each other? She was seethed with rage.

The man's evasiveness angered her more as she forced herself to cool off, however, as soon as she gained control her nostril snorted flaming in frustration. She had the time; she climbed into her car and waited for the little red car to return; she would be waiting for her all night if she had to, she has the time.

Less than an hour the little red car came bearing down the entrance of the retirement community. Sanari had her car parked with the air conditioning on; she was ready to roll, following the little red car. The hit-and-run driver had to stop to insert her card at the gate to open for her to drive through.

Anger build inside Sanari as she waited a few seconds for the gate to open and off she went following the little red car. It served, zing and zagging its way to a stop. The woman was a fucker of a hit and run.

Sanari trailed her back to building 1009 and confronted her. She was drunk as a skunk and denied everything. She even went further calling her a liar. She stood there in shock as the driver of the red car vanished into the building. She turned to the red car to see whether there were any black marks and found none. She walked two cars down to hers and her astonishment found no dent or marks on hers either.

What the fuck just happened? Sanari took the car to the body shop and was told that the dent pushed itself back into place. A magnifying glass is needed to see any scratches; there were two tiny ones, nothing to make a fuss about. She let it be and stayed away from the driver of the little red car whenever she saw her coming towards her.

Two weeks later she ran into the driver of the little red car again at the post office without her recalling Sanari much less the incident. She smiled so sweetly, introduced herself as Asa, and talked none stop about everyone and nothing in particular. Sanari realized that Asa had no sense of her own identity and was a copycat of others' behaviors.

Asa was a doctor, a drunken one that is, and who used people in a desperate attempt to define herself. She was clingy, demanding, and needed others' admiration and affection to justify her persona. "A drunken doctor, well.... I wouldn't want her to operate on me, Sanari silently admitted to herself. She would rather die as she looked and listened to this Asa person talk and talk and talk....non-stop. Certainly, a run-on sentence with no logic, all myth and lies, and deception.

As she listened, she realized that Asa used everyone in her life as a mirror in which she could see her reflection as a friend, daughter, sister, and lover. Without those definitions, she was lost because there was nothing in her only a void. an emptiness that accompanied her everywhere she went. She filled the gap with anything present to avoid her pain and truth.

Sanari's anger dissipated and pity came into play. She realized that this woman needed compassion, heaps of it. She pinned a little note in the back of some thoughts to remember to do some meditation for her-the hit and run drunken doctor.

Who is she? Little does Sanari know that this was the beginning of a whole lot of trouble and a little bit of hell which is about to interrupt the flow of her wonderful life on Planet Earth.

Fiona, on the other hand, was saddened that Asa had to die the way she did and was very grateful for the help she had from her-more grateful than she realized before this moment. She had first met her at the pool chatting away with Mrs. Gina Razzista when she joined them. She realized that she could not get a word in, besides Asa was gossiping and very good friends with Mrs. Gina Razzista. She met her a few times drunk or driving so fast that the tire of her red car always left a skid mark of burnt tire scent in the air.

A flash of anger stroked Fiona's face for a brief moment, only for a very brief moment. She couldn't fathom what sprung the new tears probably from a mysterious wound she fought to forget, nonetheless, old wounds did throb.

What a nihilist? Asa packed a bullet of meaning into that, the syllable of every word she spoke. She pushed conditions to the far end of the spectrum to show who is in control even if it means hijacking people's biography. So much power lay within the bits of Asa. It took others to show her a light that can give her the lasting fulfillment and enjoyment of life; she refused it. She let go of the past that held the bridge of her life in place; the post broke and the bridge fell.

Who is this woman? A smile tucked on Fiona's and Sanari's lips with a sigh of relief hit both girls upon the freedom they realized they now have from the death of Asa. The rain had slowed a bit, however, lightning was quicker than before; a sign of relief came forth from both of them as they considered themselves above unkind gossip. The ladies sat in utter silence in remembrance of Asa, the village gossip.

3

"She's dead. I had to come to see it for myself." Sanari told Fiona.

"This is the last of death for a while. They say it comes in threes." Fiona informed her as they passed Mrs. Razzista lying dead in her eighteen-gauge presidential casket in pink; it was on clearance.

Gina Razzista was an old haggard patronized American white woman with Italian heritage who defined herself through her two dead husbands. She was an angry bitch who hated her two husbands for dying and leaving her to live life alone. She was a racist and would tolerate every other nationality besides African American. The dead flap of skin hanging under her arms can knock anyone unconscious.

There was not much to her life that both husbands are dead, buried in a solid oak casket with white velvet interior while she buried herself in a cheap imitation of good stuff; not that she couldn't afford it? She retired with a good pension and joined her last husband's investments. Fiona saw her bank statement and mentioned it to Sanari.

Mrs. Gina Razzista believed that she doesn't deserve anything luxurious; she placed more value on males than she does females much less herself. She was conditioned this way by her parents, culture, and religion.

Gina spent her retiring days watching reruns of old series and movies, News Channel that broadcasted only half-truth that bitched about life. She was a Republican and bitched about the Democrats. Eighty-six years she was for her five-foot, one ninety-five pounds, however, cruel and mean-spirited she was to the core of her being. No wonder her children and grandchildren rarely visit.

Mrs. Razzista hated one of her daughters who is gay and refused to speak with and/or about her. She swam in the summer, played card games at the clubhouse on Fridays, and cook awful Italian food the rest of the days of the week. She doesn't talk about her gay daughter nor does she speak of the half black, half Italian granddaughter. She righteously goes to her Catholic Church every Saturday afternoon and sins the rest of the week.

It's not as if the Catholic Church would expose every headache and demon from Gina Razzista or whatever inhabited her human psyche; the Catholic Church more likely aided her in hiding it. What with all the Priests' sexual abuse over the centuries on the rise and the Nuns hiding their pregnancy; it's no wonder why she's angry. The very thing she believed in has betrayed her and she has no one or nowhere to turn to for comfort. Her confession is made up of thoughts of killing the President and colored people. As hateful as she was she cannot see beyond anything else.

Mrs. Gina Razzista wouldn't talk about her first husband's nephew, Ricardo who was in the Italian Mafia because her first husband whose name was also Ricardo was murdered by the opposition.

Ricardo, the nephew refused to repay a debt of one million dollars to the opposition-the people he owed; they killed her husband while he was at the dentist. It's never a good idea to tick off the person who can drill your mouth one week and use a gun to blow your brains out the next.

Ricardo had never liked his nephew much less him having his name. He despised his sister for naming her son after him and avoided all family affairs that included them which were about every event.

Mrs. Razzista was left with two young girls to support. The insurance money from her husband's death soon ran out due to bad money management and forced Mrs. Razzista to find work. She had to leave her two daughters with her mother who resented the intrusion.

What choice did she have? A wave of steady growing anger notched up her spine and a sense of hate entered the picture of her life. Not long after about, two years after the murder of her husband, Ricardo she and the priest of her Catholic Church fell in love, well so she tells the story. Peter conveniently left the church for her and never let her forget it.

Verbal abuse and chain-smoking were Peter's main course of the day. The anger in his voice as he swore at her was overwhelming, however, real as a physical wind hitting her in the face on a cold winter morning.

Anger would often cross Gina's face and she would turn away choosing to hide it from him. It became Gina's life and she lived through it and delivered a healthy baby boy on one of those same cold winter mornings, one year into marriage. Gina never once suspected that Peter was looking for a way out of the Catholic Church long before she became a widow.

Then a nasty storm blew in as Peter, an old man who took their grandson to fish by the lake. Gina begged him not to go because the wind was becoming uncontrollable. Peter, however, has a large inflated ego and went fishing. He didn't see any danger as the distance between the condominium and the lake was a few feet and as he looked up he saw wispy cloud passing.

The wind picked up speed, Peter realized that his wife was right and refused to give her credit because he left the priesthood for her only to live in the shadow of Ricardo. Peter remembered the first flare of anguish in her deep grey eyes that ripped right through him and stayed in his heart when he made love to her and she called out Ricardo's name instead of his, Peter.

Peter junior was conceived and knowing this had tampered with his relationship with his only child, his only son. To top it all, he was a virgin, his very first experience and he was a substitute for a murdered man! Jealousy ran through him for a long time before he banished it. He confronted Gina about calling him Ricardo she called him a liar. Anger wobbled in her face and regardless of the evidence of love he had for her, she chose her life of anger because of who she loved. He didn't make love to her again and sought comfort elsewhere known or unknown to her he didn't care. The swelled of life for her was gone from him. Fiercely guarded the depth of his emotions, anger diffused his pain of being second and not loved by Gina.

Smuggling against the panic that threatened to collapse his ferociously secured feelings, his nerve endings popped and his body clenched. Discarding his defeat as meaningless, he held his breath a minute too long and a strong gale of wind picked him from off his feet and landed him on his only grandson, burying his body beneath his large frame. He was holding his grandson, Peter's hand when his heart gave out and his knees buckled falling on the little two years old, taking his only and the very last heir of his generation with him. His son Peter jr., died in a car crash several years ago, leaving a pregnant wife behind.

Peter had lived many years with hate, he let it out just before he died. Gina's name slipped off his lips in disbelief, bending myriad emotions of shock, surprise, and anger then joy slipped into his heart.

Gina saw the whole incident. By the time she arrived at the scene both her husband and grandson were dead. Alarm flared through anger in her eyes as her heart pondered. She was ashamed to admit what plagued her, what sins behold her to drive two males to their deaths. Grief suddenly overwhelmed her. She wept and screamed, yelling to God for mercy. The rain fell going unnoticed as grief pushed her into collapsing on the ground over the bodies of her husband and grandson.

Neighbors came running to the rescue. It was after the burial service, sitting alone, weeping profoundly that Gina realized the years of hate she had allowed to consume her, inflicting poison into her soul. She knew if she had gotten rid of the grief she carried for her dead first husband she could've walked through the other side of love, nevertheless, grief to her was not a tangible corridor. She remained trapped in her resentment and she spoke more with hate than anger.

Forgiveness was not within Gina Razzista beliefs nor is she lightly to ever love herself. Bought up in the conservative traditional life of giving and loving others and being defined by those who she married she lived in the shadows of religion and culture, a life of being nothing, hiding her beauty that lies undercover within her soul. The fact remained when she put into perspective this hateful nature of hers and the length she carried the hate; it was astonishing to see diseased thoughts that constantly preoccupied her.

Yet, every night Gina says goodnight to both of her husbands' framed photographs standing on her chest of drawers next to her bed. Her son and grandson were long forgotten. The treasuring of the male's species and the denial of the females' self-worth is how she lived her life. The denial of females' worth ran deep into her soul and she refused to see anything else. Self-worth was not hers to keep as it belongs to her husband, son, and grandson.

Gina's jealousy of others' relationship with Asa foreclosed any argument of justice to what she would say and do to others, distancing them from Asa. Not that Asa hasn't done the same to Gina, when others became close to Gina, Asa is known to have put some facts and fiction together to push others away from Gina, particularly when Gina used the jealousy card against Asa with others. They behave as mother and daughter with a killer instinct that kicked in on both sides. Yes, they were that jealous of people who they think would be a threat to their jealous relationship. The game of forsaken jealousy bonded these two women.

One day innocently a neighbor, Jenna Ferguson was out of food and came down the rotten steel steps all thirty of them to ask Gina if she had any spare can of food. She will pay for them when her disability check arrives on Wednesday. It was Monday, two days to go. Gina with the help of Asa gave her breakfast, lunch, and dinner with a huge smile.

Poor Jenna Ferguson she didn't know how vindictive the pair was until she asked them how much she owned them. She was shocked because those two charged her double the price for a can of chicken noodle soup, more than the supermarket prices. She didn't even like the soup; she was hungry, she took it.

As if that was not good enough Gina and Asa opened their big mouths and told the landlady that she cooked meals on the stove. The landlady had asked Jenna Ferguson not to cook on the broken stove until she can have it replaced in a few days when her retirement check was deposited into her account. The landlady kicked her out in the heart of winter!

Gina and Asa saw her moving with bare necessity.

"What is happening?" Asa boldly and innocently asked her as she stepped off the last stairs.

"Someone told the landlady that I was cooking on the broken stove and she kicked me out." Jenna conveyed tearfully.

"Gina did it." Asa happily informed her.

"Why?" Jenna wanted to know, quivering with anger. She was surprised to see Gina's head pushed through the door and as bold as Asa happily told her, "I don't like niggers." Gina taunted.

Jenna Ferguson's anger rippled the air around her, distributing an abdication of mixed emotions which slowly amounted to resentment. As Asa watched with a tiny smile on her thin lips, Gina's hate in her wrinkled dark almost black eyes send vulnerable Jenna into an emotional suicide mood.

Gina's hard-boned rugged face with skin shaking under her neck and mouth set a high volume in her voice that doubtfully hated as she glared at the poor homeless black girl. The heat of fire radiated from her stare and Jenna's flinched with shock.

A burning sensation surfaced in the back of Jenna's black eyes. Tears brimmed on her lashes as she stood there in disbelief. She walked away because she refused to give either of those spiteful hateful bitches any satisfaction that what they told her hurt so badly.

A few veins popped up as Jenna put distance between the bitches, walking towards the exit of the retirement compound. Tears brimmed over and fell on her cheeks. She wiped it away. Soon more tears came, stumbling over into a crying spell of disgust. One tear burst forth as she tripped on the speed bump on the road; that one drop of tear fell into the palm of her hand and she closed her fingers over it.

Fiona and Sanari were innocently caught between these two

hateful bitches. Innocently or not the visits from Fiona and Sanari were manipulated by Gina when she deliberately played the jealous card of how much time they visited her from Asa, who rarely visit. In the long run, Asa told her half lies mixed with some facts about the two, confusing poor old hateful Gina. Gina became verbally abusive toward Sanari. Why Sanari? Sanari was olive skin while Fiona was of white skin.

Racism was the issue here. Sanari, who at one time, not so long ago, gave Gina old romance books to read; Gina also bought romance novels in huge bulk from the library. Gina and Sanari would sit and chat about the stories by the pool in the afternoons. This experience was tossed aside the day Asa pulled the jealousy card and played it. Now, that's no longer possible particularly when Gina happily told Sanari and Fiona what Asa did to Jenna. She purposely left out her role in the incident.

What Gina didn't know was that Fiona saw Jenna trip while driving that cold winter day. She stopped and upon seeing Jenna's tears took her into her apartment and gave her the spare room until she found a place to live. Within a week Jenna was sharing a two-bedroom apartment with another female on the opposite side of the retired community.

Nothing pleasant ever left Gina's mouth except for Fiona, Asa, and the male species. When Anna Fairmont, the new African heritage lady joined the group sitting by the pool in the afternoon, Gina was rude. She pulled her whole body further to the other side of the chair making sure everyone noticed her resentment toward Anna. Gina believed the stories of Sanari that Asa told her and began a hateful pitch about colored people, worse than Hitler himself! Gina confessed to Fiona one day that she never liked Sanari. What she liked was her company. Yes, the books were an excuse to get her to visit her at home particularly at night because she was lonely and bored. Soon Sanari quit visiting her. Fiona, however, reduced the visits to Gina. She would occasionally take her out for pizza.

Asa on the other hand, whenever Gina gave her food she would take it over to Sanari's flat to be given to the wild pig, Puggna who lived in the swamp area not far from the compound. No one truly cared for Gina's baked brownies. She would take a plate of them to anyone who was in or at the pool. Those who tasted real brownies usually refuse while those who don't know the difference between good and awful brownies would eat them.

Gina thought that God loved her exclusively until she fainted and fell by the mailbox one hot summer day. How long Gina Razzista lay in the hot ninety-five-degree heat, is a good guess. Upon awaking she dragged her body on the black tar parking lot into her house.

What happened next was a little bit of hell on Planet Earth for poor old racist hateful Gina. She had layers of skin peeled off when her knees touched the tar and her shoulder broken in two places.

As if that was not good enough Gina had a nasty concussion where bits of memory were lost and reality was fused into fantasy. She was emotionally broken and more bodily damaged than ever.

Gina walked forward with her back crocked, yelling at everyone when they let the pool gate close or when the rope across the pool that separated the children from the adults' side was not hooked on either side of the pool. Although she lost a good part of her memory, it didn't stop her from being hateful; she's more verbally abusive now than before the accident; even though she forgets more than she remembered if that's possible.

In the months that followed, Gina refused to go to the hospital and refused any type of treatment even those that were administrated by Fiona and Asa. She even refused to eat and lay comatose for days at a time. Hate and racism coupled together kept her alive. It's a wonder she survived; did she really? The hate became larger than her life as the jealousy ran ramp to those who have more than she does in life.

To top that, many times Gina was bedazzled by confusion, saying that she lost all her money in the bank and forget where she lived. The chaos of confusion upon thinking she lost her money, the delirious moments she knocked on Sanari's door bringing her trash bags and saying she lost her money. The delusional days came as to what time it is, what food items she is buying, or where she is going is a wonder; she still drives.

Gina's daughter, Ana, and husband Frank visited her once a month to pay her bills. Frank sometimes would collect her to see the grandchildren over in Clear Waters. She would spend a few days with them. In the stretch of her life, nothing made sense anymore; everything flew over her thoughts as her mental processing system and cognition kept spiraling downward. Hate would do that to anyone.

The ambiguity is Gina sat all alone pondering what happened to her life.

Few gave her the time of day because hate penetrated deeply into her voice and no one wanted to have any type of conversation with Gina Razzista certainly not Asa; only Fiona.

The musty rusty brownish reddish short hair girl was weird and controlling. Asa Fleischer better known as Doc Fleisch lived in building ten zero nine apartment eleven ninety. She knew everyone's business and very little is known about her or what is known is partly truth and partly fabrications. Whenever questions were addressed to her somehow the conversation turned quickly to something else, therefore very little is known about the nosy Dr. Fleisch.

Standing tall at four feet two inches, thin as a string bean, freckles on her face dominated the high narrowed cheekbones and its large pointed nose. To accompany light blue eyes, was a pair of blue tattooed eyebrows. Asa battled anorexia and is a full-blown long-standing alcoholic. Retired from doctoring, as told by her, due to an accident and memory loss, nevertheless whether fake or real, her certificates are plastered all over the wall in her den.

The apartment Asa lived in is tucked away from the view of residents with a sparkling view of the lake. Although few had seen her place, those who did, mentioned that it was closed with hurricane shutters and very dark.

Asa rarely invited anyone in and rarely give any invitation. No one ever ventured further than the door unless it was the repair service. She was weird, weird, weird, and controlling.

Asa's days are spent walking in the evening at the mall, visiting people, and creating chaos. She rarely surfaced before the afternoon and have supper at midnight. She eats the same food day in and day out and refused the dishes that were given to her. No one cared; they offered anyway. Behind closed doors and according to James, her lover, she drank after she goes in for the night vodka and Fresca; sometimes it was just plain old vodka.

Asa's voice was loud and extremely high pitched which sail above everyone else. In other words, she demanded attention because she navigated people, places, and things with an advanced type of radar, for her pleasure. People with short attention spans don't fit into the profile or see others' happiness.

According to Asa, short attention span and happiness that flood into people's life is due to the enduring breakdown of diplomatic relations with God. She told Sanari this particularly when people don't listen to her. Very little logic pertained to her thinking and feelings.

There isn't anywhere to go with the conversation with her unless it is about a topic she likes or about gossip. Asa's thoughts always seemed to wrap around something vindictive as if it is a flag in the high wind, thinking about who would be her next victim to extort money from, particularly those who wouldn't go to the police. She's well aware that she doesn't give any emotionally strong people the attention; only the very vulnerable will work, someone who has something to hide.

This meant that it would be easy to extract money from them; not a lot of money only a little at a time. Small amounts create less attention than large amounts of money. It seemed that everyone she meets has to pay a huge price for the pain she carried on her poor tiny frame, no more than eighty pounds. Between Asa and her brother James, yes, the same name as her lover, the residents wondered who is more spoiled and emotionally immature.

Regret pumped through her fragile body as if it was adrenaline shooting through her veins. Asa's mouth became a brass drum thudding loud with rage and spreading layers of stuffy attitude over people, places, and things. She deliberately and incorrectly interpreted others while they are speaking. Upon repeating what they say, she twisted and turned the words into a completely different sentence that suited her limited vocabulary.

Asa constantly repeated details of every incident over again, even six months later. She forged no language in managing conflicts and she incorrectly interrupted calmly while her manner bordered on hostile. Talked about walking right into stupid!

Beneath the surface of everything she does and messages conveyed, she was well dressed. She lived her life and refused to budge to accommodate others except for Fiona and Sanari. She tried to live their life because they are always laughing and having fun. She aimed for laughter.

Asa followed Sanari and Fiona everywhere they went, leaving no stone unturned. She seemed to have their schedule memorized to the last stitch of activities because she was always there even when there was a change with the date. It was as if she was some sort of physic who can foretell the future. It's a wonder someone put a stop to it all. Who? Who saved them all from Hell?

Dr. Asa Fleisch was born of dawn and died in dawn so was the meaning of her name and the report of her death. She died in the wee hours of dawn about five in the morning. Her ethnicity was somehow connected to oriental heritage, the shape of her eyes spoke, however, the color of her skin and hair spell some level of Caucasian in her. Her parents are pure all-American Caucasians without any trace of oriental.

Which one of Asa's parents is oriental and which one is white is unknown? Everyone wondered about the connection as she confessed to pure Caucasians. Asa ignored it. She doesn't want to know whether she was her parents' child or adopted, nonetheless she constantly referred to her brother, James adoption, and whenever she meets anyone new she let them know she is adopted. She kept people deliberately confused; confusion will keep people vulnerable, and easy to manipulate.

Asa wanted to be a gymnast when she was young. Her parents let her practice with the understanding that it's a sport; she has to be a doctor. Many nights she faithfully practiced her jump shot until she began suffering from anorexia; she had to give it up. She ached to experience it again; only now she does through the light of the school's gymnasium whenever she passed through for therapy for her eating disorder.

After recovery, Asa wanted to be a tennis champ and would secretly practice at college. She kept this side of her persona hidden from her parents because it would disrupt the designed life her parents had drafted for her in very clear terms. They paid the bill for her to be a doctor. She suppressed the painful experiences of her life and tucked them away where they cannot be heard or seen. She began to drink and soon her desire of wanting to be a tennis champ was suppressed so deep that she had forgotten all about it.

One day while practicing tennis, a ball hit the rim of her net and sliced in the air, boomeranging into her forehead knocking her unconscious. In the hospital when her parents questioned her, she lied to them and told them that she was stressed out about getting a B in her math class and was taking her anger out on court. They accepted that and told her that having a B is acceptable. Asa laid down her studying habits and took up repertoire number two, partying and drinking.

One winter night when the shadows waited for spring to come again, Asa was navigating her way through the goldfield of people as she called them at the Grand Central Station she fainted. She was returning from a college party and was heavily intoxicated. This time, she told her parents that simultaneously a thousand people, mothers with children and women with shopping and drunk men were trying to get off the train and twice that many were trying to get on; that the old train rolled on rock n' roll with no place to sit and hardly a place to stand.

Asa was avoiding a drunken man who was inappropriately touching her. A vacation to Barbados was paid for, a whole two weeks she had all to herself and her then-lover Millie. So what.... she's bisexual, she likes both genders.

For whatever it's worth, the musty rusty brown hair girl was short and thin and faithfully goes to the salon every week to perk up her hair and every other week for her pedicure and manicure. Not that it did much good to Asa fifty-four tried wrinkled skin and heavy-duty sunspots from excessively tanning in a booth drunk on vodka. She knew there were solutions to life with surprises when she can get her alcohol-soaked brain to focus on figuring out what it is and where the complication lies. It's not her fault that she's where she is in life, that her parents were unhappy with her.

Dead they may be, Asa's parents certainly cut her out of the will. They left her share with dear brother James. Oh, how she despised him. She only kept good with him because she convinced him to leave all the millions of dollars to her when he died. He did because he too craved companionship and Asa is his sister, after all, his adopted sister.

Deep-rooted anger is still embedded in Asa's persona and no matter how much money she spends on the beauty pallor wrinkles kept popping up each time she blackmails someone; adding to that the prescription drugs and sleeping pills she took on top of it all made her looked more seventy and failing. Very fragile indeed and hell on wheels or more bat out of hell.

For Doctor Asa Fleischer, life is simple. All she has to know is people's rules and beliefs then she would break them. It gave her pleasure to break rules and she pompously bragged about it. When people mentioned to her that they broke a law it was known throughout the retirement community within hours.

The residents are going to be leaving the church smiling, each carrying their memories and secret of Asa Fleischer to their dying days. After the second meeting, everyone avoided her as if she had the plague. Ah, she was the bloody plague, the black plague for what it's worth.

Asa Fleischer was the juggernaut-a massive inexorable force of pure hell on wheels. She was unstoppable and mercilessly destructive with a metaphorical force of a tornado and a hail storm in one. It's no wonder someone put a bullet in her.

The effects of Asa's blackmail dangerously played havoc on her thoughts. Thinking about wild sex was indifferent to what she had been through with her anorexia. She screamed aloud with a combination of fear, anger, and pleasure; she was a woman who had gone before without a sensual frontier. A good fuck melted her brain and turned it into jelly while every nerve in her body went on high alert blocking out her real pain.

The pain, the pleasure, the blackmailing, and meaningless sex were a series of events that created a chain reaction in Asa's life. The more money she obtained the more wild sex she demanded which rectitude with no conclusion having reached with her lover James.

So, at last, the six times that Asa admitted cheating with other men who were very good to her and such fun, faded quickly. The yearning had neither die nor the desire for the combination of pain and pleasure.

Every day is a new day for Asa as it brought with it the fundamental shift in underlying expectations for her. What Asa didn't know is that high expectations delivered reality and on the heels of reality followed disappointments-huge disappointments. She hopefully found that out before her untimely death. Bull's-eye! Ouch! Everyone who knew Asa wondered what she was thinking when did she become a bitch? Guess it was a surprise to her parents when they overheard people calling her a bitch; Asa couldn't explain; she was speechless. Asa speechless! That would be impossible. The woman is petite, small in everything, yet she talked in run-on sentences, forever! Boom! Asa is dead! Well, with more of a Bang you bitch.

A man who she caught cheating on his wife and was paying her money with every paycheck to keep her quiet so his wife didn't find out smiled as he passed her coffin. Doggone it, no suffering. She should've suffered for all the nasty things she did to others, especially the blackmailing part. What a waste of life? Ha, no one is going to miss her! It's a bet that Asa's brother is smiling too. He was the very same as she was, twins metaphorically of course. The question remains, who put a bullet in her forehead and why? She had been edgy and irritated lately. Her relationship with James Asher, who has a daughter is tedious. She had broken off with him two days ago.

Did he shoot her? Hardly as James is a pure simple drunk and wouldn't know the difference between the barrel of a loaded gun and the trigger. Most likely he would have killed himself if he had pulled the trigger.

Well, whoever did the wonderful deed of taking Asa away from Planet Earth did everyone a favor. She had created more conflicts and hell for everyone living at Helenville.

None of this explained why there is a bullet in her head. She must have ticked off someone very badly. Rumors had it that she blackmailed others to pay her mortgage and maintenance fees. Her ailing aunt paid the rest plus all the inheritances she received from her deceased father's relatives who had no children and willed their money to her and James, the brother.

So, who killed Dr. Asa Fleisch? There's no doubt that many people wanted her dead, however, the question is who did it and why; not that anyone cared a rat's ass, they are just happy she's dead. It would be interesting to know who relieved the world of such a hopeless inhumane narcissistic bitch.

The celebration is in order and a massive thank you to the one who ended the bitch from hell life. God blessed poor old hateful Gina Razzista and Asa, hopefully, there's something their God can find to bless them or he might just toss them into Hell!

5

The rain halted. The thunder and lightning continued. Piercing the lighting sky, the clouds hovered way above as if they are protecting something. This was cloud-to-cloud lightning. The thunder roared; its voice traveling deeply into the homes, into the citizen of people in Seminole County, Florida.

Cars pulled over to the side of the road with the hazard lights on, too dangerous to drive, waiting for the storm to run its course. Within ten minutes, they moved the vehicles into traffic onwards to their destination.

Fiona and Sanari made a run for it between thundering and lightning, unaware of the car that pulled up next to them. A flash of light and thunder roared as they entered the bar for the usual drink of rum with coke. They sat upon the very stools that stood empty as if the stools were expecting them even though it was not their usual Saturday afternoon leisure time.

"Tell me what happened before this fear I am having spread to the rest of my body?" Fiona wanted assurance because she was waiting for Asa to blackmail her and the waiting was killing her, slowly. Asa is dead. She let out a deep long breath that spelled a sign of relief. Her face turned from flush pink to bright red as goosebumps circled her body. The hair on the back of her neck stood straight and warm feelings flooded her heart. A huge sense of relief washed over her. She let another; rather a few more breaths go before she felt a calm feeling surge through her.

The room at The Twixt Peach was filled with the rustling of paper and the keys clicking of a portable computer. A young girl no older than sixteen with short bright red hair and a gothic look chomped on a worn gum that kept the gap of her mouth opening blind.

A huge wet circle under both of her arms indicated the sweat pouring out from her; not because it was hot in the bar since the air conditioning was on high and the place was cool everywhere.

A short fat man came and sat beside her, pushing the glasses up onto the bridge of his nose. They probably came from the neighborhood of small homes that tucked hidden, half a mile behind Interstate four.

The smell from the kitchen teased the air as thick as oppressive smog on a very hot day. The few regulars chatted away eating burgers and fries, the most popular food on the menu. A family of six walked in from Helenville and nodded to Fiona and Sanari as they walked in and sat at their usual place.

Anyone who doesn't know them would think that the bar stool has their name on it. Maybe it does, because the second week of The Twixt Peach opening the blonde and dark hair girls walked in and claimed it. They had seen a few men sitting right there and Fiona kindly requested in a soft echoing voice that bridged on sexy.

"Gentleman, those two seats belong to us." What would the hillbillies do? Except get up very quietly, smiled at the ladies, and took two other seats on the opposite side of the bar. They wanted a good view of the girls. The men were left with no choice; no one ever addressed them as gentlemen. They have a new norm to live up to and they are obliged.

The bartender looked up with his usual grin. Upon seeing them he said boldly, "You had to bring the rain with you, huh?" A little drift of gold dust came into the blue of his eyes and a smile appeared as he executed the space between him from behind the bar and where the girls sat.

Fiona and Sanari never missed the striking tone of his physique; his male was born sexy and charming. His mouth dropped open in surprise to see them without a third party. It's not their usual day for drinking and they missed it last week. He wondered what gives, too much rain perhaps. He picked up two glasses and fixed them to the usual drink; a beer for Fiona, rum, and come for Sanari with

Mount Gay rum from Barbados.

Sanari had bought the bartender a bottle of Mount Gay Rum the second time she came in and requested that he used this particular rum with her soda. He ordered the rum and never ran out of it. He even had a bottle for himself and occasionally had a shot of it. He set the drink in front of them and the extra one for Asa. He leaned his head toward the drink with a quiet voice "where is she?"

"Dead." They both answered simultaneously.

"Yrrrph." The reply came from Ryan working a muscle in his square jaw as his face color changed from a slight tan to hot red. His brow furrowed, and the blood drained from his face leaving it white. A rock band jammed inside his head made his head incapable of linear thoughts.

Excessive thoughts ripped through Ryan, circling his logic and making him dizzy. He doesn't want to think as thinking brought up too many memories; memories that he is trying his darndest to forget. He pulled the air phone out and hit the stop button on his thoughts.

Ryan, the bartender of some ten years took the vodka and tonic he had set out for Asa and swallowed it in one gulp. He was tall and handsome in his mid-thirties. A veteran from Afghanistan with four tours and some was honorable discharged due to a busted knee. His smile vanished and his broad-shouldered turned lean and weary.

The bartender tended the bar for seven of the ten years Fiona and Sanari became permanent residents there. His eyes were sparkling blue and sexy with wore outfitted jeans. He would chat with the ladies until Asa started to join them, then he was silent and watchful. Now, they watched him, and as if they can read his thoughts. The girls wondered what were the add-ons to his lineage making him so sexy.

"Bullet to the head." Both girls belted out together, trying to keep the irritation out of their voices, and pointed to the center of the forehead. They proceeded to take a sip from their drinks.

Ryan pulled a candle from under the bar and lit it. The light shimmied and tossed out a shadow that landed momentarily on his frowned brow. He paused for dramatic effect and his voice shook. "In memory of your friend who lived on, in the memories of those of us who were blessed because of her." He added with a shrug then continued, "May she rest in peace."

"The terminology in such a situation is "hope she rots in Hell," Sanari whispered.

All of Ryan's growing years and experiences didn't provide him with knowledge of how to respond to anyone who rejoiced in someone's death. He passed through this experience with the expression with his mouth sprang opened and he guffawed and worked a muscle in his jaw, his voice choked, nonetheless defiant.

"Come on ladies, give her a break. What did she do to deserve such language?" He asked in surprise as he rested both of his muscled arms on the counter of the bar. He lifted an eyebrow and they didn't argue. He could hear the happiness in their voice.

"She blackmails people and followed us around as a lost puppy." Sanari furrowed a brow with a wary tone to hear a whispered voice.

Granted in agreement Fiona arched an eyebrow and recalled, "She volunteered to help people in crisis then turn around and blackmail them. She is a nasty bitch and she deserved to die. People aren't crying, they are partying, even her brother." Her face blushed and flushed.

"Oh." Ryan's blue eyes narrowed. His reaction was not reflected in them. He turned and walked to his office. No disease can survive from laughter or the joy of death. He tried to grasp his failed memory of her and the story just told. He's trying to think objectively and was unsuccessful. He guessed the girls' quirks of Asa married their experiences with hers or something else, he can't figure out.

The girls' words tumbled out, powered by the joy of talking of Asa's wicked deeds. All that was left for Ryan to do was to walk away. He's reserving judgment on the wisdom of saving himself for saying something thoughtlessly. He mused. What else can he say? This was an unusual experience, his first.

Silence prelude as Fiona and Sanari ordered the third round of drinks followed by coffee accompanied with vegetarian appetizers to munch on before they became drunk. As much as they wanted to celebrate, they wanted to be sober doing it. Asa's death deserved to be celebrated; they would until they died.

The girls were unaware of a stranger looking at them from two stools down the bar. An eyebrow rose in recognition of the sole behavior of the killer of Asa Fleischer. This was easy to figure out how the difficult part of the job, collecting evidence.

A shadow fell across the bar as Ryan stepped out from his office just as Sanari paid the bill while the stranger left five dollars on the bar counter more than enough to cover her half glass of tap beer and a tip. He watched the stranger follow the ladies out and stood by the door leading to the parking lot. He knew she was some kind of law.

Ryan prided himself in sniffing them out in his bar. This one had the marking and behavior of an investigator. She suddenly turned and blue eyes collided with blue eyes. The stranger had walked through the door, all thirty-five years of her while he was talking to Fiona and Sanari.

Juan, the other bartender served the stranger with Gin and tonic. She was planning an escape route in case she was questioned while taking a long slow swallow of her drink. He had studied her on the monitor in his office. He admired her long legs under the black narrow knee skirt and boots she wore, nevertheless, it didn't disguise her. He would've guessed as much anyway.

Sensations started to hum in his heart and it escalated into a symphonic scream. He doesn't want to turn it off because it made him come alive. His mouth fell open as his eyes came to rest on her breast and with that, he felt a kind of pull resulting in his jeans. Tedious questions plunged into his thoughts. He had never experienced gallant sexual energy. He looked at her with knowing twinkling eyes.

The stranger was as attracted to him as he was to her. She had a warmth to sell and more, much, much, much more Ryan observed. Feelings and affection replaced the intense passion that had engulfed him. She was letting him have her speed of light and sandstorm message while she was hitting him with a no trespassed sign allowed. He understood her message. No attachment; sex would be quick. She doesn't want to be involved with anyone.

Some sex is better than none, Ryan thought. He is overdue for some fun in his den of hay, and bed. For a long hot rude minute life stood still and slowly she blinked, disappearing into the wet afternoon. Ryan let out his breath and a shifter ran up his spine. She took her warmth with her and he didn't like that one bit. He felt cold and turned to take an order from a familiar face.

"Hey, are you alright?" The man exhaled a slow breath as he drew a shaking hand over his wet sleepy tousled hair and then down his damp whiskers face. Green paint covered his fingernails. The painting was a means to keep him busy.

Ryan smiled at him and knew that he suffered from Alzheimer's and painted the same thing every day because he can't remember whether he painted the wall yesterday. He came in with fresh green paint on those same nails for the past six months. With his failing eyesight and no one to tell him, he paints and has his meals here. The smell of food guided him to the bar every day at the same time. Where he lived is everyone's best guess. Ryan fed him every day for free.

"Yep, the weather always gets to me," Ryan said softly.

The tall tanned, leaned once dark brown hair man raised his eyebrow in wonderment. The lightning and thundering had ceased an hour ago. Everyone knew that even he, so what's the fuck? Realizing this, the man stared at Ryan. He continued to defend his actions.

"My mother died after such a wicked storm. What gives?" He lied to the once dark brown hair man.

"Scotch straight up." Not believing a word the bartender expressed, he sat his ass on the stool looking at Ryan as he poured the drink. He took two big gulps, the scotch disappeared down his throat.

"Keep them coming." The once handsome dark brown hair man ordered Ryan.

Ryan watched him drink half bottle of scotch in half an hour before he rolled over and died. Well, he fell backward and didn't move.

Ryan pulled his cell phone from his back pocket, dialing the emergency number while running the short distance between him and the tall once handsome dark brown-haired man's side. He put his two fingers to check the pulse on his neck. Finding none, he yelled to the audience in the bar. "Someone called 911." "I taught you are doing that." The waitress who dressed as a gypsy stated.

"Oh, damn it, I forgot."

"Here, let's have it." Taking the cell phone from Ryan, she spoke to the operator. She hung up and dials another number. "There's no pulse, send an ambulance and Charlie coz we don't know him." Charlie is the police officer who did investigations into unusual deaths in this part of the county.

"I think he's dead. Nothing is coming from him. Call Charlie, will you Melly." "I did."

"Oh, hell this is terrible. Anyone knows him." Ryan looked around at the faces of the onlookers and everyone shook their head in the answer to "no." It was the paramedics and police car that Sanari and Fiona heard as they pulled off the road. For some reason, they knew it was The Twixt Peach. Several pairs of eyes followed the vehicles as they drove past the Jag and into the driveway of the bar.

"Who died?" Sanari asked about the damped air.

"Oh, hell bells another death! I don't know if I can take any more of this." Fiona let out a long breath. "Drive, will you. Take me home. I had enough for a lifetime."

The weather was gloomy and murky, however, late into the August afternoon. Sanari pulled into the parking lot of Fiona's building and followed her into the elevator to her apartment. Fiona then proceeded to remove the bug that was placed in a vase with artificial flowers.

It was placed there by Asa a few years ago and was discovered by Fiona's brother, Roland who is a retired police officer upon a visit to her. They had then checked Sanari's apartment and discovered the same, only it was placed under her breakfast table. Roland had it analyzed and traced it to Asa Fleischer.

A further investigation named Asa as a drunken doctor whose name was attached to a misguided surgery under the influence of alcohol in a New York hospital. Her license was revoked and she was barred from ever practicing medicine again. She soon packed up and drifted from town to town talking to whoever listened about how she left her job because of politics and prejudice.

Finally, she settled in Helenville, too close to her parents and brother.

6

A thick layer of fog was quickly moving in, bringing with it a swamp scent. Another thick fog lay low while yet another banked which had rolled in from the sea carrying with it a light almost white grey mist that blew in from the Atlantic at four in the morning, a very short time before the crack of dawn show its' face.

The fog lifted its veil and the mist lay still, only for a few minutes. The sunlight burst through the clouds and elevated some of the haze. The sun slid behind tall buildings sending a chill in the air, more fog drifted in, this time it stayed and melted the fog and dried the mist.

As dawn broke into the darkness, a little bit of light shone through to reveal what was sitting around the lake. It doesn't freeze in winter and thaw in spring. The excess water from this lake joined by rivers flowed into a larger one and then vanished into the ocean.

This body of water that accepted the raindrops is tucked in among hundreds of tall green trees that blocked the view of the deadly swamp hollowed behind the apartments. Come evening as the sun is about to set, lovers and families strolled along the broad walk; the lake breathes from the heat of the day.

Buildings loomed suddenly from the disappearing fog. The newly built walls stopped the flow of excess water from flooding into the land, curved in the distance, and disappeared moments later in the aftermath of the fogged morning. Headlights of several cars appeared and cut through haze that drifted across the old trees next to the asphalt road.

Sitting around the ridge of a massive lake in the heart of Seminole County, Florida nestled a retirement community on the edge of the northern border of Deltona. It was built with an eye for drama. The Sussex Apartments complex is situated in Helenville, which is neatly tucked far away from the other retirement homes. Twenty buildings painted brown, green, and yellow stood out on the structure giving the compound the air of happy-go-lucky residents. The color was voted by the retirees to emphasize their dramatic flair for entertainment, more for gossiping and death.

Each building housed twenty-four either one or two-bedroom apartments on eight levels. These self-contained units have their washer and dryer with the conveniences of modern living. It was upgraded to accommodate the disabled as well as senior citizens and is taken care of by ten full-time maintenance crew who work round the clock.

The buildings have an innocent idyllic air setting, which was conveniently snuggled into every green landscape with a souring forest at its back. Swampland surrounded the community on the left, a sinkhole in the middle, and a drainage pond on the right. Dramatic looking as it did, palm trees outline the point of land overlooking the lake where various water vehicles docked.

A little less than a thousand singles, couples, and families resided, who assorted the daily life in this old retirement community. The fog was completely lifted, and sunlight dappled on the roof and the concrete walls of the buildings. On the lake, shadows were cast from the trees and buildings as bugs fell prey to the frogs sitting on the smooth water of the lake. As the sun rose, the reflections of its light danced with glittering motion on the water and shun into the stretch of windows on the east of the buildings.

A light wind played through the top branches of the Palm and Elm trees. On the low-lying branches, early morning birds sang their song of love while the squirrel danced all around. The ducks' swan and quacked as the branches swayed as the wind blew. The sunlight cast shadows on the grass and water sparkled in the lake and pools.

As the sun gained strength and becomes warmer, other life forms, insects and small animals found shelter in the earth and surfaced for food in the seemingly lifeless ground. The outside residents that drove past the compound usually experienced a kind of unreliable frequency on a cloudy day, a Brigadoon moment as if the place made an appearance every hundred years.

It gives off an eerie feeling and is usually ignored by tourists and locals. Very few know or remember its existence except of course for its inhabitants. The multifaceted that housed the elderly and young are haunted by many deep dark secrets that sweep through the crack ever so often.

Today is often, one of those days, a female stood her five feet six inches with one hundred and thirty pounds on tiptoes, stretching her neck to see whether there was anything, floating in the lake. Upon finding nothing, she rattled her brain wondering whether she dreamt, imagined it, and questioned if it was real, sending her emotional index into orbit.

"No, I know it was real." She whispered to herself. "I saw it. I know what I saw. It was real." Sanari stood at the water's edge surveying the lake trying to see the debris that stood floating. Did she see what she thought she saw last night, no not last night, in the early hours of this morning, three thirty-five to be exact? Was a man truly throwing a bag over in the middle of the lake? Was she dreaming again? She curbed into her memory and traced it to when the fog lifted for a few seconds when she saw the structure of a boat and a man throwing something into the lake. The tear was sealed by the fog, and the pair-the boat and the man faded from her vision.

The treacherous fog that had robbed her of sight now upset her further into a deep intuitive level. Disappointment shafted through her and she stepped from the edge of the water away from the sensed danger that she feared would be sprung upon her.

Sanari's stomach crunched and her instinct kicked in as the thought surfaced, did she see a murder? This is worse than Mr. Gray pinching her backside every time she met him at social events. Her hand automatically reacted and touched the exact spot that was pinched as reality hit again, she covered the shock on her face with both hands. Her eyes expanded into tremors as the sensations in her stomach did several summersaults before it contacted in to respond to her deplorable revelation.

Dawn broke through the mist of sun rays and the man standing without a shirt dripping with the lake's water raise a hand in acknowledging her. A bug stung his fangs into her leg; she was quite unaware of both, the man and the bug. The grass under her feet was wet and cold; she began to shudder and felt the chill inside of her. Her hands were crossed over her legs and her breast was folded over the other as if it would keep the cold out. She tried to comfort herself and stop the profound trembling.

The man turned and stared at Sanari as if he saw her for the first time. Becoming aware of a presence that she was no longer alone, Sanari looked up still shivering from the aftermath of her murdered question, she held his eyes. Ty, the man who loved her, and she couldn't love him. Being awakened by dreams she rather forgets was the reason why she was up so early and now, confused scared feelings daunting over her present moment.

Painful memories, Sanari feared she never access usually surfaced as dreams and triggered tension in her body. Being scared ticked her off more often than she wanted to admit; being ticked off made her cranky. She usually does something to release the pressure from the crankiness. Massages usually work. This chain reaction has wound itself around her for years. It's simply getting worse with the dream of becoming intensified. She meditated the dream and memory away for the crankiness to subside and her day can be productive.

Sometimes her thoughts tiptoed through the welter of memories and she survived the night without dreaming. Sanari had to bring her personal history into this morning event, why? Until she can have some solutions, the past is where she seemed to live. She felt wounded by it, the shocking reality of murder in the present. Although she had accepted and tried to look beyond the reality of her past, she couldn't, therefore she can't move forward until she let go or work through those haunting memories.

Seeing the mask on Ty's face this morning was not reassuring either. It wasn't the answer Sanari sought. She focused on the voices in her dream remembering who she was thinking of when she was releasing the tension of memories through a scream. She fixated her thoughts on capturing the memories that were teasing the edge of her brain since she came to the lake this morning.

As the mush surrounding the memories in the dream cleared, Sanari realized the man, her past lover, Ty was in her; she shivered more upon remembering. She was using his image as she cultivated herself at that hour in the morning to release the tension in her body. This cannot be because she had only met Ty in the last six years and the dreams that haunted her were before she came to the United States. It had died down for many years, however, it surfaced again more intense with Ty's admission of what he did in Afghanistan.

Ty had told Fiona of his time spent there, unknowingly setting the dream and images of her past in perspective. The silence that hung heavy between her and this man for months, vibrated with regret of not being able to express herself of her shady past and running away from her family. She pulled herself onto her trembling feet turning to go and upon seeing the man leaving, she stayed.

As Sanari sat on the almost dry lawn, twirling a bead of grass through her fingers, she wondered what other females were doing around the world. What are her brothers and sisters doing right now? Where are they? She let her imagination run wild threading across the basin around the town where she was born in another time zone. The fog had lifted and the sun was out. She remembered the dark chill of fire and sea.

The resilient smell of the Ocean carried the shoddy tendrils of fog except that it was greyer than the one that sat on the lake moments ago. A great span of white sand and rocks covered the hills, grasslands, and valleys where people, her family, and some of her cousins lived in tents. The land gushed from mountains that were topped with snow and continued down to rest at the bottom of a stream.

From this stretch of the desert came new species of life forms, changing the landscape forever. A few times, one of her cousins, Iffy had lit a fire for a group of them to stay warm as he relayed ghost stories. The ghastly images sprung open with laughter and sometimes let the darkness of the tale in for weeks. Out from the fire on those nights, they cuddled together until morning broke.

Despite Sanari's best effort to stop the memory of her past from surfacing, wispy recollections drifted through her thoughts as if they were flotsam in a lazy aquatic. Females, her mother, and sisters particularly were sewing, cooking, and sowing seeds to plant come spring. In another time zone, males are designing gowns for a formal dance and writing useless laws. Girls are given no choices in marriages to older and abusive males. Babies are being born, carrying on the tradition. Life goes on.

What would her family say of her life now? Sanari thought about the meaning of her name, sweet and beautiful. She felt sweet and beautiful every day; she knew that her family wouldn't think she was sweet and beautiful considering she's divorced, fifty-two, and a sex therapist. Never mind, she worked more as a consultant in sexual abuse and rape cases than an actual therapist.

Indian and Arab with a Muslim heritage and Islam for her religion was her ethnicity. Sanari knew she was an outcast from her sect. What did her cousin call her, nihilist-destroyer? Was she a rebel, a nihilist-a destroyer? She was the outspoken one in the family and refused to obey the laws of anything. Her motto in life was, "listen to the laws and then break them" and that was exactly what she did according to her parents from birth. A thought rolled out of another person who did the same. Was she at the same level of life as Asa?

Sanari found her peace here in her heart a long time ago when the first sexual abuse case came to her attention as an intern for a private company that represented the victim. She was consulted on the case and refused to keep the victim in therapy longer than necessary.

Agency keeps victims for the insurance money and government funding. It's horrific to see an agency that is supposed to help victims move into a healthy life hold on to them for a long time in the name of money. She walked out, opened her consulting company, and never looked back.

It has been so long since Sanari arrived here on that cold brutal winter morning; a refugee on her birthday of sweet sixteen many cold winters ago. Refugees, who fled the civil wars in their countries found shelter in a camp just across the border in Jordan. In an off-kilter moment, she did something else that still haunts her.

It was cruel and brutal to the point that she had to run from her family to figure out her life and purpose. Her journey was one of chaos with disturbing dreams, day in and day out for the better part of her twenty years. The marriage was short and bittersweet, sweet for him and bitter for her, nonetheless, she became allergic to marriages. It was no different than her family, possession, and ownership!

Living in building ten zero three, apartment ten seven-two was where she called home for the last ten years. After gaining her doctorate in educational counseling and divorce soon after she set up her practice in a rural county, where the poor lived in inhabited and unprecedented conditions.

Sanari Amani never settled in one area for too long. She became restless and moved again setting up counseling services for the poor and misfortunate of society.

The jackasses of racists don't know the differences between a person who has an Arabic name and isn't a terrorist from one who has an Arabic name and isn't a terrorist. The second there is a question about her and her life, Sanari sold her practice and left, settling in a different state. How many states has it been? Too early to count and too cold to think about the wide variety of places lived.

Sanari felt fit in somehow in the retirement community, regardless of the accumulated wealth she tossed out when she abandoned her birthplace or the wealth she had accrued presently through hard work and excellent investments. Irrespective of some abuse, racism, and minor other challenges she loved it here.

The residents tend to draw her into controversial topics. She had learned to resist and see the signposts before arguments and gossip spread.

Whenever the argument flared, it had an effect of a spectacular fireworks display; Sanari avoided it at all costs. The people here are too bored with retirement and create drama so they can be entertained while they sit and wait for death to come to visit. She felt settled and secured even though she has a fear that people would find out that her father was...still a terrorist!

7

A continuous blanket of sun-baked the sea moisture and raised its power onto the weather of Planet Earth. Summer was leaving, burning itself out, and slopped into autumn. The sun is up demanding more practical pursuit from the moisture, however, since it wouldn't rise to the challenge, the solar shun with a fireball in the sky making the last days of August heavy with heat. The ray of light rolled back the years spent in the back of the old sandy town.

The midmorning sunlight spread ruthlessly. In the sun-kissed clearing of the county, the sun trigged the cycles of the engine into life. Footprints can be seen rising from the black shadowy fissures that led to Lake Monroe.

Wildflowers cloaked the path with green, yellow, white, and orange on the cliff towards Interstate 4. Trees were caught in a wind surge that moved toward the East.

A mother and daughter walked slowly along the mud path of the lake which formed a straight road. The dust covered their feet from the morning breeze and lifted their hair covering half of the mother's and all of the daughter's face. Her son leaned against the tree and her husband was studying the faces of his loved ones for the sign of peril. People traveling in traffic on 1792 signed internally, while practicing patience as vehicles cruised in the heat of an accident, slowing the space of drivers.

The juvenile probation officer felt for the first time something beyond the whiter flower due to a case of sexual abuse, boggling his mind that landed on his desk this morning. The social worker's thoughts ran to the waterfall in Jamaica where she met a hunk of a man, the all-American male. Imagine that, she had to leave her hometown and travel to Jamaica to meet the man of her dreams who lived right under her nose-two miles down the street from

Longwood where she lived.

The juvenile delinquent who was caught smoking a marijuana joint now sat in the back of the law enforcement officer's curser on the way to be processed at the Juvenile Assessment Center. The officers had said it a hundred times to parents. Maybe this time he will when he hears it from the anger counselor. Don't parents realize that children required direction for their talent, a place to develop, otherwise they wouldn't know where to go?

The youths know where to go, into the arms of illegal activities. The delinquent high on a joint of marijuana was thinking about the old Darwinian shuffle that had a few steps he had not known before and had found out this afternoon. He admired the sound of evolution over the idea of God.

Cars were heading southbound on highway Interstate 4 and others climbed homeward. Blue, white, black and many types of vehicles cruised along elliptical driveways in the shadowed corner of neighborhoods, some of them routed to Helenville. One person was driving and thinking of how drivers carelessly killed people; how people forget to have dreamed was astonishing to her. The female wheeled the car toward the retirement complex and pointed it towards the closed gate.

A male gunned his truck across the dusty, pot-holed road towards the swamp. The blue sedan came around the corner in a maddening skid, the wheels squealed without warning, catching Anton's pants on a bumper, stripping and throwing him against a street light. A white car with a passenger shouting out the window came barreling around the corner behind the car. Another stopped in the opposite direction, avoiding a collision.

Anton lay there naked from the waist down completely in shock. He felt the warm air on his penis and then his erection. He tried to move his hand to cover this part of him and found out that he couldn't move. He tried to lift his head and couldn't move either. He lay back down and closed his eyes as if he had lost consciousness.

The old lady in the blue sedan jammed the overheated transmission into gear and floored the accelerator. A loud explosion rocked into her ear and a crash waved through every inch of her followed by another one that rapidly took control of her thoughts. Holding on to the steering wheel sternly, she watched through the bursting windshield as the trees in front of her swung insanely upside down. She didn't know how that happened because she had stepped onto the brake pads. How did the sky change places with the ground? After a dozen thoughts, the driver realized that she had hit the wrong pedal, the accelerator. Oh, God what a mess? She always had an overwhelming fear that she was going to make an accident happen and it often consumed her. In reality, it followed her all her life. She had run through the worst-case scenario' drills throughout her driving life. Her parents had driven it into her thoughts every time she was driving somewhere. In her imaginary test environment, she would run through accident scenarios not realizing that idea was built into her. She was an accident waiting to happen.

The driver heard the engine of her car die which means her headlights would be off. It would be dark soon. Is it daytime or is it soon to be night? Confused she tried to think happy thoughts, none came, the pain kicked in from somewhere, everywhere it seemed. A hissing sound came from somewhere. Her lungs burst for air; she suddenly needed to breathe. She tried to lift her neck and felt a quick jerk of sharp pain.

She tried to scream for help and couldn't bring her voice to express a sound. The driver remained silent hoping someone will come to her rescue. Words piled upon other words making it difficult to speak. As much as she wanted to scream "help" she couldn't, she started to think of something that would tear the blockade of thinking of the accident she created and couldn't come up with any. Reality was a painful barrier to fantasy at this moment in time.

She was occupied with her thoughts that she didn't notice whether anyone was about the complex. Surely someone heard the 'Big Bang' unless she's dead and waiting, waiting for what? The woman who lay upside down in her blue sedan, the very one who created the accident went into panic mode.

"Accidents are vital to working. They are nothing, only your carelessness. Your thoughts and feelings were organized out of the unconscious, the awareness spontaneously unleashed on you, and whoever was in your path." An inner voice was quietly informing her.

"Am I in hell or heaven? And you figured this out when?" The woman who created the accident wanted to know. "Get up and face your truth." The inner voice whispered in a higher tone than normal. "And you want me to do what? Is that you God talking to me?"She captured a giggle before it escaped.

"Am I in heaven or hell? Please let it be a haven. I only cheated on Andy six times. He wasn't a good lover and I need someone to love me. He's cold. Please forgive me. Let me into heaven. I'll be good." She heard the ambulance reeling before she fainted.

Children, teenagers, and adults stopped what they were doing and stared at the startled Anton Soto who lay flat on his back, dazed and confused. Someone ran and covered him with a t-shirt from prying eyes.

A man checked his pulse at his neck, found a beat, and let out a breath of relief. He rubbed at the taut muscles across his nape trying to figure out what to do next when Anton opened his eyes and softly whispered in a coarse voice, "Thank you, Mrrr...Fields."

All eyes, including Anton's, were following the car that plowed into a curb and bounced off the pool's fence before it came to a solid stop against the street light, upside down. The driver had laid her head against the seat and one arm dangled aimlessly; the other one Anton couldn't see from where he was laying. He tried to see who caused him this disgrace and couldn't move due to excessive pain in his body.

A man ran over and opened the door of the woman who caused the crash. He received no response from her and looking at the door figured he best wait for the fire department and ambulance. He went around the car checking for fuel leakage. About six people had called the emergency number.

Anger hit Anton, not that he was slow in thought; he was in shock which was no different than everyone who saw the accident. The ticing of a pulse in the hollow of his throat sprung alive and beat rapidly. He couldn't move and didn't want to think the worse; he closed his eyes. There was dead silence before another man stepped up and ran to Anton, breathlessly asking Mr. Fields if he was "okay." "I am not the one hurt, he is," pointing to Anton lying on the grass. The man, Gordon Phillips who lived across the street had witnessed the whole accident. He was the first to call "911" and was still on his cell with the emergency operator. He became aware that the victim was naked, even his boxers were gone.

Mr. Gordon Phillips looked around to see where it lay and saw it wrapped around the bumper of the crashed car. He realized that Mr. Fields had taken off his t-shirt and laid it upon Anton's uncovered body. His eyes were surveying the surroundings, informing the emergency operator. He rubbed at the taut characteristic muscles on his overnight shadow and ran his hand over the black kink of his hair.

Anton tried to pick himself up, however, a surge of pain hit him hard and he collapsed backward on the grass. He closed his eyes as a tear fell. His entire body hurts.

"Lie still, the ambulance is on its way. Don't try to move." Mr. Fields ordered Anton. Something akin to anger flooded into his deep voice. He saw fear in the child's hazel eyes and his black skin change color. Red marks began to appear on Anton's arms as he opened his eyes to acknowledge Mr. Fields only to shut them quickly again. Blood appeared out from somewhere and leaked into the grass to the already shocked onlookers watching two feet away.

The man, Gordon Phillips didn't introduce himself, however, he had stopped talking to the emergency operator. He heard the children gasping and upon seeing the blood he fainted. He lay next to Anton's body. The emergency operator was taking to the air for a few minutes before five-year-old Catherine Adair picked up Gordon Phillips' cell phone and started to speak to the operator.

"He's dead. He's dead." She yelled into the speaker and closed the phone.

Anton heard her, opened his eyes, and started to ask God not to take his life as he's only fourteen years old. Then he started to bargain with God that he was good and upon realizing that he was good tried to come up with another bargaining chip. He couldn't think of any, he closed his eyes and think about all the candy he had eaten and wanted to eat. He was going to die before he had a chance to live and see the world. This was where the ambulance responders and law enforcement officers found him. They performed emergency training, checking him out and keeping him from going into a coma.

All Anton was thinking about was that he had no underwear and wondered who saw him as he was lifted onto the gurney. Gordon Phillips was also on a gurney, now awakened from his moment of unawareness zone. He was thinking that he was too old for this excitement and here he thought that retirement would be quiet. It hadn't been quiet since he moved here a year ago after he had lost his wife to cancer. The twin girls were married with a family of their own; his days loomed long and lonely before he moved here.

On the other side of the street, a few feet away, where the blue sedan came to a sudden halt, old Mrs. Asby started to laugh hysterically. At the same time, Mr. Fields and a few onlookers reached Anton Soto, Mr. and Mrs. Dujon as well as Olympia Van Amstel the FBI that is investigating Asa Fleischer's murder, arrived upon Mrs. Asby. They all stood there watching Mrs. Asby's hysteria as she ignored Mrs. Dujon's help who was on the cell phone talking to another emergency operator.

For whatever its worth, Mrs. Asby was truly upset and extremely emotional. What could have made her so upset? The silent question was asked by everyone who watched as the scene unfolded. Mrs. Asby was in her eighty and has a slender body with few wrinkles. She was widowed and lived for her children, and grand and great-grandchildren visits. They were scattered all over the world and she often visited them. The photographs adored her apartment and the funny thing is she can remember every moment and gave details of each photograph.

Well, the truth of the matter is, there is no knowledge of her family around so there is nothing to validate the information given. Everyone just believed her. Mrs. Asby kept mumbling about something at her age. It seems that her doctor from the old Sanford town that she had visited a week ago had called her while she was in the supermarket.

The doctor's office had forgotten to take enough blood for the cholesterol test and need more. She was on her way to his office to have more blood work done and for some forsaken reason, stop at the supermarket.

The doctor was congratulating her on the result of the blood test. She had told the doctor that the results were incorrect and she demanded a new blood test. She reminded the doctor of her age and why this is impossible, on all accounts considering it's been plus ten years since she had sex. Doctor Mortenson realized that this was indeed a mistake, and began to apologize sincerely.

Hearing Mrs. Asby's anger, he wanted to be far away from his office right now. He decided that it is time to retire. Retirement seems a wonderful place to be. He rubbed his chin and hung the phone on its receiver.

Mrs. Asby was so angry she drove home very unaware of her driving. She stepped on the gas pedal instead of the brake when she drove around the corner from the gates. Regardless of her status quo and being short a few French fries of a happy meal, she was told by the doc that she is pregnant!

The Special Agent from the Federal Bureau of Investigation found herself walking away from the scene of the accident. She was as quiet as a lamb; her feet took her to the swamp behind building one thousand and five in her apartment complex. She glanced up at apartment number two hundred and four overlooking the lake.

It was dark which meant that her lover had moved out. She smiled. The Special Agent had left the apartment to give Andre time to move his belonging to his new place. She was talking to Mr. Pinthouse, a retired Chief of Police when the accident occurred. Shock shook her body as she watched the whole scene unfold with the accident. She needed time to gain control of her emotions. This is where she usually hid when she needed to be alone.

The practice of Buddhism taught her how to be quiet, particularly in the midst of chaos. This aspect of quietness or rather a stillness in her life she can't seem to acquire. She craved stillness because with mental silence comes peace. Peace of her past and longing for peace in her present life is what keeps FBI special agent Olympia Van Amstel spacing her wooden floors at night.

Although the applications of solving problems were already built into her software; Olympia can run them mentally, with a double click in the memory, anytime she wished, she is too vulnerable at this time in her life to see live action. The accident scene was under control. It doesn't require the presence of an FBI agent. Normally her victims are dead; live actions are a rare occurrence, especially where she's involved. She moved into a jog of fear and some anger with no relief in sight.

Guilt and fear have been in Olympia's company for a long time now; the very same two emotions that destroy her relationships due to her being emotionally bankrupt. There are too many questions to ask with little or no acute answers. One floated into her thoughts, why did her parents give her up for adoption? Who are her parents? Where are her parents? This was the reason why she became an agent in the Federal Bureau of Investigation, to have access to records at her convenience and to find her birth parents. The records were tightly sealed and vanish when she tried to discover who they are at age eighteen.

Years have flown by and still, there were no answers. It was a lead she was working on that made her so vulnerable because at the same time the puzzlement of her birth came to play and she lost focus on the present moment. She had fixed a few pieces of the puzzle of being born to a young mother of sixteen to a married politician of thirty. Who they are is unknown and the reason for her being given up for adoption is common sense.

The young mother has an affair with a married man who had no intention of leaving his wife and kids for her. Who knows? All Olympia can do is hazard a guess and play a zillion different scenarios in her head as to why? What she does know is, of all the darndest things in her life she had to go and get shot in her ten years of working cold cases.

Semi-retired Olympia Van Amstel stood her full five feet six inches, one hundred and thirty-five pounds looking at the silhouette of the alligator that is currently viewing her for dinner. Her hand automatically when for her weapon that was tucked away in the small of her spine. She watched the alligator with her blue eyes until her brain reminded her that there was a fence between them and she was safe. She let out a breath she unconsciously held and took a few deep breaths to steady her nervousness.

Feeling a fool, Olympia found her bench and rested her backside upon it. How many times has she been here and yet she goes for her weapon upon sensing danger. Was it fear or her training that put her into a position of always having her weapon wherever she goes? Sometimes she felt such a coward, also having a restless feeling concerning her life's path.

Olympia Van Amstel inhaled a deep breath and wondered for

a zillion times why her adoptive parents name her Olympia. Every person who knew her, they have a different name: Limp, Offy, Imp, and plain O. She heard a loud splash in the swamp and went for her gun again. Her fingers relaxed from the weapon when she realized there was no danger that the alligator swam away looking elsewhere for dinner.

She still received a salary from the FBI as an undercover agent and her weekly column of "A whole lot of trouble with a little bit of hell" in the weekly newspaper is a smashing hit. Her editor had given her a wonderful compliment "that was a hell of an epitaph you wrote there, the best ever." The weekly column was the fragment of various short stories, a different legends that blended together with the landscape of different people. The truth was twisted a tad bit to make the characters more defined and entertaining. The blended fragments of stories have become an adventure with her audience and a very nice income. The stories were about the lives of the residents in the retirement community, a carbon copy of what's truly happening in Sussex Apartment in Helenville.

The day Olympia entered the complex the "Sus" was painted over in red leaving the title on the sign of the gated community as Sex Apartments, Helenville. She started to laugh and knew she would love living here. She figured it was the teenagers who hid behind the palm tree watching the expression of those that entered. She let it be and when she ran into the bunch of them at the pool a few days later she smiled and told them that she loved the sign. She watched their puzzled expressions and the question of what was next. Fear was written on all of the four teenagers, fear as eyes followed her into the pool. When she surfaced from her dive they were all gone. She belted out loud laughter.

What's her fear? The edge of the emotion whispered through her and she felt it. She's not that old, only forty years, why are these emotions currently surfacing? The freak accident of forbidden love was long over. It has been five long years and also the present one when she found out that he cheated on her. Karma is a bitch! The question again was: what is her fear? There it is again; fear piercing through her. She had inhaled fear along with oxygen for too many years. Time to let it go; ah, there it goes pinpricking of fear needling her spine.

Olympia reflected briefly on the love affair with a married agent whose wife found out and took his gun and shot her upon discovery. They covered it up as an accident because they were partners working on a cold case. This was the same time she fixed a piece of the puzzle on her birth parents.

For a split minute, she lost her focus on the woman pointing a gun at her and instead of shooting her, she was shot. She never knew her partner's wife; it was a good thing she was shot, otherwise, if she had done the shooting there would have been an investigation and truth behold it would have come out and disaster would be the case.

She laughed out loud again for a different reason. She remembered the experience and the lies told in the inquiry. Fear covered the stutter of electricity during the investigation of being shot. The fear she had held on to, by lowering her standards; she had an affair, something she had promised never to do. Her heart was aching because she felt abandoned. The shock drove her thoughts to a standstill; she answered her fears with the emotion of anger denting her dreams to live a moral life.

The affair was not even loved, a mere accident that they began sleeping together. It was a bitterly cold winter day deep undercover in a cold case and both fell into bed to keep warm because the heater was broken. One thing led to the next four years. Marriage or moving in was not mentioned nor divorcing his wife, Marian.

It was one of those things that happened and continued until his wife followed them on the job. The confrontation was not pretty. She appeared and attacked both of them for cheating on her. She ran to Phil Massy, her husband pulled his gun and shot her, Olympia in the breast. Pow! Chilly, chilly bang bang!

The Gods were with them that day and it was a challenge in her performance to lie as if her life depended on it. Her life did depend on it. Nope, it didn't ....she could have survived by writing her column in the newspaper and also a Blog. She had to lose herself to discover who she is, except it was a harsh reality in how she found out her truth.

Since it was the job that she was shot, it was easy to cover up the shooting and what followed was the typical procedure with Phil and her saying that the gun accidentally went off when Phil thought he saw the suspect running toward them. The funny thing about that is the suspect's shoe print was left on the earth. The Gods were with them.

Phil threatened his wife with divorce if she ever came clean plus she would be arrested. He would divorce her and have full custody of their three children who were six, eight, and ten years of age. Yep. She kept her mouth shut.

Phil had decided to divorce her as soon as the children were of age. The marriage was over a long time ago when he found out the firstborn was not his; the blood test didn't match. Mitch was in the hospital after falling off his bike and breaking his arm. He had lost a lot of blood due to a cut on his left leg before he was discovered by the neighbor Mr. McLeod. He ordered a DNA test and discovered that the son he thought was his was not; he kept quiet and did an investigation only to discover that Mitch was his best friend Ian's son. The other two children are his and were already born upon this discovery of Mitch, nevertheless, he loves Mitch as a son. None of the children deserved to know until they can manage the truth. He knows Marian continued to have affairs because he hadn't had sex with "the bitch" as he referred to her since he found out four years ago and he has no intention of ever having sex with her again.

Sometime or the other, the suspect Floyd Mayflower had made the journey, and who knew whether he saw Phil's big fat wife Marian entering the building and decided to follow her, leaving his footprint in the mud. He probably saw the whole thing take place. They would never know because he was arrested the next day for driving out of state. He was wearing the same shoe that made the print, however, he never mentioned the incident.

Olympia guessed he was too involved in being charged with the murders of his sister, Martha, and her lover including his girlfriend Wanda. He confessed to the murders that he committed ten years ago. He's a dying man because he has terminal cancer.

Guilt would do that to a person.

The thought of the bartender flashed across her and images of the silent exchange came through as her memory software gave her a full-frontal view. Walking into the path of love again she had given up, was scary. She had covered the distance when both eyes collided and mated in that brief moment. She took with her the complete understanding of the exceptional meaning of the word love and with its meaning, the lasting peacefulness. She had been more nervous than a frog on a trampoline when she realized that the fusion of love had slowly come around to her and of all things with a bartender!

She had to let her lover go because it's pointless to have him think that there's a future when she fell head over heels for the first time in her life with Ryan Reyes. She wasn't going to keep Andre around knowing he cheated on her, anyway. There was no judgment, however, after the heated moment with the bartender Andre was no longer appealing. It was a mutual agreement. The cheating wasn't even addressed. Why bother!

She couldn't keep her heart out of this equation even if she tried because her heartbeat kicked up a few knots. She realized that the past heartbeats were an illusion and that she loved her past lovers, however, her heart never beat that quickly; the truth is solid as anything debatable contained myths. Thoughts drifted back to the moment shared. Her gaze smacked right into his and sparks danced in her blue eyes as his sensually soft eyes found her cold ones.

There's a mystic influence in the air that tied them together and threw love around their hearts. This new relationship will give birth to something she had never experienced in her life. Eyes had looked at her then straight upward as the thunder of passion rolled within her. Time went back to a country of long-lasting love where no one had ever ventured with her.

In her peripheral vision came fruition with the awesome power of wanting to know his character, to be absorbed by his warmth, and to have the courage to say how she felt. She wanted to have a conversation that fired him with admiration and gallantly sarcastically intervened. She wanted to experience life with him, yes, the bartender!

Olympia's nerves that were hot-wired to her spine rise and light her feelings on fire as shyness stunned her in a paralyzing fog. Fear didn't step in when their mating eyes electrified the air with its pretense. Surprise filled her blue eyes making them warm in his, her eyes gleamed behind him, chasing out every emotion permitting true love to stride in. She felt it and she knew he did too.

A sudden light sparkled and twinkled in his eyes, transplant gallantry that diluted his serious lips into a smile he gave her which was utterly gorgeous utterly beautiful. The grin twisted into a crooked smile, a smile that ended in his teasing her. She sealed that precious moment of pure pleasure into her memory.

She stopped deliberately thinking of Ryan Reyes and turned her thoughts to her job. She was the femme fatale in her active FBI days. The other agents told her that her seductive walk was of ninety-nine points, nine percent all female, and a little bit of nitro, whatever that means. The guilt surfaced and Olympia examined the emotion thoroughly and finally realized that the two secrets are creating her edginess and irritation of being an undercover agent including an undercover writer.

She never shared this with anyone and now as age became hers; she wanted to scream it out and let it go. Her biggest fear was her girlfriends of childhood finding out and abandoning her about the affair and the undercover work. More so, the accompanying lies she told them to keep the undercover work undercover. If they knew about the undercover writer and the stories she wrote they would definitely abandon her.

Her adoptive parents did.

9

Zilch........the imp of my life! Asa is dead! He's not sorry, not that he didn't think of it, killing her; he did think of it, plenty of times, especially when she would beat on him-the fucking wicked witch of the north, north where, north whore, hoe who the fuck cares? Huh? Good for the wicked bitch. She deserved it. God, how he has learned to despise her, the anorexia alcoholic backstabbing two-faced bitch fucking around on him.

James Asher thinks he knew it all. The problem with this was he knew it all only when he was drunk as a skunk. Today, he's drunk as a skunk and decided to show everyone what a smart ass he is or he thinks he is in this retirement community. After all, he's a retired businessman and he's entitled to do whatever the fuck he desires and whenever he desires it to be because he erranded it. This is exactly the conclusion he came to about life in general.

He's the Alpha male that had remained stoic to Asa and listened to her, swallowing every word she spoke, watching her panting for breath from their pain and pleasure sex life. Hate tightened his features and a sudden rigidity vibrated in him.

James had noticed for the first time the early line of age coming to her face some years ago. Asa didn't age well and wrinkles splattered across her face as if she was a bullmastiff dog. A bully abusive bitch she was; one who was soaked with rage and blamed everyone for her misfortune. He deliberately left vague answers wanting her to squirm. Anger being her operative word and anything else was a disclaimer, rather than his disclaimer.

"Why are you asking?" He wanted to know each time she ventures into his past life. "To justify what you are saying about me and define what you believe?" This would be his question and answer to her prying eyes on a life he doesn't live anymore much less think about.

Asa's words were pregnant with a carefully considered revelation of sarcasm; he didn't tone down his either as they escalated into huge fights only to have violent makeup sex later.

Makeup sex was the only thing they had going for them because everything else was dead. He pretended to sleep and roll over when she demanded him to sexually perform or when she was intoxicated not just with cheap beer; by her closeness and the smell of her high-powered collogue. She had gone to bed with him on the night when spring was high on the mixed smell of blossom flowers that rode on the wind of Helenville. Those nights smelled of flowery rosy scent, mixed with sexual mist that ran its course. They had turned sour on the first night when she wanted pain and pleasure mixed with sex.

Asa had tried to explain why she liked pain and pleasure sex to him and he had cut her word off and replied, "if you are into erotic fine, your choice. Do not define, justify, validate, or explain to me through romance. Erotic is pain and pleasure and people who are into erotica are in pain and pleasure. You would think that you have to inflict pain to get pleasure? Gentleness is not erotica, Asa." She flung away from him and sulkily told him, "You don't have the credentials to perform, I've to teach you. Don't be so dammed cute you giant. If you love me you would oblige me."

He had changed the conversation and she deliberately altered it back to erotica. He had talked himself into the belief that she needed him; he gave in and actually liked erotica. Well, not really, his need to have someone in his life is greater than having pain and pleasure sex. Besides, they both are always drunk anyway. There's no feeling attached, therefore he tolerated it. The sexual performances sometimes were an unpleasant duty, instead of satisfaction, and since they couldn't always get it together, Asa wandered around for a quick fix whenever she could.

James knew this because he followed Asa and saw her having sex in the wood with some guy she picked up from somewhere. He hardly seemed to notice at first until she was bent on some inner contemplation as she requested "good fucking here and some there and with a threesome?" Curiously he did have sex with another man she chose. His experiences with the threesome rankled into jealousy while Asa loved it all. He had no idea why and he had no intention of figuring it out.

There was a thought of impulsively punishing her for putting him through the ordeal. He gave into temptation and soon became high-octane fuel shooting with a few blanks in her cylinder which became a knotty problem apparently from her rigid expression. James's lips twisted into a grimace; he was thick smog running on empty and formulated gas. He was impotent. He let her be and then one day she told him that she was pregnant with his child and wanted to get married. He believed her for a few seconds because her voice was so shaky that it changed from a high to a low pitch on the tune of the word marriage.

"No." He replied tripping over his tongue.

"Then we never had this conversation." She said with impatience.

"What conversation?" He answered candidly. Asa's proposal was sincere and one day when she was drunk she told him that she was never pregnant and called pride to her defense in offering marriage to him.

"Marriage was supposed to be part of my life." She yelled out at him, tears flowing down her cheeks.

"Marriage is an endangered institution." He had replied unmoved by her tears.

"Your personal veracity needs an overall." She had defended her actions. "Veracity" she was shocked at her speech. Where did that come from? What's does it mean? She was too drunk to think logically and drop the thought.

"I doubt you taught of me in marriage and how we'll make it work. It explained why we don't discuss the future sober." James broke off the lid of the beer can he held in his hands. He was out of vodka and this will do. He sold it, well borrowed from his lover, Asa's friend Fiona and Sanari. Hell, she's not even going to miss it.

He had planned the bugs as Asa has asked many light years ago. He pretended that he was drunk and knocked on their door, they opened it, and he asked for some sugar. He planted it while they were getting it from the kitchen. He did that on two different days and no one suspected anything. They didn't even mention it to his bitch of a girlfriend when they saw her.

Asa is dead! Hell, she hated sex yet she loved to watch erotic movies with him. Voyeur, she is and dead as sea salt in bed. Is sea salt dead? What the fuck, who cares? He wickedly smiled on his remembrance of how he went to her apartment two days ago with Asa drunk and fuck the living daylights out of her. He was an excellent lover and cannot imagine why she doesn't like sex without pain and pleasure.

James took a sip from the can, then had second thoughts about it and drained the remaining in his mouth. He waded to and from a few times as he emptied the last bit of beer. He crushed the can and threw it on the lawn. He burped loudly and received a high on the control he thinks he has over everyone and life itself. He looked around at the compound and smiled wickedly. Then as a thought formed more vividly he grinned, his lips showed his semi-white teeth. His grin became wider and then broke into a silent laugh.

Asa dead! God how he's going to miss that bitch. Not...never will. Good for her. Everyone showed up at the funeral just to be sure that she was dead. He wouldn't believe the secret smile on people's faces as they viewed her dead body in the casket. They all left soon after. No one was at the burial site, not even him, well, her parents in spirit and brother, maybe. He would never know because her family doesn't like him since they blamed him for her being an alcoholic. He had met them a few years before they died six months apart from each other.

Alcoholic and a looser they called him to his face. He, James Asher, the businessman was a drinker and not yet an alcoholic. It was her that drank into senselessness and pulled him into her shadow. He watched her every night lay drunk on the carpet floor then somehow slowly he became one too. He was the neon.....an amateur to her alcoholism. She always has to bitch about some fucking trash that has no bearing on reality.

James rubbed his crooked nose and ran his hand through his

grayish brownish hair. He looked at his white wrinkled skin and the need for a tan fell upon some other random thought. Why do white people always want a tan? Another corroded thought slipped through his cracked brain cells and his dormant emotions kicked in, arousing his desires to do something hellish. He mused over the thought as it formed fully and transform from fantasy to reality. He liked it very much.

What now? James pulled his six feet to a full length and swayed a little. He giggled and then found the sofa falling into it. He mentally spoke to himself not to get the nymph as doubt dipped in his idea. He pushed it aside as a physical rim of life hit him that he would be celebrating life without Asa. He was going to urinate on her grave. He started to laugh hysterically. He remembered how they met at the hospital where she has fired for drunken surgery some decades or more ago. He was in there for food poisoning and overheard the nurses gossiping about her.

After he was released he sought after her, following her into a bar and letting her believe that it was a coincidence. It took exactly two days before he made headway into her affection and another day to fuck her. She was vulnerable and easy to bed. Manipulation was how he survived and run on.

Asa the bitch was dead. He was free. Free to do what he wanted and then a remembrance struck him. She had transferred all of her money to him. He was drunk when she came to him in the dawn six months ago and asked him to sign the paper. She left and came back two days later and gave him a copy.

Essentially, she left it in the drawer in the kitchen where she had her bills kept in her apartment. He slowly picked himself up and walked to the drawer. He pulled the envelope out and looked at the copy. Yep...it was her money in his name alright. How much was a guess? He chuckled; his sight was too blurred to read the numbers. He blinked a few times, rubbed his eyes, and pulled the paper closer and further away. He couldn't make out the numbers or was it that he can't believe what he was seeing one million dollars!

Now he sank to the tile floor with the documentation in his

hands, the pieces fell into place. Blackmail! The bugs were placed into people's apartments to hear their secrets then Asa blackmailed them. He was the one who placed the bugs and became known as Asa's drunken boyfriend. "Oh, God! Those poor people and Asa! What a mess?" He spoke out loud. There are tapes, where are those tapes? Where would Asa keep tapes? It had to be here somewhere in his apartment. Why transfer the money to him? She was being blackmailed or IRS was on her ass for tax evasion? This was her place and he had a key. He lived a mile from Helenville and she had a key to his apartment and ample time to come and hide her blackmailing tapes. His body slid to the floor and he lay there for a very long time, trying to put the pieces together. James fell asleep and awoke some hours later with a nasty headache. He thought he was at his apartment. He groaned and opened his green eyes looking at the ceiling.

A piece was cut and oh, god........the tapes. She hid the tapes in the ceiling in his place because she taught him that he would never look up. What a stupid bitch? He rose to his feet and walked out the door. He was so high on his discovery of being so smart that he was at a loss in what he was doing; out the front door walking down the stairs upon the lawn in the bright southern light of September.

The new moon blinked at James who winked at it laughing. He was in a drunken mood and there was no stopping him. He was on top of the world as his penis stood erect. He lifted a hand and held it as he began to empty himself on the newly mowed lawn. He was in so much of himself he began to laugh out loudly. It was not loud laughter; it was ten after three in the breezing morning of fall.

He stood there for what seemed forever which would validate the amount of alcohol he had consumed. His body was too exhausted from the abuse and can no longer maintain his six feet structure swayed back and forth as he hosed the hibiscus plant with his urine. What James didn't realize was as he enjoyed his escapade, he was at Asa's apartment and he was naked!

10

Fiona Blanchard age fifty-five was taking the stairs two at a time to check on Craig Altner who lived in the building next to Asa. She was asked by the director to see if he was alive because he wasn't seen him in months and they were concerned. She had phoned him with no reply, now a visit is due.

Fiona does this often with a few other neighbors, after all this is a retirement community, therefore checking on the residents is a regular occurrence. People died just about every day here. It's normal to check on them even if she never met or know them. She knew it was late, however, it was now or never.

In addition, it's known that Craig is usually up at this time plus a light shuns through the window leading to the lake. He never sleeps; visiting him at three in the morning was not a conflict. She was on her way home when she decided to go and see him. It was a spur-of-the-moment decision. This is the only time she has because she was helping Lance Jeffery with his catering service.

One of his servers called in sick, therefore she worked that shift and was going home to sleep; She has her regular job in seven hours at the hotel.

The key didn't turn in the lock, which meant that he had changed it. Fiona drew in her breath and turned slowly, walking down the stairs. There's nothing to do except report it to the front office. They can check on him. She wasn't too fervent to see him; he gave her the creeps and her instinct warned her that he was dangerous. How she knew this she doesn't know, from her instinct perhaps and she doesn't want to know. He's dangerous and that's all.

Fiona looked up to the shy as she reached the last stairs and seeing that it was going to rain, made a quick dash across Asa's building to her car. She longed for the quiet of her apartment and sleep. She sensed someone present and turned to look around her, resuming her surveillance of the sky and the coastal route to the lake. She stood her five feet six inches, one hundred and forty pounds looking at the back of a spectral shape man standing naked on the lawn urinating. Who could that be? Who would do such a disgusting thing to the poor hibiscus plant? Upon recognizing James, she turned and walked to her car. In minutes, she was driving to her building while making a mental note to convey what she saw to Asa. Asa had to do something and she was confident that she would do the right thing, dump James. She was completely aghast having run into him, well seeing him naked!

"Oh, hell Asa is dead!"

Those two, Asa and James had hacked themselves toward each other through violence using the old thicket of ignorance that usually separated strangers, it had bought them glued together as Siamese twins.

Fiona realized that her thoughts about them were pertinence and factored in insignificance. She smiled to herself and figured she might fall into the stomach of hell for her thoughts, nonetheless, she can find her way out by church time on Sunday. Isn't why they have the church beg for forgiveness? She giggled aloud. Fiona reflected that James was smiling showing his semi-white teeth; at least he had his teeth in his mouth. There were times when she saw him without them. There was when he visited her pretending to be drunk and asked for sugar. He did that to Sanari too. It was two weeks later when her brother visited that they realized that Asa had planted the bugs. James did it!

James and Asa often were drunk come six in the evening. Alcoholics were to the core of their being. Asa had jumped up and left when she and Sanari turned the conversation to alcohol and alcoholics. It was a flash of brilliance to manipulate the conversation hoping Asa will seek help. Alcoholism is desperation to cover up insecurities, however, it's only brought out the worse in them compared to when they were without alcohol.

Alcoholism isn't a disease; it's a need, therefore a need isn't a disease, or is it? Is alcoholism a disease? With the influx of abundance of incidents concerning alcohol this century, alcoholism was an old habit that was declared a disease.

Upon hearing the word alcoholics as if Asa didn't what to hear it nor did she like it; she did abhor it, smoldering with rage amongst other things was her excuse. Soft or sweet was not the word that readily comes to anyone's thoughts when they think of James and Asa.

Fiona took the conversation with herself to her building, ten-ten apartment twelve forty. Thunder and lightning pelted cold rain from the sky. She stepped into her flat and the shower. Images of her past life floated in front of her as she closed her eyes and allowed the warm water to run on her face and tan body. She wished that the water would take the images of her rape to the distant space and leave her alone.

Married and divorce didn't heal these vivid images that plagued her from time to time. When she was occupied with married life they left her alone. She was never certain when they would pop up only that they do and she let them flow. No one knew except Sanari. Confiding in someone is different from privacy and she likes her solitude. Her fear concerns the rapist coming looking for her and that her two children and five grandchildren would discover her secret.

When she counted the things she has going for her, she has more than what she doesn't have including her children and grandchildren. Why spoil it by telling them about her horrific past?

It was prudent to keep it from her family because her children knew the rapist and it would change their life which she wouldn't do to them. Her withdrawal and divorce were a slap to her children's father who never once thought much of her anyway.

After all these years, she still has doubts about how to proceed. She refused to degrade herself while she was working through the pain. There has to be hope at the end of her rainbow; she has yet to see it. Even a dirty martini or wild sex can never take the images away. She remembered that windy day when she was married to Alex when the rape occurred.

Alex was in bed with their 6-month-old daughter Alexia asleep. She had arrived home from work at ten that night and was shocked when someone put a knife to her throat as she stepped into the kitchen from the garage. The rapist told her to be quiet or he would kill them all moving his head in the direction of the rooms. She dropped her handbag and pinpricks of fury needled her skin.

Who's he? His voice sounded different, his breath stunk of alcohol and he knew her and her family. She wished she had put the lights on when she walked into the kitchen.

"Don't do this; you'll regret it." Fiona pleaded with him as sorrow entered her voice, however, it didn't stop his anger from roaring through her.

"Do you have any idea the hell havoc you gave me?" The rapist's shallow breath fanned her cheeks and his lightly parted lips touched the corner of her mouth; his eyes gleamed. The heat from his body pulsed against her same as a furnace. He pushed her onto the kitchen table. The stuff set off his shoulders telegraphing the pain and anger he was feeling.

"What are you talking about?" Confusion flared into anger. A sharp pain lodged between her ribs. His knife played with her throat. She spoke with an inflection of anger in her voice; unrelated her tone was low and soft.

"I am going to fuck you, bitch. Seeing you every day fucking my best friend. He doesn't deserve you. I saw you first remember but you choose him, him over me." Profanity quelled the building anger in his voice. She recognized his voice. The rapist had no idea what he was saying because she didn't meet him first she met her husband long before he introduced her to him and his other low-life friends.

Anger began to simmer in her. "I am going to make you feel really good tonight. You're not going to want that husband of yours after I am done with you." Intense anger merged with his sarcasm. His scornful tone for her husband tripped through her anger. "You like playing with my emotions, Fi hon?" Sarcastic needling tone left a little mistake in the meaning of the scornful barbs. "You're going to like what I'm going to give you." He opened the zipper on his jeans and pulled out his package still holding the knife against her throat.

He pushed her legs apart and moved the knife against her ribs. With one forceful move, he opened her jeans and yanked them to her knees. Even in the dark, she could see his anger. The lack of a speck of cantankerousness in his face of her anger piqued her into pity for him.

"Just the sight of you throb my blood fucking hot. A heatwave baby, I wanted you for so long." He pushed her panties aside as if he had done this a hundred times before this moment. Bitter and angry until it had eaten away his happiness all these years of wanting her came forth fury that was sitting idle rise inside him, bubbling dangerously to the surface.

Wanting her assurance, the rapist said, "You're going to like it." With an angry scowl, scorching his face with rage which he thought he had carefully banked flared. He wanted to comfort her with affection only to add to her anger which he didn't want. Uncontrollable wrath toppled out from him and he was too drunk and stoned from sniffing cocaine to care.

The rapist wanted Fiona to protest; he became enraged about her not fighting him, of her not begging him to stop. He didn't expect her to be agreeable to his raping her. He had lost his need to have sex with her. He tried to summon some more anger and couldn't find any. He took to profanity.

The whole thing didn't have any intellectual. He saw the last remnant of anger leave her expression and was replaced with hate for him. He was quickly losing his erection. He didn't enjoy it anymore and began hating himself for Fiona seeing his impotency. He didn't bargain on it. He fantasized about her enjoying it as much as he did, nevertheless, it was nothing of what he imagined.

Reality hit him as a fat rage surged in him. His green eyes never left her once he had her attention. The fear he saw in her blue eyes and his voice was a hard whisper vibrating with fury.

"You're going to like it." He forcefully entered and brutally raped her.

Fiona had sent her a message with an inflection of hate. A hot spike of rage had subsided; an old pattern of old anger that she had locked away was driven by an urgency bordered by depression climax into her body. She closed her eyes the minute she figured that he enjoyed the contact. She refused to oblige to his wishes. She might fuel the flames of his anger. She knew he doesn't hate her, however, she wanted him to hate himself for what he is doing to her. She wanted to take the joy out of the rape. She hoped she had succeeded.

The rapist's first reaction was amusement; his second was more fury. Wild rage rode in his eyes as he took her, his head snapped back, eyes still looking at her; he bit into his lip tasting blood that fed into his wrath. Red hot anger drowned out her pain as he continued with his invasion.

A sharp knife pain jabbered in her with each brutal entry as her body yelled louder to stop, and her knees buckled. Her body consumed with the agony of pain refused to let up as her features pinched with agony. She fought down the ache followed by fury and couldn't figure out whether the pain she is experiencing is from the rape or her anger.

Fiona got a grimace before he stepped into the night. She brushed her eyes with the back of her hand impatient with the emotions that authorized themselves to flow her with tears. She sat there on the kitchen table with her clothes still the way he left her, in shock emotionally exhausted. She wasn't sure what emotions she wanted to see on his face, regret came, however, she knew she wouldn't get it.

Sick feelings oozed through her body. Fiona searched for her voice and couldn't find it. When she felt the blade of the knife against her ribs, she knew she wanted to live for her children. She pulled her clothes together and walked into the bedroom where her husband, Alex drunk as usual was asleep, including the children.

Fiona took a long hot shower and said to the water, "you're going to pay for this." She didn't know how, she just knew it. When she spoke, she discovered she found that her voice was only a whispering fragment. She wasn't certain how to identify with this experience except for each time it surfaced her emotions were suspended for a short while pending more facts. To know so little was to feel insignificant and a little insane with rage and madness.

Fury rolled through her. She was sizzling with anger; she had held on to her anger and it had controlled her turning into depression, illness, and disease. She thought that she had recognized her rapist's voice, however, it was foggy.

In the months that followed, she suspected that it was one of Alex's drinking buddies, John who lusted after her and made several attempts of kissing her. When he'd spoken to her, trying to intimidate her she knew it was him by the way he pronounced certain words. He was delirious with jealous and found out that Alex had discussed their sex life with all of his friends when they were drunk.

She fucked Alex the next night just so he can share it with "his buddies." She wanted John to know that his raping her didn't affect her. It did anger him because he showed up the next day in rage; She wasn't alone and never was again.

She switched her hours from evenings to days and always made sure that someone was with her or she was in the company of others whenever John showed up. The honor was the cornerstone of her character and she kept it by holding her head high and putting a smile on her lips. She always pretended that nothing happened and was thinking of having a divorce when she found out she was pregnant.

She knew it was John's child and sure enough, the results from the DNA came back positive. She waited until Alex came home drunk one day and filed for divorce. She knew that John would know, would figure that Lexi was his and Alex would never believe that she was raped by him. No man wanted to believe that his wife was raped, much less admitted that one of his lifelong drinking buddies was the rapist. Honestly, where's the value in that, particularly when she needed it, to be valuable the most in the aftermath of being raped.

She moved soon after and never saw any one of them again. When the children were old enough she told them that their father was an alcoholic. He wasn't then; nonetheless, he was heading on that path. When the children were eighteen and sixteen, she took them to meet him. He was an alcoholic. He couldn't care less and all he wanted was money. They didn't see John; he didn't know that he had a son from the rape.

"Don't let the behavior of others disturb your inner peace, Fiona." Sanari had counseled her. She had explained that the origin of fury lay in the rapist's life due to accumulated disappointments and in his corroded beliefs, he thought he found the antidote that transformed his disappointments into poison, rape. He transferred this poison upon her. He didn't understand his feelings and never sought help to discover solutions to managing those feelings.

Sanari had told her that when she confided in her. She packed up her anger with its fury and told it that it no longer resided at this address. Balance and harmony are active and because of it, she's happy.

Fiona was silently crying, she always had a fear that her children particularly her son would discover the truth and would quit having her in his life. She couldn't live with it. She screamed some more and with that let the water wash away her tears.

11

He heard the door's knob turned and peeked through the hole to see who it was to decide whether he should open the door or walk away. He had a grimace at her before the night turned into daylight. He had just finished jerking off upon images of her and there she is standing at his door. He was glad when she broke it off because he always had an emergency landing with her and was embarrassed.

Who the fuck does she think she is? The thought ran through freely. He's a man with principles no one comes knocking without calling first. He hated that when someone just thinks they have the right to show up without calling. He was in seclusion for a reason and don't want to be disturbed.

Another thought flew into him that she did call him and decided that it doesn't matter. He turned and walked to his bedroom lying on the semen that covered the other dried ones that were left there when he had sex with Sanari in his bed. The smell of the rankness infused the room with a scent that sent his nostrils wild for blood. Oh, how he wanted blood again, very soon, he comforted himself.

Only last night Craig had watched the three girls, Fiona, Sanari, and Asa sitting across from him enjoying a meal and wine. They can't see him because he had chosen a place where he can see them. The huge fake palm tree was in front of him covering his face and most of his body, not that Sanari would recognize his body. They always had sex under the covers because he was ashamed of his body. He knew what was there and that was good enough. No one ever has to see his body and he rarely looked at it. He wished he had bionic ears to hear what they were talking about because he thinks they are discussing him.

He may be labeled disabled by the psychiatrist as paranoid schizophrenia. His insanity and paranoia is not open question because he knew what and why he thinks the way he does, he cannot separate the two, because they looked the same to him. His psychological gratification is ejaculation while watching others having sex. His uncle, however, was worse than that and no one ever labeled him. Uncle Pete as he called him had other thoughts of gratification.

Remembrance came to play in his thoughts as it dribbled on the day he and Sanari met. He was sunbathing on a lounge chair when she approached him. She spoke into his ear calling his name and as the warmth of her breath touched his ear, a sound of vibration went through him giving him an erection. He was sure about the significance of it because the broken way in how his name spilled from her jacked him into overdrive. His pulse rate with high and the sensation of hearing her voice sends him into sexual bliss.

Her laughter was contagious; he adored the devilish smile and the primal mar in how she flirted with him. Sanari had pushed him towards the frontier of creativity and creativity he had plenty of, too much that it had boiled in him for years. He had allowed them to move freely in his thoughts forming a picture of what he had to do; he had found a way to release it.

He allowed his thoughts to recede all of his creativity as he approached them carefully just enough so he can chase them. The cat and mouse game he played with his creativity entertained him as he lay lifeless in bed thinking about her. Two months later, the smile that she usually summoned to his lips whenever he thought of her died a quick death as soon as he saw who came to collect her. She was the one he was meant to spring with not him. What is she thinking? She lied to him, a cheater. The angst that was part of his personality showed its true colors that cruel day when Sanari climb aboard his bike.

As the shock of seeing them together began to wear off, anger moved in rapidly. For weeks to come he restrained the anger that had rolled through him threatening to explode, nonetheless he was growing angrier by the second. Anger had somehow coiled the same as a rattler in his chest and rage consumed his eyes. A thick thread of dark pain turned his anger into a weary resignation of them together.

At the sight of Sanari, more anger was evoked and as much as he let go of his memories of her on his bike, the anger came with a reminder. The anger that flashed in his eyes stayed permanently. A red mist of anger that had hazed his vision erupted in him. They are all of the same element of cloth, all of them. His anger was apparent to all females now.

The doctors have said that he's impotent, has deep-rooted anger, and has a tendency for violence. He never hurt anyone in his life although he can only have an erection under certain conditions. He admitted to having auditory hallucinations, and he hears voices what's the big deal? What was his uncle hearing, the devil? The only place he liked to touch is his penis. He doesn't like kissing and on more than one occasion he had suicidal thoughts. He cannot feel anything since he was five and that was because his drunken father belted him one day leaving those scars on his back. His mother watched and did nothing, however it was his uncle Craig James Altner who stopped the beating. He told his father if he ever did it again he would call the police.

His father never touched him again, nonetheless, the verbal abuse was constant and his mother hated him for whatever reason beyond him. He is angry alright and has emotionally distanced himself from everyone and everything except sex. Even now as he watched those girls sitting there he can hear the voices telling him to go and jerk off. He wouldn't not after last night and she was watching the lake. Does she know? Did she see him? He watched her watching the lake through his binoculars. He had to get rid of her, soon.

Craig smiled and wanted to kiss himself for being so smart. He's only thirty-eight and can figure things out for himself without help. He had quit taking his medication. He doesn't need them. He liked the voices because they keep him company and he was never alone. For crying out loud, he even named the voices. Yes, each voice has a name, all twelve of them. He had fancy naming them when he discovered the photographs.

Every night for a long time one of the voices would have sex with the photographs. It was trilling until it got old and the excitement rare off and nothing happened for months until he met her, Sanari; Sanari with her big appetite for sex that he couldn't give her. She wanted it all, the romance, the touching, and the kissing. How grossed that is for him.

Delusion is an understatement where Craig Peter Altner was concerned. He never met Sanari or Fiona, however, he did meet Asa and chose to stay far away from her. She was too scary for him. Sanari, however, was his perfect mate so Craig Peter Altner conjured all different types of fantasy every night and ejaculated. He's confused with Fiona and Sanari and often mistakenly takes Fiona for Sanari.

At first, he hated Fiona because she took Sanari from him with what he assumed that Fiona demanded Sanari time when Sanari should be with him. As time passed, Craig Peter Altner became more delusional. He blended his twisted thoughts of Fiona and Sanari as one. Fantasy is what he lived by and maintained with all the manufactured stories of various women and men he fancies. Rarely does he blend a man or a woman together, however, it is known that he had done it, had sex with a man before his uncle died, at least twice?

Craig admired Gilles de Rais and Steven Brian Pennell only because he met them through the uncle of his namesake, Craig Peter Altner. As a young boy growing up, he used to wonder what his uncle was doing in the woods so late in the night. When he was thirteen years old he waited until his parents were asleep and followed his uncle who was living with them at the time.

Over the years that followed he took to the ritual and rather found that he enjoyed what he saw and look forward to his uncle's sexual activities. He became a voyeur and would wait until the same day at the same time as his uncle was having sex with the newest girlfriend to watch and then jerk off with him. This continued for years until he moved out on his own.

He waited when the sheep lamb in the spring to have his first girlfriend and took her into the wooded area behind his house and had sex with her. It was a disappointment and broke up with Adriana Morrison blaming her for not being excited. He next had sex with a gay boy his age and that too was a disappointment. The service they produced was inadequate. It did nothing for him....until Sanari.

Craig found out he had more fun watching his uncle and his girlfriends, however, since his uncle had moved out three years prior he was trying to recreate the excitement and loss.

There was no sexual excitement when he had sex with either a boy or a girl. He couldn't figure it out. He even tried watching his parents having sex and that didn't do anything for him. He went over to his neighbor's house and hit in their closet only to be stiff from the long hours of standing quietly. Zilch!

Upon this uncle's death five years ago he inherited his condominium and moved here. Cleaning out his room to make a place for his things he discovered fifty photographs of young girls some he recognized from those distant years when he used to watch his uncle having sex with them in the woods. He started to use them to create his sexual excitement, ejaculating in the process only to become disappointed.

Sometimes, he would have a male or female over after he had created his sexual excitement to have sex with them. It didn't work either. They were too drugged to do much anyway. They had to go and go they went into the lake. They knew too much about him.

A year into living there he discovered in the mattress a flash drive and then it hit him what his uncle was doing with the girls. Many girls had such a violent death; he became excited with the blood covering their bodies. He had to jerk off. According to the law, his uncle Craig James Altner aka the black water killer was named a serial killer because he had killed the girls, had sex with them, and dumped their bodies in Black Water Creek.

All of the killings were videotaped including his uncle having sex with them. What was so exciting to him was the watching, how was he to know that his uncle was raping dead women!

12

"Alright, I had it. I have a feeling someone is watching us." Sanari belted out after half an hour into dinner. Frantic electric sensations screamed through her heart zinging straight to her toes then up her spine and felt a shaft of heat scorching her skin. Her thoughts flowed back to the conversation earlier checking to see what they were talking about as if that was the reason she felt spooked.

"I thought it was Mrs. Gray and those other widows she had for the company. They kept looking this way at us." Asa answered quickly, knowing very well that she felt nothing. She wanted to be part of the conversation.

"So, you feel the energy of being watched?" Sanari more or less asked no one in particular. "We just don't know who?"

Fiona took a sip from her white wine and said, "I know someone is watching because my hair has been standing on my neck since I got here."

The topic of conversation was dropped and forgotten as they looked from one to the other. Sanari lifted a brow looking at Fiona in question as they tuned into their sensations. They ignored Asa. Several minutes passed quietly as they stayed focused on their instinct that is trying to tell them something. Who is watching them? Which one of them is he or she interested in?

Three females different from oil to water and night to day lived an intriguing life in a retirement complex. They met at the annual Christmas party and became fast friends well Sanari and Fiona did, Asa is a whole different matter. They have had dinner once a month for the last ten years at the same time and the same day of every month at the same restaurant across the road from the retirement compound.

Well, Sanari and Fiona did until Asa followed them there and pretended to bump into them. She pulled a chair and joined in the conversation ordering dinner. That was four years ago.

They dressed for the occasion. No casual clothing worked here because this was their niggling day off. Except for Asa; she doesn't want to dress up because she doesn't know how to manage it gracefully; jeans and a t-shirt were her attire, always. On this day, they talked about everyone and everything, well almost. They used to until Asa started on her rant gossiping about everyone; they listened and listened they did, knowing about the latest in nothing. Some women can talk a whole bunch of nonsense for no reason. Asa did.

She picked herself up and left the table which is common to Fiona and Sanari who used the time to talk about what mattered most to them. Today, they were focusing on the people around the restaurant trying to figure out who is watching them and why. They were still at it when Asa returned and took up her seat again reaching for her drink of vodka and tonic.

After a well-deserved sip, she belted out in her squeezing voice, her lips twitching periodically. "I saw Charles Callahan and Craig Altner from apartment twelve forty sitting at the bar."

"Together?" Sanari asked. A frown appeared above her left brow.

"No, opposite each other; Craig's hiding behind a palm tree with a sandwich and beer. Charles's munching on wings and fries and beer." Asa informed them quite happy with herself for her detective work.

"The office asked me to check on Craig, they haven't heard or was he seen in a month. I did and the locks were changed. I must inform the office that he's alive." She concluded.

"Craig sent me candy, flowers, and even called a few times. He had all the right moves for asking me out except that I've never met him. I just didn't realize the wrong man was behind the gifts and he does sound sexy. You think he's following us." The smile on Sanari's face was touched with regret for accepting the gifts.

"You're so........." Fiona's sentence was cut through by Asa's question.

"How do you know that it was Craig who sent the gifts?"

"I have caller ID and I asked the florist who told me who paid for them."

"As I was saying you're so lucky. Remember that guy who bought you duck eggs, then tomatoes, eggplant, and that broadleaf thyme me thinks you called it?" Fiona was laughing.

"Oh yes, Edmund. That was a long time ago." A silence stretched between them and Sanari for a few minutes. Sanari didn't mention that she stole his tomato plants and planted them in Fiona's garden. She even invited him one evening while they were all sitting by the pool chatting to have a look at her tomato plants.

Fiona was laughing so loud she wouldn't have been surprised if the window had cracked. Sanari let her she will have her laughs later. Feeling uncomfortable she broke the uneasiness and fell back on asking questions, starting with an all-purpose one to Asa, to cover the fact that she was not welcome here with her and Fiona. She became distracted and uneasy from being watched she forgot what she was going to ask and said instead. "You know that Mr. Gray had pinched my backside many times." Sanari finally broke the silence.

"Arrah, yes I know he did with others as I saw him. I didn't know one of his victims was you." Fiona admitted with a frown then she giggled.

"You know who I feel sorry for, Anton Soto." Asa chipped into the conversation deliberately changing it.

"Why? He's alright and will get a lot of money from the insurance," Sanari asked and answered her at the same time.

"How was he?" Asa asked Fiona ignoring Sanari because she knew that Fiona visited the hospital and probably seen him.

"Oh, yes him, Anton I saw him when I went to see Mrs. Asby," Fiona informed them. "He's happy and recovering well. I am told by his mother."

"He's fine and would be home in two days. As for Mrs. Asby, the psychologist was examining her head while I was there. This morning she found out that the lab tech made a mistake with her blood work." Fiona said.

"Is that so?" Sanari asked as her brow rose in surprise.

"Yes, they got the two Mrs. Asby mixed up. Her daughter-in-law is pregnant."

Asa hated that they knew more than she did and as much as she wanted to change the subject again she stayed silent. It was slowly killing her.

"That's a bloody expensive pregnancy. I hope she has money coz she's going to be paying out a lot of it." Sanari informed them.

"Naw, ah, her insurance would, and if that ran out she has her husband's insurance money from his death," Asa said.

"Asa, how are you doing with your breakup with James?" Fiona asked as she looked at her knowing full well that she and James are still together. They both knew that she lied to them and that she and James had gone their separated paths.

"The truth, I was trying to dumb him a long time ago but I didn't know how." Asa boldly admitted not realizing that Sanari and Fiona saw them together a few nights ago in the parking lot of the supermarket at two in the morning while sitting eating ice cream in Fiona's car. They saw her and James kissing while putting the groceries bag in Asa's car.

A slice of the new moon hung forty degrees to the left in the direction of Helenville, while billowing clouds sat in the blue sky. The warm passing glow of dusk had long gone taking the fragrance of roses with it.

"So, it worked out." Sanari more or less mentioned as she rubbed her neck hoping to remove the buildup sensations that lodged there from being watched. She felt queasy and her past flashed before her. She guessed it was to remind her of who she was and what she can hold on to or maybe who she is now, what she has become in the present. Hell, if she knew.

Her father's last ringing words, "You are nothing without a man and marriage." His expression was demanding and fear had poured into her. With this unknown person watching them, she felt that same shock of fear she felt so long ago for the first time.

Asa ventured in and reminded them of the last Memorial Day they had with the veteran Jane Gibson who was honorarily released from the army due to her shaking disease of Toilette's syndrome. They had found a real live veteran of war at the pool one day while barbequing. She had inherited her father's apartment who was a veteran in the Air Force. It meant a special moment to have her over on Memorial Day.

They deliberately left Asa out and told her it was a spur-of-the-moment thing. Fiona intervened and filled them in with the food served of hot dogs and chips with beer. Asa had passed and heard them laughing and was furious for not inviting her. She had heard them through the bug she had placed.

"Oh, JG was such a sport. She saved my life." Sanari added to the conversation making Asa more furious. She wanted them to feel guilty for not inviting her. She knew she spoke in anger due to the pondering of her heart. Shame surfaced and plagued her feelings because she couldn't evoke guilt from either of them.

Shame for losing her cool and sight of what she wanted from them, friendship. She was thinking of a hateful response that would release the shame before it cascaded into anger. It didn't work.

Nothing is working tonight. Asa felt such a loser and they make her feel worse by not including her in their life. She wished they would invite her instead of her inviting herself. "They only catch a broken branch. Don't make such a big deal out of it." An inner voice spoke as outrage twisted on Asa's face. Both Sanari and Fiona felt the fury vibrating through her and saw the pain and rage fused in a hot tangle in her chest sending it to heave heavily.

Fiona laughed when Sanari reminded her of the time when she asked her to make some rum balls for her. "Fiona, you took my one hundred and fifty years old Barbados rum and I didn't see her for a week. Finally, when you turned up you only had the empty bottle and told me that there are rum balls in the fridge and that it tasted not so good."

Fiona laughed more and it took a few minutes for her to add, "Asa you should've seen her face." It was hilarious. The narration of the story didn't touch Asa. She was seeing red with anger in the sea of uncertainty about this monthly dinner. She had changed her drink to Sanari's rum and fruit punch followed with a martini hoping it would quiet her, however, she seemed to be living in these two writers' fantasy as they control the conversation.

Silence prevailed upon the group. Tension mounted. Resentment flared from Sanari and Fiona to Asa for her intrusion. Emotions ranked high among the three females as contempt was more than a small amount of anger. Irritation warred with pity and frustration from Fiona and Sanari to Asa.

Asa doesn't want to think because her thoughts kept giving her a headache. Whenever she found she was thinking she drank it away, and poof it disappeared.

Frustration, anger, and heartbreak all collided because one emotion overwhelmed the other and a surge of the three sprang forward, fused, and slapped Fiona and Sanari in the face as hate. Protesting the anger that is building, rebellion melted in the rush of falling and began to vibrate between them.

Asa picked herself up and walked away. Her eye bright with an emotion she couldn't recognize Sanari laughed out loud and that sound followed Asa as she stepped through the restroom door. Sanari and Fiona both let out a breath they held on whenever Asa was around. It smoothly left them as Sanari recalled an event with Asa.

"Fiona, two days ago Asa called me when I was shopping. When I answered she was in bed with her lover James. I was in Wal-Mart on the speaker and it took me a minute to realize that somehow, she dialed me unknowingly. I still can't figure out how she called me when she was huffing and puffing so profusely. It was worse than an erotica movie, I tell you.

"I was standing there trying to figure out what the fuck was going on. It took me another minute to realize that people had to stop to listen to them fucking each other. When I realized that I held the phone up and told them if they want to hear more pay up to five dollars. I got five hundred dollars before I got escorted out from well, kicked out by security. No worries, I donated the money to the children's fund you know the one that sends orphans to college." They were both laughing when Fiona went sober and said, "I have to tell you something important. I want you to listen. I think this feeling we are experiencing is about me. I....I was...mmm I was raped eons ago by someone who's now in town.

"Oh my God!" Asa expressed her shock at Fiona's admission as she sat in her chair upon returning from the restroom. Asa felt her pain because she too was raped by a priest and a nun in a Catholic school.

"Oh fuck." Sanari followed Asa's shocked face and then realized that it wasn't meant for Asa's ears. They were taken up with laughter and the the seriousness that fell upon Fiona's face that they didn't see her approaching.

"No, Sanari, I wasn't fuck, I was rape." Fiona smiled at her friend's expression, realizing it was too late for Asa's ears.

Sanari gulped at her reckless expression and was about to apologize when Asa asked, "How long ago was that? How old were you? How did it happen? Did you report it to the police?"

"Girlfriend, if I didn't know better I say you are an FBI agent or something." Fiona's brow joined in a frown and her few wrinkles were vivid as her eyes moved from Asa to her friend. "I came home one day and my ex-husband's friend raped me. My son is his and I never told anyone. That's not important. He's here now and he wants to meet." She admitted. While she spoke, she was thinking about her children and grandchildren and how much it would destroy her son if he found out, more so than the rest of her family.

"Meet with him and then let's beat the mother fucker to a pulp." Asa expressed her intensified anger.

"Asa!" Sanari and Fiona said simultaneously.

"Look, the way I see it he didn't get punished for it. You didn't get justice. What is it he wants with you now? Have you healed?" Asa wanted to know.

"If you meet with him he'll stick around you and bleed you to death. He'll emotionally destroy you once and for all." Sanari said to both of them. Fiona shook her head, ridding herself away from the whispering word of "no" echoing in her head.

"Rape never goes away, Sanari. Some days it spirals on every nerve I have and then it lay to sleep until some incident sprung up. I meet it again and sometimes I relive it. I should've gone for counseling. I was very scared and ashamed. I tried to come to terms with it as I met others who were raped. I keep carrying it around in my thoughts. I have nightmares sometimes for weeks then I confront it whenever it surfaced with a hot shower. I cry. It hasn't gone away." Fiona winched.

Sanari gripped her upper arms and said, "Let's do it." Talking business had taken a seed at the table this moonlight night. She agreed.

"What a capital idea, let's beat the son of bitch up. Maybe we can injure his penis so he can't do it again." Asa nodded to Sanari in agreement.

"What?" Fiona looked at her two friends in shock. "Have you gone mad? We couldn't get away with it."

"If you think like that then we will get caught. If we plan it well we wouldn't. Besides he deserves it." Sanari said as Asa nodded in agreement and charmed in with a wide grin.

"Miracles are a sideline of mine. Anything else you want to say would be the time to say it. I know exactly how to do it and we will get away with it. I had planned to do it to my rapists and never had the guts to follow through." Asa charmed in.

"Huh?" Fiona looked in complete astonishment.

"Leave it to me. I will plan it all without leaving any fingerprints.' Asa cantankerous informed them. Fiona and Sanari kept puzzled faces looking at Asa in amazement, who loved the attention she was receiving.

Little did Asa know that she was being manipulated very cleverly by Fiona and Sanari, both were fully aware that she was raped. This was going to be an amazing twist when the event came in less than a month.

13

"Ki what?" The FBI technician asked never shocked as to what would roll out of Olympia Van Amstel's mouth.

"Kibosh," Olympia replied. "It means something that served as a stop to something from happening."

"And what are you stopping from happening." "Oh! I wish I knew."

"Oh come, Olie give me more than that."

"Oh, Randy baby, I wish I could. I gave you all I can already."

"I want more, lots more."

"Why am I having this feeling we are talking about two different things."

"Ah-ha, I was seeing if you were paying attention. You seemed so far away."

"I am far away, old goat. You are in Langley and me in Florida."

"You're in a different world."

"Yes, I am and the thing is this Asa Fleischer is a piece of …."

"Art?" "No, Randy everything else except. She was dabbling in everything except honesty. undeniably no beacon in the night." Olympia informed him.

"Oomph!" came back from the other side of the speaker.

"Okay, you ask for it. Once upon a time in a galaxy far away there…

"Seriously, that's what you got?"

"There lived a boy and a girl….."

"Come on seriously this is torture I'm not listening!" The comment came with sadness.

"Alright. You asked for it. I don't have all the evidence yet, just my intuition."

"Hit me. That never let you down before Olie."

"I know. The prototype is of a sphinx and an oracle all in constant motion with each person's perception and moving in and out of sync with Fleischer. There're so many factors that are coming into play presently. I can't seem to breathe. It's a maze that's unraveling slowly. Then there is serendipity, synchronicity, and karma all wrapped into one."

"Every single person I mentioned."

"Mmmm except one."

"Pizzazz who?"

"Sanari Amani."

"Why am I not surprised. No fingerprints, huh?"

"Zilish, as if she doesn't exist."

"I had a funny feeling when I saw her. This makes my job harder."

"Ha. you'll get her."

"Yep, I usually do what a zig-zag mess? Fleischer made her fortune at the expense of others; where's the money?" Olympia asked him.

"I'm going to have to get back to you on that. It'll take some time to get that information with this little to go on. Also that Amani girl."

"You are getting technical on me." Randy Pillsworth said softly and sweetly into the speaker.

"Serendipity is chance, fate, or coincidence, finding something that I was not expecting to find. I didn't expect that from a short anorexia girl with a bullet in the forehead dead smack in the middle. Synchronicity is having the experience of two or more unrelated events occurring together by chance which I'm beginning to observe with Fleischer with loads of meaning. Karma is what goes around comes around."

"Mmmmm....are you putting me through a test to see how smart I am or are you exercising your right to speak freely? You got a lot on your plate there Olie?" A grinning voice answered.

"Oh Randy, you don't know the half of it."

"Age doesn't define you, Olie, you define the age." He teased undauntedly.

"Are you saying that I'm too old?"

"No darlin' you are experienced enough to figure it out.

Serendipity, Synchronicity, and Karma are too much for me to grasp. I'll leave you to figure it all out then you can explain it all to me over drinks."

Olympia and Randy were once partners as rookies and when Randy was shot in the leg by a delinquent female he took the data research job. They would go out once a week for dinner and drinks talking and sharing everything. They had a good relationship and sometimes his girlfriend, Lila joined them.

"Yep, that's what I always say. I love that synchronicity, a true niche in life. It put a zing in my window of opportunity, Randy. Every time I have evidence to back up Asa's murder a new and different plot surfaces and I'm back to zilch. It's so frustrating." She signed.

"Sending the info, you requested darlin'."

With an elixir of delight and elegance, Olympia disconnected the speaker and sat silently for a long while in her apartment. She closed her eyes and lay her head on the rim of her white sofa thundering through the voices of thoughts trying desperately to sift through the zing and zang of the Fleischer's case.

Stirring the flow of energy to tap into the sizzling juices of creativity, she stumbled on an opening and wondered what Amani and Blanchard have to do with the murder of Fleischer or the bartender Ryan Reyes.

What happened to Amani's identity? Who is Asa blackmailing? How many? She stood up and walked to the patio where the failing light of the September evening melted the shadow on the lake. She was glad to have something as concrete as her laundry and groceries to do to anchor her to reality.

The dark essence of the water on the lake was foreboding. The sun was setting in a huge ball of orange, red, and a few other colors making a magnificent picture. The smell from the barbeque cruise teased the air thick with oppressive smog on a very warm day. She allowed the possibility of dreaming of Ryan Reyes to seep into her thoughts just as a golden light swept over the ridge of the swamp laying a carbon copy of itself on the water in the swamp. The sun was below the horizon and darkness fell.

Olympia yawned at the cozy feeling the last thought inspired. She admired the well-muscled arms and want to have them wrapped around her body. She felt his gaze on her every time she entered The Twixt Peach for dinner at the same time every day. She gently cultivated his strength as sultry warmth enveloped her. She knew that she would bed him as soon as the report gave an all-clear.

For now, she silently flirted with him letting him know that she is interested. Ryan's blue eyes pinned her every day and every day he told her silently that he'll wait. He's ready to romance her. Her lush lips parted invitingly and she gingerly ran the tip of her tongue over them making his eyes twinkle. He gave her a wide smile and she matched it with a firm grin. The sensuous profile he appended her with chiseled through her heart into pure love.

The earth that stretched out rich with their mating evolved with a fragrant that awaited his touch against her skin. Every one of their eye contacts has a symphony; a symphony they had silently orchestrated was a new one neither of them had ever experienced. "One day soon, Ryan one day soon," Olympia whispered to the wind. She deliberately turned her thoughts back to the Fleischer case.

The FBI was called in to investigate the death of disappearing couples in the area several years ago. Since she was a cold case investigator and on leave in Florida, they found her a vacant apartment number twelve forty-nine in building ten eleven.

This was five years ago and no one expected that the state of a disappearing couple's affair would last this long. She was undercover as a realtor which explained her various hours. She had a view of the lake and its activities and saw someone dumping bags in the morning and knew that Amani saw it too.

Olympia was up writing her column for the newspaper with the sliding doors open when she heard the splash too big for a fish and as a true investigator she went out on the patio looking. She didn't see anyone, however, the next morning she saw Sanari Amani standing looking at the lake.

Someone threw something in the lake in the wee hours of the morning because they didn't want anyone to know what they are hiding. Based on the loudness of the splash, she knew that Amani wasn't that someone because she can't lift that much weight.

It had to be a well-muscled strong person, a man to lift a bag that made such a splash while throwing it in the lake. She also figured that he did it deliberately to fool anyone who might be up that it was a fish.

Dumping the bag into the lake and making it sound as if it was a big fish took some calculating. What he didn't figure out was that two or more people in this community wasn't too old to figure out what he was doing; they weren't old, grey, and senile compared to most of the resident in the retirement community.

What puzzled Olympia was the location of the drop? She wasn't sure where it went down because by the time she walked to the patio she only heard someone paddling away from the spot where he did his dirty deed. It had to be a male; a female would make that much of a big splash unless she had a large built body. She couldn't put the lights on or go down to investigate that would be too obvious and she didn't want anyone suspecting that she knew the lake was a dumping ground for something; bodies she guessed, the missing couples?

Olympia had a camera planted in Fleischer's apartment and knew that James Asher had taken permanent residents there. She saw him finding some tapes in the ceiling in the kitchen and planned to steal them tonight from him. Sliding the chess pieces of intrigue into place, Asher was a professional con artist, and he conned Fleischer, into having him as a boyfriend letting her think that she did it.

Asher's crime went far back into his juvenile days and presently a warrant is out for child support from his wife with his two children. What was he doing with all that money in his account and what was on the tape? His dysfunctional family didn't prepare him for a long-term relationship with anyone nor did they ever instill in him a desire to be a father. He didn't allow any cold fur to cloud his thinking when it came to his con artist business.

He was a pro at what he did which made Fleischer an amateur. She walked inside her desk and closed her laptop. She had planned her move tonight into building ten zero nine apartment eleven ninety. It would be easy because Asher will be drunk by ten-twenty and asleep by eleven. She would enter quickly and remove the tapes without being noticed.

Olympia smiled as her thought ran into a future image of Asher going to retrieve the tapes and finding none. He would be thinking that he dreamt it. Piece of cake, her job is, yep piece of cake, blueberry to that piece of cake.

14

The all-American Caucasian two-hundred and fifty pounds computer programmer forty-eight-year-old male sat his five feet ten inches on the bar stool sipping his beer. He was looking at the waitress, well more undressing them with his bedroom eyes. He took a drink from the bottle of tap beer and waited for the assemblage to move on for him to see the other people. He can see what matters more with greater importance.

His blue eyes rested upon the Caucasian waiter as his thoughts led him to undress the fine form of a man. He is obsessive, compulsive, and has a disorder. He knew this and took full advantage of using his disorder sexually. It gave him great pleasure to do everything in sixes. Six times he undressed a guy, six times he undressed a girl, and six times he would have sex with them. Six times he would check his door to see whether he locked it. He's known to purchase everything in sixes.

The number six intruded on him immensely. He's obsessive with six; he's compulsive with the number six and cannot fathom why. He has six guns and six cats among other things. He is already on his third beer and three more to go before heading to the stripper club and then jerking off later after six-lap dances. Since stripper clubs were all closed due to the county's new law most of the parties are private.

He paid his fee, got a girl to give him a lap dance, and then he hit Orange Blossom Trail for a nice young male for the night, some nights he would have a threesome. This one woman at the club was stripping for him when she asked him to dance with her, his control slipped and since he was bound by circumstances to be polite he quickened his pace and hopped onto his feet dancing the night away.

He saw what he liked and the thing was, he had to convince her that he wanted what he saw in front of him. She hooked him for a hundred dollars and before she knew what was happening he fitted her into the backside of his car and fucked her brain out. Indignation was her name for a week because she was laid up in pain.

Then the man who he picked up from a different bar in Orlando on an afternoon felt the sun sinking into his skin. On this swell try afternoon where the wind ceases to roar less through the open window of his Toyota truck, he had the best blow job. The sun's ray spilled on the floor at the back of his truck, the very spot that he had laid in the aftermath of having sex with two women some weeks ago.

The lake was out in the woods in Chuluota where he often goes with various males and/or females. It's his sexing ground where nobody knew his name and he can skinny dip in the lake. He knew the tall pine tree would keep his secret. He has been coming here for years with potential lovers who can smoke a joint of marijuana and drink his six beers without law enforcement gunning them down.

Charles Callahan doesn't like aftershave and has a rank male aura that generated a pungent scent of musky. It's hard to miss. He liked the variety in both males and females. He grinned when he thought about those varieties and a wide smile reached from ear to ear. He liked sitting on his sofa naked watching pornography movies and yes, he watched six movies at a time.

He had picked it up since he was six and his mother spanked him for eating all the chocolate chip cookies. He ran from her after the six spanks on his backside and hid from her under his bed till the next morning. He had an erection for a long time. He liked being spanked, however, he doesn't enjoy spanking.

Oh, she apologized the next morning; hugging and kissing him, nonetheless he was a changed man. Today, his mother is suffering from Alzheimer's and his sister is an ignorant fool who's after her money. There countless days she was lost trying to find where he lived.

Sanari would bring her to him. She was always in the right place at the right time guiding his mother to him considering they all lived in different buildings. His mother, Janice separated from his father for some twenty years and lived in building ten zero four. He smiled when he remembered teasing Sanari two weeks ago when they were in the supermarket and stumbled upon Fiona with Sanari saying about some topic, "the fat one."

"Oh yea, thank you."

"Oh." Upon recognizing him she continued, "we were talking about pencils for her granddaughter, the big fat ones." Sanari explained, cheeks flushed and a bit embarrassed. Charles is fat and he knew it. His stomach is pointing outwards to the point that his belt is not holding his pants in place.

"Uh-huh." He was not sure what to say because he was joking with her and the joke went haywire.

"Honest." Sanari gave him eye contact letting him know that she wasn't talking about or referring to him

"That's the point." Fiona was laughing and poor Sanari was left with her mouth opened before she realized the teasing. For some reason, he likes them both because they listened and don't judge him. They chat for lengths of time whenever he bumped into either of them. Very few people knew about this disorder and his neighbor, Sanari was the only one. His thoughts drifted to another moment in time.

"That's the whole point." He had to protect her now that he saw that man watching her at the bar. "The thing about it is and the point to be said, she and her friend, Fiona should be protected." He carried his concealed weapon with him wherever he goes and he touched it as he whispered in his drink. He wouldn't and he mentally repeated that he wouldn't protect that bitch Asa. The point was there where no point that can obstruct his decision.

All this talking from the bitch was just a verbal prop to camouflage her pain. The therapist told him that when he was in the sixth grade and was bullied by a girl. The point of it is, that she doesn't deserve anything from him because she made it quite clear on their first meeting when she speeds past him by the entrance to Helenville.

"The thing that gets me is that she gets away with it all. A doctor she is as rumor has it. I wouldn't let her operate on me by the looks of her." The bartender Jim looked at him as he whispered again to his drink. Guess he'll have to do it six more times Jim thought before he paid and leave. He's used to him doing this every week and he's an awful tipper.

Charles was looking at a waitress that was taking orders from a couple. His eyes followed her and lay upon another waitress that his eyes followed. This was how it was for him as he nursed his fourth beer. His eyes were following one waitress when they lay upon his neighbor above him at the bar. He was about to walk over to say "hi" when his instinct kicked in and shot off a warning bell in him.

He froze in time and watched his neighbor watching something.......someone, who? It took him a few minutes to follow his eyes and pinpoint who he was observing, more spying on. The expression on his face told Charles that this was intense and his emotion was blank. He knew from doing the math that this is no ordinary admiration. According to the intensity and his instinct, it was hate. Why?

"That's the thing," he whispered into his beer, "If you want to harbor on hate go ahead. Don't harbor it on Sanari. You got me to deal with and I am a whole lot of trouble with a little bit of hell." Charles's tight hand automatically left his beer and lower it to the steel in his pocket. With satisfaction that his gun made him feel secure, he smiled. He has nothing to lose and someone has to protect Sanari. He's unemployed anyway, he has the time. Why is his neighbor watching those three ladies? He knew them well especially Asa as he lived in the next building from her really building ten zero six, apartment eleven thirty-six. He knew Fiona too, what gives? What's going on here? He left his stomach crunched and knew that this is bigger than what he wanted to believe. He's going to have to mention to Sanari what he observed because his instinct is telling him to be on alert. The question is, why is his neighbor watching them with so much intense hate? What is going on here? Many times, he was over at the pool with Fiona and Sanari chatting with them when Asa appeared. He swore that she was spying on them because she always showed up exactly when they are together, never separated. Does Asa have anything to do with that creepy guy?

The village gossip as she is named doesn't fit in with anyone at the complex. He's very careful what he communicated when she's around. God damn it, that woman can talk, non-stop. She carried on a conversation all by herself.

Sanari and Fiona always included him in their conversations and say "Hi" to him when they saw him. That bitch pretended not to see him and looked in every direction except at him. The whole of Helenville knew that Asa followed Sanari and Fiona where ever they go. She is the village gossip as everyone called her and much more; she is a whole lot of hell.

Washed out drunken doctor with no purpose or nothing to do, is what Asa is about. Oh hell, she's involved with the swindler James with no purpose. At least Charles convinced himself that he has a purpose, unemployed he may be, nonetheless, he admired nice-looking males and females. That's a purpose.

Charles smiled and lost interest as his eyes followed a waiter who winked at him as she passed and he chuckled. His cheeks turned pink and he turned in his seat following her with his eyes. He stopped suddenly and stared at this neighbor as his eyes connected with his green ones. A staring match began quickly and lasted only a few seconds, nonetheless, the messages were clear for both men.

Charles chiseled into granite eyes that studied him with contempt and rage that bored into his neighbor Craig's cold eyes. He gave him back the same, hoping he knew just how fond he was of Sanari and Fiona. He didn't care a damn who his idiot thought of him, he wanted him to know that he was aware that he was looking at Fiona and Sanari.

What if he's wrong and it's Asa he's attracted to, that he's watching. A smile curled on the bottom of his lips and he silently told Craig through his thoughts that he was welcome to her any time.

The village gossip has an admirer. Well, what do you know?

Someone actually likes Asa besides that loser of a boyfriend she had around her. Good for her; they suit each other. Hate will carry them far into each other arms.

Another smile tugged at Charles's lips as he took some bills out of his wallet and laid them on the bar. He turned to look at Craig who had long lost interest and was watching the girls again. Neither Charles nor Craig is afraid nor intimated by the other. One was a killer and the other a protector; one is defined by a knife and the other by a gun.

15

It was a rainy night and most of the retirement community was attending the monthly association meeting. Everyone was displeased with the current management team as well as the board of directors. They all sat paying attention to what was being said, listening to the lies and corruption being told only to cover up the misuse of money, their money.

A lone figure stood by the lake admiring his handy work of sinking the bags in the water. He had waited until daylight turned into the darkness to step out so he can stand here without anyone noticing him.

The last girl was saltier as her descent was more pungent to an aromatic favor as his tongue touched her dark olive skin. The Spanish blood oozed freely with the blade of his knife. Her aromatic was of melon due to an earlier mixed with something spicy in the earth from which it had sprung.

She had left nothing to be missed only the moonlight that had streamed through the window showing her naked body. The slat of moonlight had stripped his bed and she lay there smiling at him enjoying the brutal ride he gave her after her body was drained of blood. The light from the bright moon had washed through the opened visors tinting their silhouette with silver, gliding her hair to sparkle as he raped her dead body.

How he loved them when they don't talk back to him. He didn't know her name nor does he care. The killing was more important. This one fought back and he was hurt and had to silence her before his ritual was completed. He touched his chest where her nails had left marks and as he played the images again, tremors worked through his body. Agony bored deep into his face and injured shoulder as sweat rolled off his forehead into his eyes.

"Bitch, you got what you deserve."His tone simmered with frustration and anger. The memories came rushing in as he wiped them away with his hands. The images never came without the familiar regret of his past and the anger that had built over the years. He was punished for his parents' anger and only his anger helped him survive life. She exercised her anger when she fought him.

A voice came through to him and voiced its opinion. "You aren't punished for your anger only by your anger." He didn't want to hear this one voice that would make him wrong and he doesn't what to be wrong; he told the voice who he named Kimberly to "shut the fuck up."

With the rain clouds drifting through, a little illumination came from the moon above now craved a shapely shadow upon the water. The palm and pine trees filtered with whatever little moonlight the clouds ate through, glittering with raindrops. The moon dust silvered in the early hour of the night. The moonlight softened the blunt angles of his stubble jaw as he stared at his reflection upon the water; a smile slowly tugged his chapped lips.

The killer turned around and cut through the foliage with the white shape of a man-made waterfall that led to the building where the meeting was held. The owners of the apartments were retired with a fixed income, therefore how can they raise the maintenance fee so ridiculously high? Many owners are having difficulty in paying, they let the payment slide until it goes into foreclosure or they gave up and abundant their property. Even the ones without any mortgage are having a tremendous struggle in making the maintenance payment. Where are they going to get the money from?

The others who aren't retired either inherited the apartment or it was sold to them by the heirs of the retiree. They are the working bunch and if they too cannot afford it how can the retirees? The owners who are walking off are leaving for less expensive places while the ones who remain have a larger maintenance fee to cover the loss of the ones who left. This isn't right nor is it fair. What's it that they don't understand? Trap within their youths, darkness had fallen swiftly upon the room of angry owners. A silver moonlight shuns through the windows casting a shadow on the tiny room. The management deliberately used this room and adjusted the lighting hoping those who cannot sit will leave and they would have fewer questions to answer. They were little light to see the expression on the board members' faces. Everyone was asking questions and the board is not responding to any. They sat there watching the audience.

Where's the money going to? Who knew how long the night will last, hopefully not until a new day dawned. Through the windows, hazy moonlight filtered in, mixed with a fresh scent from the rain. Kissed by the light from the moon shadows, it had fallen to rest on the residents of Helenville.

In the midst of the listening, anger, and objections from the attendees, sat Craig Altner whose eyes were permanently fixed on the three ladies he saw a few days earlier at the bar. Unknowingly to him, sitting behind him is Charles Callahan who is watching him watching the ladies. All other eyes, including the three ladies, were on one woman, Caroline Waters. She's the bitch that caused all of this because she has a trust fund and can afford it. She figured out a way to financially rape these poor elders and the few young. She also has someone in Tallahassee who she paid thousands of dollars to sign her documents whenever there was someone who reported her.

This is a company that is hiding behind another company, that wants this particular property because the son of a bitch has some pitiful dream to build a better more modern complex where he can charge more and become richer; he paid thousands of dollars to the board members of Helenville to "get rid" of the residents.

Who puts that Walters woman on the board? She was the one who misused the money. She took the money as the treasurer of the board and redecorated her apartment, pre-paying the painters who were her friends.

There's this massive mortgage on the property to the bank and the building still needs painting. The company of the painters filed for bankruptcy and disappeared from view. This is what the residents are demanding to know?

Craig is vexed, vexed to the bone about the mistreatment of people by others who are inhumane. Scum bags people are greedy, greedy scum bags he thought as he watched everyone in front of him. He was having a mental debate about whether he should voice his thoughts of anger when he saw the moonlight on Sanari's face.

Craig Altner studied her as his face transformed in the moonlight dazzling him and creating shadows that discerned the color of his pale blond hair. She glanced up quickly; her black eyes met his blue ones throwing sparks at him. He smiled big and she smiled back as she moved her eyes acknowledging others. That was good enough for him. He then turned around in his chair coming eye to eye with that man again from the restaurant!

The blood ran out of Craig Peter Altner as he stared at Charles Callahan. God help him, the man is staring at him. A wicked smile came out of Craig Altner's mouth as his thoughts ran rapidly slicing him into shreds and dumping him into the lake. His smile became wider and he turned into his seat still smiling an etched deep line on his face. He pulled his six feet frame with one hundred and sixty pounds onto his feet and left abruptly. No one noticed him leaving, not even Charles Callahan nor was he missed.

Craig had enough. Besides he wanted his thoughts to formulate how he is going to slice that ugly-looking man who stared at him. His need to kill is coming up in his stomach again. He received no satisfaction from the last bitch that left marks on his torso. He demanded satisfaction, after all, that is why he killed to have self-satisfaction. Soon, very soon he comforted his stomach with several rubs and touched the pain that poured out from his shoulders and chest.

Back at the meeting, Charles Callahan complimented himself with aplomb and on behalf of his mother. His smile widened as Fiona and Sanari turned and waved at him. His poise was shattered. Two beautiful ladies acknowledged him; they waved at him and no one else. This is huge for him and he felt more of a man than ever before in his adult life. This is what he always wanted to be accepted and acknowledged by the opposite sex.

Fiona and Sanari have done that, not Asa. All attention was drawn to the president of the association who concluded the meeting with a promise to address all complaints. The residents were disappointed as they left the building.

Charles Callahan sat there wondering what he can do or whether he should let it go. He already asked his mother for money to pay his mortgage until he can find a computer technician job. He emptied his 401K and halfway through his savings that went to support him and the lap dances. He's going to have to give his pleasure up because it's too expensive and settled for pornography.

He must remember to close his blinds because Asa caught him sitting naked on the sofa giving himself a hand job. She told everyone who would listen and if he didn't overhear her he would never have found out what a bitchy gossiper she was as if she is any different than him. What did her boyfriend tell him that she's into pain and wild sex?

Charles Callahan shoved those sexual thoughts aside for later and bought his thoughts back to the meeting he left a moment ago. Caroline Walters was speaking to the President of Helenville. He guessed they didn't realize that he was still sitting in his seat with the dim lights blocking his silhouette from them or maybe his shape had been blended with the shadows of the moonlight. Who cares a fuck? He can't remember much of the meeting anyway. He had other important things on his mind, only if he could remember what. Anger was mixed with astonishment making the bitch from hell voice raise, he heard the whole conversation. Caroline Waters' voice cracked from rage provoking the others to her anger. She couldn't keep her anger from her voice much less her squeeze clean image she portrayed to everyone else except the resident of Helenville who knew her true colors.

The anger had taken a few moments to hit the others who had no choice other than to listen to her and when they did from what he can see in the dim light they were scared. When the anger came from the others, however, it came at the same moment she was yelling in a rage about who was in charge.

An angry yelling match erupted as everyone was saying what

they think and felt. Distracted by the group's anger coupled with greed Charles Callahan heard names of who she knew and who she paid and how much each of the board members was paid to get "these ignorant fools to leave." Let them assume what they wanted because facts will be falling upon them soon. Wait till the others hear what he heard.

Charles Callahan's anger dissipated and he tried to summon some anger and none surfaced; not even a little agitation. Something is going to have to give and right now it looked as if people are going to be without homes come Christmas.

The lawyer is a piece of trash because she was representing the community last week and switched and presently representing Caroline Waters to stay on the board. They somehow paid the personnel in Tallahassee to switch to their side and the government is against retirement communities.

Conspiracy and fraud are everywhere and there's no one it seemed that cares about the people. What can he do? He is an unemployed man with no money to seek help. No one would help them with this problem and no one wanted to take on a case for free. He cannot ask the community to pool their money together to hire a lawyer. They have none.

This is Florida, one of the retirement states, and no legislation to protect them. Everyone even the retirement homes is ripping the retiree off their money. There is no justice. God help the United States of America.

16

Madre de Dior! She did it! She stole the tapes from James Asher right under his nose. When she entered Asa's apartment with her tools he was passed out drunk on the floor with the tapes in his hand and the statement that had the transfer of Asa's money to him. She took them both and left.

Piece of cake, who would've thought that her job was so easy? Relief left her light-headed as Olympia Van Amstel settled into her apartment. Her undercover is over as everyone in the complex knows that she is working on the Fleischer murder. They all have a story of destruction about Asa.

She heard it all except for those two females, Sanari and Fiona. Time to hear what input they have in this entire ethos. Asa Fleischer's philosophy was conning and blackmail. What are theirs and Ryan Reyes? She hadn't interviewed Ryan as yet because she's trying to bring herself under control as a result her professionalism would be intact.

Right now, it's not where she is a concern. Suddenly she felt a peace being stirred between them and realized it wouldn't be difficult to question him. What is her problem?

Olympia felt sensations run down her spine and up into her brain making her dizzy thinking about Ryan. She wondered what he thought of her yesterday when she walked in without the usual FBI attire and donned a dress with heels. She knew what she was doing and hope he didn't figure it out. She wanted him to come to her instead of standing giving her a cool smile, a smile that chased her sadness away. Her lips had echoed his smile, a teasing smile.

She had taken her time in dressing. When she finished marketing herself in the mirror, she was confident that she'll have the highest bidder, Ryan. With a twist seductive smile on her light red lips, she glanced for the last time into the mirror liking her black short backless dress with her red stiletto. She decided to take her FBI jacket, he will think that she was working, she hoped.

Olympia gave herself a wink in the rearview mirror of her car before she entered The Twixt Peach. She had asked all law enforcement to call her at this time, she would look extra busy and on the job. She ordered steak, potatoes, and broccoli instead of her usual burger and fries. She was busy as well imagined and was even surprised when a few of the officers joined her for dinner giving her the latest development on the murder of Asa Fleischer. She soon had forgotten all about Ryan, focusing on the case. She wondered what he had thought.

At one time when she stood up to maneuver Officer Gross to her table, she thought that he hid a smile. She did see a grin that nipped at the corner of his mouth when Officer White with the corner report entered looking for her, however, she refused to look at him to confirm it.

Little did she know that her dress with heels and warm smile ignited a fire in the pit of Ryan's stomach and set his heart burning with love. He liked what he saw and knew that she was for keeps, however, he decided he has to figure out how to let her know his feelings for her.

Olympia was on her patio with a beer, munching on a bag of stale and soft potato chips. She was tired and surviving on little sleep because she had to be alert to enter Asa's apartment.

James Asher didn't fall asleep till three in the morning. She was up listening to the bug she placed and had to wait until there was no more cursing except his snoring. This morning for a moment, she watched a gigantic black cloud gather over her and Asa's apartment and rolled off towards the lake. Lemon permeated the air and she figured that someone has a tree somewhere close. The clouds had hung low in the sky with a light breeze tossing all things light to dance. She could have sworn that she saw a hooded man ascending the path to the lake, however, he vanished into the grey mist. She couldn't follow him because she was on a mission. She glanced at her sofa and at the bag of tapes, she has carefully released from Asher's hand.

There were about two hundred various recordings of people's apartments she bugged. Her choices reflected who she was, a bitter spiteful, hateful bitch. She had something on almost everyone in the retirement complex, except for Amani and Blanchard. Why is that so strange? Something very fishy here, she can smell it.

There is no cobweb of innocence with those two, Asa and James. The tapes from their collection apartment were all pornography. The conversation of Sanari and Fiona was nothing of importance as if they knew of Asa's bugs. Why keep the tapes? "Oof! Doc, you tell him! You go girl, tell him what's what? Keep him in line. Just don't ride him so hard that he'll leave town." The laughter came through from the tape with a sound from Fleischer, Amani, and Blanchard.

Someone else was there, who? What was in the conversation for that person to say that to them? She had replayed the tape six more times before she recognized a male's voice. "I know that voice! Where did I hear it from?" Olympia's enunciation was with a frown, a frown that etched into her brow for so long that she was rubbing it when there was a knock on her door. She automatically went for her weapon which was on the glass top table by the lamp. There was no light on only a candle burning from the further side of the living room.

She let out a breath and walked lightly to the door peeking through the hole to see who was there. No one! What in the world? Who would do this to an FBI agent at five o'clock in the morning? Did the person leave a package? Olympia glanced at the active laptop left on the sofa. She closed in a few feet of distance and punched in the file for the cameras. She had installed cameras in and around her apartment for safety. She pulled up her door camera and saw the schizzy silhouette of Craig Altner.

Her stomach growled into the action of warning and she pulled the paperwork off the floor of every person's profile and interview she did, looking for his folder. She turned on the lamp beside her and looked for his photograph stapled on the information sheet. She looked for his name and her instinct kicked in rapidly. "Schizoid, oh hell, this is trouble! I can feel it! What does he want from or with her?" She picked up her gun and opened the door retrieving the package left there.

Since he was wearing gloves she knew that there were no fingerprints, however, to be on the safe side she put a pair on and slowly opened the package praying that it was not a bombing device. She was shocked at the photographs that tumbled out from the package. Clearly, he was unaware of the camera and didn't know that she would be up.

Who raped, tortured, and murdered all those women? How many are there? Why did he deliver them unless he wanted to be caught? Did Craig Altner murder these women? Where are they now? Are they in the lake? Was he the one dumping....something in the lake? She'll have to put a surveillance team on him.

Olympia pulled his profiled sheet and read the report that was given to her and his activities when Fleischer was murdered. He stated that he was sleeping, however, she thinks differently. If he's up at three in the morning he wasn't sleeping on the night Fleischer received a bullet in her head. Oh no, he wants me to investigate him then that's what he'll get, a thorough investigation. She picked her cell up and hit number two on the redial buttons.

"Pillsworth, don't you ever sleep?"

"No."

"I do. I was," came from the sleepy voice on the other end.

"You do sound sexy," Olympia whispered in the receiver.

"I am wide awake. Tell me your troubles. I'm all yours darlin'."

Laughter rang out deep from her and she bluntly and boldly asked. "Anything on Amani, Randy?"

"I love it when you talk dirty. No, and yes. She arrived as a referee from an unknown Middle Eastern country and is listed that she's from Jordan. Her name was Farfanzi and that's it. The photos were an identical match. She changed her name when she was twenty-five. Is Farfanzi or Sanari her real name? I don't know. She unquestionably has an Eastern heritage. She worked and paid her taxes and invested in various legal stuff. She is legit. Can I go back to sleep, pretty please?"

"Check out Craig Altner, e-mailing the dynamics." She heard a clicked on the other end and hung up. Her thoughts ran amok with the remembrance of her exile to this outland retirement compound. Eloquently, she slid her body off the sofa and folded her arms over the folded knee, burying her head into her arms. "I was not the only one who ran away, you did too, Amani. We found different places to hide." They were all running from someone or something, even Asa Fleischer. She was running from pain and ran into more pain and had pleasure inflicting pain.

The affair with her partner was vivid as she fastidiously permitted her thoughts to flow before inhaling several breaths and gaining control. She needed to discipline her passion for being involved with the wrong men. Is Ryan Reyes the wrong man? Denial of her choosing the wrong man won over the curiosity of wanting to know him as she continued to comfort herself.

In the saga of her life, it seemed that she is always separating the paddy from the rice, the wheat from the chaff between her perfect neatnik world of the FBI, and her personal life. Here is the Sussex place with its secrets.

Everyone is hiding something. The communication snafu was muddled in every aspect with her one, mmm no two investigations of Fleischer and Altner. Presently, she felt that she is throwing her precious energy around willy-nilly. What a frightful mess!

17

"Oh, Sanari can you help me, please?" Sanari lying by the pool, upon hearing her name raised her semi-tanned body off the chair. She looked around to see who called her. Upon seeing Janet Lorrison holding groceries bags and breathless, she pushed to her feet, covering the short distance to her, relieving the weight of the groceries bags from her.

Janet Lorrison was a sixty-two Caucasian female who was disabled and lived in the same building ten zero three, apartment number ten fifty-six. Before her forced retirement, she was a manager for an electronic company, divorced with two children. She stood five feet three inches, one hundred and sixty-five pounds with more health issues than anyone Sanari knew living in Sussex Place.

As Sanari took her shopping bags and walked with her, listening to her talking about her pacemaker batteries going dead, how she missed the first surgery and she's on a standby list, waiting for the doctor to call her and tell her when they will replace the pacemaker. She's watching death closing in on her.

In the meantime, she can die. She felt that her life is on standby and that at any minute she can be expired. To top this, her mother of ninety-two is in the hospital, not doing good. Neither one of her children had even bothered to call her in the last month nor does she feel loved. Needless to say, she was in tears.

Sanari was used to her complaints as she heard them on numerous occasions and always gave her compassion. She understood Janet and as she listened to her, she realized how much they have in common. She wished she could contact her family and see what they are up to; not her dad, her mother, brothers, and sister.

Ingenuity, she couldn't and had to continue living life wondering about them in the same way that water flows uninterrupted. She did something she rarely does; she leaned in and kissed Janet on her checks.

A wide smile lit her face as well as her light blue eyes. She had a lot to thank her for after all; she is healthy and has good friends with much to be grateful for in her life here.

Janet's mother Pia demanded custody of her two children from Janet. The Sate was giving her money to maintain the children, Pia wanted the money. The daughter, Anna left as soon as she turned sixteen and never contacted Janet or her grandmother Pia. Pia had conveniently forgotten to notify the State that Anna left. Anna did, however, contact the State and the money stopped.

Pia kept asking Janet for money. Pia turned Todd into a disabled so that she can continue receiving the money from the state. Todd became aggressive toward this mother, Janet, and remained in Pia's care until she broke her hip and went into a retirement home. Todd was in the hospital for unknown reasons as no one can figure out what is wrong with him. Of course, the hospital kept him as long as they can for the money from Medicaid.

Janet suffered tremendously upon the death of her last daughter Bea who died from drowning. She was on the phone talking to Pia when Bea aged two wandered outside and walked into the pool. Janet found her some hours later. The death of her child had become a nasty promise for her future, not just a horrible memory of the past.

Pia never let Janet forget what a horrible mother she is and held her captive with a treat. Janet sank into a depression and slipped into chronic depression when she found out that her husband Todd was cheating, however, she did nothing about it and maintained the status quo. Todd divorced her the second he found out that she knew and married his lover. He died five years later from a massive heart attack.

With depression sinking her into despair, divorce over, and the loss of her children to her mother, Janet buried herself in her work and made money. Pia used every wimped she has to pull out as much money from her as she can and what Pia wanted Pia gets. This tugged love-hate relationship between mother and daughter survived the rigors of years and has flowed as pain in the body of Pia, Janet, and Todd.

They all have some disorders and diseases consuming a massive amount of prescription drugs. In the years that followed, Janet worked and party heavy. She saved and invested her money and bought into the Sussex complex by a flux. A client had inherited the apartment and Janet capitalized on it. She continued her lifestyle for years and gave into her mother's money demand often. She contacted her daughter who refused to have a relationship with her. She lost all contact with Anna and her grandson, Andrew.

Money and karma became her sanctuary. She blamed and prayed and complained to Sanari who listened since they met some five years ago. As groceries were laid on the floor of Janet's apartment, Sanari stood listening to the various complaints and helplessness that Janet kept babbling about. She smiled and gave Janet eye contact and the comfort she required, however, the minute Sanari left all was forgotten.

Sanari had no desire to remember anything because she had heard it a million times before and would no doubt hear it again a million times more. Janet, Sanari concluded was a beautiful woman with the best smooth complexion and skin in the complex. As aged as she looked presently, the beauty laid in her face which can still be seen upon close inspection, along with the once kindness held in her eyes.

In the midst of all of her troubles, she was given a final blow to her life's existence. Her body sagged from the condor of her reality the day she was raped by one of her dates. The attacker is running loose while Janet is still paid dearly for the repercussion of the loss of her children and being raped.

Janet helped Fiona make the final decision about her rapist. Sanari told Fiona about Janet's rape and gave her the final push she needed about what to do with her rapist.

As Sanari swam laps in the pool, Craig Altner walked by as she pulled her body still on the six feet depth of the pool. She held on to the rim for support when he said to her. "Nice day. You look nice." His voice was sharp with anger and squeaky from drinking excessively while his eyes which color she could not see from the distance between them drop as if he was high on smoking a joint of marijuana.

Unsettled by his compliment, she dropped her eyes from his to the onyx of his t-shirt. With a forced smile on her lips and having no intention of replying, she swam away from him continuing unnecessary laps. She saw when he left on her third lap and waited until he disappeared around the corner of the next building before she pulled her exhausted body out of the pool and flopped into her chair.

She felt Craig's anger and his hate riding off his body. She can tell that he lives in his anger and required revenge. The flare-up of his anger must be tremendously violent and she can see from his misdemeanor that when it swept him up in a swirl of rage and confusion he often loses control. Sanari caught him many times looking at her, more or less lusting after her. He's committed some sort of fantasy that included her or Fiona or both.

This particular man has something working up a storm in his thought; whatever it is, it's giving her violent vibes of energy that spell murder. Maybe he was the one dumping bodies in the lake. Who would believe her, besides Fiona? It was distasteful the way he would sneak up on her when she least expected it.

Today was no coincidence; he knew she would be here; he pretended to pass by. Everyone around here knew each other schedules. She usually is here with Fiona except that she had to work today and she came anyway to do her laps.

Anger was about to surface and burst out of her when she thought of how stupid men are when they wanted her attention. She needed to release this anger she picked up from him before she consults tomorrow.

A visit to her Zen teacher this afternoon looked promising. A smile tucked on her lips she retrieves her things and walked the short distance to her apartment. Her contentedness with Zen practice took place by accident. She was looking for a place to find inner peace from her past when a client told her that he practiced meditation. She began visiting various palaces and was looking for a center that was holding meditation when she walked into a building asking for direction.

It was a Zen center and decided to stay and experience what they were practicing. Zen practice is of awareness of the present moment; just as it is and with whatever is there in existence. It is comprised of taking the energy of the body and thoughts that are habitually used to create and maintain the self. It focused the self in the present on the moment in time as it is and does not interact with what is taking place.

Meditation and soul-searching are certainly back in vogue as she found out just how many people are doing what she is seeking. Ubiquitous is everywhere. Possibilities are everywhere. This universe contained with everyone, within them, lay infinity of energy. She learned how to develop direct awareness in herself as well as with people, places, and things and at the same time attempt to gain calm and patience within her being.

Most important she gained knowledge on how to fully bring this awareness to every moment of her life; a dawning of new awareness and consciousness working together for her. She had crossed through a place of darkness and as much as a new day dawned, she still experienced nightmares from her past. She had witnessed a major spiritual transformation occurring on each first light as a new day broke over the horizon. She's working with her teacher on her last bit of fear that kept her awake after the reoccurrence of the same old nightmares. Although she had graduated summa cum laude she felt she has a long way to go with Zen practice.

Sanari showered and drove to her Zen teacher, Noshi for mediation. After an hour of bringing her thoughts into awareness and a lengthy chat with Noshi, she nosed her Jag to The Twixt Peach where she would be meeting Fiona for dinner. It was strange to be there without Asa, their second drink without the constant chatter of their bat out of hell, their living nightmare for the last five years. She smiled at the irony of having nightmares every night and living with one every day.

"One down, one more to go." Her words were an ere whisper of a bittersweet moment of nothing.

18

The unparalleled journey of heartbreak lured in the distant summer as fall turned into winter. The sun cleansed the arctic tundra as the moon shone full on this October night before Halloween.

A Spider had set up housekeeping in various dark corners of the house. In the door jamb, the eggs hatched as the mother watched the other inhabitant spaced the carpet floor a thousand times.

Another sleepless night and how many was this? Mother spider watched as each of her babies came through the eggs. She had discreetly made her home here disguising her eggs, watching the huge predator spaced the floor for what seemed forever. His giant hunter made Darth Vader show up as Pollyanna.

With her babies safely born she guided them under the sofa. She peeked from under her new home and watched the movement of the spacer for a second or two before venturing into safety. Whatever he is, he's no gatekeeper of good because she sensed evil from within, no softness, only hardness, no love, only hate.

The other humanoid that came through his threshold vanished into thin air; she never saw anyone twice visiting him. She saw them all once and never again. She can sense his desperation; desperate doesn't look good on him. None of her business; she has her children to think about.

Despite the dust and neglect, Craig Altner found warmth in the fading magazine's pages, books all on erotic and murders, particularly various cuttings of murders taped to the wall and cupboards. Even the photo of the young girl, his grandmother that was mirrored in the crowded bookshelf gave him comfort.

The pocket of masculinity in a lifeless house showed some sorrow as to what he is currently experiencing. There was a hint of intensified anger in the air.

With the inert movement of Craig swayed a little to the right as he stumbled on the telephone white pages left there since he inherited the apartment some three years. A single note of paper slipped through the crack of pages and Craig stood still for a long time looking at it. Eventually coming out from this irritation he was in the present moment realizing that the paper he recognized as well as the handwriting.

Patterns from the street lights cast dancing shadowy figures on the ceiling. His anxiety climbed with every breath he took and irritation flashed across his white blemished face and button nose. He rubbed his bald head and drank the hot beer. He spaced some more. A tidal wave of voile thoughts moved through him and he tried to tandem them and failed.

Frustration rose at his obvious attempt to say hi to her. Resentment entered with a need to see her was tapered off to stay away from her. What he had thought of her two years ago had no relevance to the moment in time. The bitch didn't even say "hi" worry ate at him and he wondered if he had said it wrong. How can anyone say "hi" wrong? The thought sat uncomfortably with him and he abandoned it.

Angry that he had gotten to her finally and received no response from her; what did he do wrong? Doesn't she know that he loved her? The thought cut his breath for a second and he exhaled loudly shaking Maude the spider awake. She peeked through from under the sofa to see grey poly daylight seeping past through the blinds falling on his pulse that sharply hammered in his temple. She pulled back into the safety net and counted her twelve babies, thinking that she will have to find a new home soon. His man is crazy, he never sleeps. Furry and terror filled the room.

With two million thoughts rushing through his day and night it pumped his adrenaline high, slowly building his intensified anger into fury. His fury was built solid for anyone who wanted his Fiona. "Fiona." He whispered. He bent and picked the paper off the carpet, opening and straightening it to its full length. He felt his energy drain from him and he was fully infused to kidnap her and bring her here.

"Murphy's Law-anything that goes wrong does go wrong." He

spoke out loud to the foul air and dragged his length to sit on the sofa. His uncle used to sing that to him whenever he has gotten something wrong.

An avalanche of emotions went into chaos and his thoughts went crazy. Not even a close association with Fiona could erase the effects of his past left behind by the memories of a tenacious goblin called the White Water Killer.

Thoughts swirled around rapidly taking him into his past and the paper with Fiona's handwriting pulling him into the present moment. He was pulled by hundreds of thoughts and emotions, even love or what he thinks love is with his twisted thoughts. When he met Fiona, he had let love guide his life and for a short time, love shone until he saw those photographs of his uncle and who he killed; the very ones he left at the door of the FBI agent.

He ended his affair with Fiona because those horrible images kept popping up whenever he made love to her. Sometimes a human emotion is caught in situations where there's no way to keep them from hurting her or/and him.

Where did he get that from? Probably from a show on the TV or a movie he rented.

"Don't you see I had to let her go or I would've killed her?" He told the paper. The shape of the emotions and desires that had surfaced when he was with Fiona gave birth to words that he had spoken to her and she had written it down.

"Love is a gift, between you and me,
An inner glow that constantly reflects Warm feelings between you and me
Love is a gift, between you and me
Two lovers share trust and care
Till we grow old
Our love is a gift."

"Lies, lies, lies, all lies...where's his woman to love him, where's his gift. Lies, lies lies, they all are liars" Several inner voices at once echoed lies so loud that Craig ran into his bedroom and threw his weight face down into the unmade bed. He buried his face into the bed where all the dead sperms lay and pulled the pillow over his head.

"Lies, lies, lies, I hate you, Fiona." He squelched and mumbled in the red sheet that covered him. The distinction between hate lies in the manner in which he emphasized the word "hate." Something was out of synch with his demeanor and it defined a comeback as a copy killer. He is on the cutting edge of a new trend with luring innocent males and females into his apartment and then killing and hiding them in what he named the island in the lake "Devil's creek."

This is what drove psychopaths, the many thoughts that were never mature or what they called "voices in the head" mixed in with the sensations of "feeling good" with fantasy. Truth is seldom acknowledged because serial killers directed personal anger at people that represented them.

This glitch is the reason they often slipped through the radar and aren't caught until they wanted to be caught.

Lying next to his bed on the carpet is a centerfold of his childhood crush "pure virgin Mary" in the latest playboy. Everyone who's impotent is jerking off watching his "Mary," the girl of his dreams and the first one he kissed. Thoughts flooded of the men and what they were doing watching Mary's full frontal view with her legs slightly spread and her hands laying right where her legs joined her body just above her pelvic. The suggestion angered Craig more than ever and he knew that some man tricked her into taking the photograph.

He refused to believe that his "Mary" would ever do such a thing and deliberately hurt him. He grabbed hold of a knife lying on the foot of the sofa and violently stabbed the inflated doll lying next to him several times. The spider jumped from a deep sleep and watched the destruction made by man. She made a mental list to find a new home. This one is not working out.

Craig Peter Altner was one hundred percent delusional. He's infatuated with Sanari as she used to say "hi" to him and asked him "how he was doing" two years ago when he first came to live here. He never replied and soon the "hi, how you are doing stopped." She began to avoid him because a high voltage charge of anger came off his body and she sensed danger.

He thinks her name is Fiona and often confused the two girls. How that happened is beyond a mentally healthy person because

Sanari has dark olive skin with black hair compared to Fiona's white tan skin and blond hair.

The note he claimed that Fiona wrote with the spoken to her was a note he found in his uncle's belonging with the females he murdered. This goes to show how delusional and confused he is about what he is seeing.

His perception is wrapped with images of hundreds of unprocessed thoughts and images he pulled from books, magazines, erotica, violent movies, and the photographs of his uncles; the very ones he gave Special Agent Olympia Van Amstel.

He couldn't stand what his uncle did to all those women; not that he does that. Denial is very much Craig Peter Altner's persona. What he does is not killing; it is emptying his anger of his childhood upon the victims he killed. His delusion is very severe that he doesn't know one color from the next and refused to acknowledge that he killed both males and females while his uncle only killed young women in the mid-twenty, twenty-five to be precise, and not one day older.

Yes, Craig James Altner hunted for females who are celebrating their twenty-fifth birthday and seduced them into him buying them a drink. At the stroke of midnight, he would enter their home and chloroform them while sleeping, picked them up as if they were a bag of potatoes, take them to the woods behind his brother's house, killed them, and then have sex with them.

He mounted a camera in the tree that automatically took the photographs. This was his reward later when he's all alone drinking his beer to celebrate what a good boy he was and what a good job he did; he was never caught.

Craig James Altner was never caught and died of alcoholism at the age of forty and was cremated. Most of his handy work was done in the woods where his nephew, a replica of looks first saw him. How many women did he kill? Fifteen, yes, that's right.

Fifteen women he killed starting on his twenty-fifth birthday when he accidentally killed his girlfriend on her twenty-fifth birthday. He was playing with his knife on her body when he had this urge to slash her throat which he did and found out he enjoyed it very much.

19

Sanari was walking to her apartment from the pool when she heard a loud noise. She stopped and followed the sound that became louder. It was a black suitcase that was dragged down the stairs from apartment ten seventy-three, right next to hers. She turned and walked away. Nothing new, it was filled with money from selling cocaine.

Diego was what everyone knew him as and no one knew the wife's name. They were Puerto Ricans and they do speak English regardless of what they said, "No English" when anyone tried to talk with them. They don't care to know anyone and avoid everyone. Very suspicious activities were vivid from ten in the night to four in the morning.

Fiona said being high on marijuana is different from being high on cocaine. He is always high and dragged that darn suitcase down those stairs every week. Both he and his wife seemed to be in their mid-thirties with the wife working and he staying home. They ran a profitable business with his cousin in apartment ten forty-nine who rented from the son of deceased Robert Matteau.

Diego and his wife telegraphing their nightly movement very carefully, however, the residents of Sussex Place in building ten zero three are well aware of their late-night activities.

What gives with them is everyone guesses except with whom Diego has in his company every day. They are loud and tried to be intimidating. Asa said that he looked like a drug distributor and the other one, his cousin is the seller. For whatever it's worth there are strange behaviors for young couples to have and maintain in a relationship.

Then again how did Asa know so much about these people? She

sounded as if she spied on them to have such accurate information. Of course, it's better to have accurate information than false ones. She had to have been spying on them. Did they kill her?

Diego was short about five feet five inches with short curly black hair, hooded black eyes, and two left feet that turned into each other. Foot curved into each other, knees knocking together as he walked. His wife is also short about five feet with bottled light brown with blond streaks in her long hair. She has a rounded figure, rounded slim shoulders with a short round nose that seemed to be stuck in the air.

There are enough people with abnormal behaviors living here than in most places. Sanari's thoughts drifted to the night not so long ago with another neighbor Hank who wanted to jerk off on her toes. Asa sent him to her knowing that she would tell him to go and not come back.

On the twist of it all, Sanari deliberately told Hank the days that Asa goes for her manicure and pedicure.

She was smiling as she opened the door to her apartment. What a life they lived here. There's no time to be bored and then there are so many secrets that are hidden behind the walls of this community.

Sanari was toweling her hair when the doorbell rang; she hurriedly ran to open the door. She expected Fiona as they were going for their usual drink at The Twixt Peach.

What she saw upon opening the door left her speechless. An all-American hunk standing there looking at her, eye contact understood. She sensed fear, scared, and honesty all mixed into one huge hunk.

Time stood still. Eyes connected and simultaneously, sensations tickled down their spine, she blushed. Then and only when her black eyes broke contact from excessively blushing and traveling the length of him that she saw his right hand covering the side of his waist and blood pouring out of him. Black eyes stopped traveling and in a flash met his gray ones filled with pain.

"I called 911." She told him and turned to get her cell phone.

"No." The hunk yelled and stepped into her pallor closing the door. Feet walked towards each other and the whisper of skin sliding along cotton brushed up against the hunk as he leaned forward in a fall. She pushed him up to stand and moved away not in fear to give them space to breathe.

Upon seeing his movement, she stopped and gave him her full attention. This required diplomatic maneuvering. Sanari stood there watching him, waiting for an explanation and surprising herself that she wasn't afraid. She wasn't afraid of him even though she knew he had a gun. What seemed ages, however, only minutes he spoke again in a whisper.

"I am looking for Falcon, he lives here." "No, he doesn't anymore. I do. He died some five years ago and his son Josh sold me this place ten years ago." Seeing his raised brow, she continued. "He was living in a retirement home." His bread was about two inches on his very tan face and his long nose flared with anger mostly pain. Light from the patio attracted itself to him.

"Uh-oh?" Came the reply with pain in his voice.

"You're hurt, let me help you. I know you don't want the police or go to the hospital. All I asked is for me to look at it." She pointed at the red mark on his white shirt with blood pouring out more rapidly. The hunk nodded. Warmth poured into his eyes and he almost stumped except this free handheld onto the wall for support.

"You've to come into this room. I am expecting someone." Sanari turned and walked the short distance into the room without looking back. She was pulling some old towels from the closet when she sensed his appearance at the door. She spread the towel on the bed and turned to look at him.

"Go sit on those and I'll get the first aid kit." She waited until he moved from the doorway then she headed into the kitchen. In minutes, she returned to the hunk of an intruder. She unbuttoned his shirt taking long strides. He had his gun out lying on the bed with his head down holding his side waiting for more instruction or merely managing the pain. He didn't look up when she entered the room only said, "The bullet is out."

"Oh." That was all she managed then on second thoughts she said, "I have to cut the t-shirt off. I want you to hold the towel where the wound is and put pressure so the bleeding can stop." She eyed the gun. She lifted the t-shirt and wrapped a towel around his waist, taking his hand and putting it over the blood, covering the wounded area, back, and front. It was all she could manage as she set to cut the t-shirt from his body.

She removed the towel and saw the bloody gash on the upper right side of his stomach and moved the towel with his hand over it while she tended to the back wound. The gunshot went right through; she gasped and looked up at him. He had his eyes closed; too much in pain to say anything, much less gave her an explanation.

Silence followed as she cleaned the wound and dressed it. She felt him flinch in pain a few times as she removed the blood and added pressure to it to stop the bleeding. She finished the back of him where the bullet either enter or left; she wasn't sure which, however, nothing major was damaged from what she could tell. She moved the bloody towel and replaced it with a fresh one with his hand still adding pressure.

The wound wouldn't stop bleeding; she left to collect some warm water to wash the blood off his hand. He was sitting right where she left him eyes closed. He wished she would hurry up and wanted to voice this to her including telling her if she cannot see he's dying, however, the words wouldn't leave his mouth.

"Ouch." He stared at the top of her head. She was kneeling and had rubbed alcohol over the wound that he had surrendered to her. Well, he didn't she removed his hand and towel. "Next time tell me, will you?" He was too tired to argue then he remembered she was doing him a favor and added, "Please."

"What's the point?" She whispered to his side as she cleaned the blood and taped it with a bandage. Next, she washed his hands clean and wiped them.

"Can you offload your gun and put it in here, please." She turned to open the drawer on the bedside table while he put the gun in it. She wiped his hands again. She preceded to unbutton his jeans and let them loose; she wiped the blood apex of his thighs as she worked his jeans off him.

Sanari looked at his closed eyes and expressionless face; her eyes quickly traveled all of him taking in his package in the black briefs. Sanari's eyes popped open when she saw his size and a smile tugged on her lips. Her attention was pulled away to his remarkable thick black ponytail and strong cheekbones that shaped his face into handsome and beyond. She stood still for a minute waiting for a micro-blast or something from him. Nothing came.

She watched him for eons of minutes as he looked as comfortable as a pickle in a jar. Suddenly a grey eye popped open then the next making her spontaneously jump. His lips widen into a smile that reached his grey eyes warming her heart.

"Ryland Cooper, I'm FBI, undercover." The hunk revealed in a deep voice, however, in pain and a whisper.

"Dandy, just sweet bliss of dandy. You should stretch out in the bed and drink this water with two painkillers. You lost a lot of blo... od." The doorbell rang.

"Ooppssshhhh Fiona." Sanari's voice was sharp with excitement extremely not from hearing the doorbell. Running to the door and swinging it open she was about to pull Fiona in when Fiona stood still looking at the path dripped in blood, leading to her door. Sanari followed her eyes.

"Oh, God! What a mess?" "What happened? Are you hurt?" Fiona looked over Sanari's body and her messy wet hair and found the blood on her white shorts.

"No. Someone else is and he's in the spear."

"I'll bleach it, hurry!" Fiona ordered her.

Fiona rushed into the kitchen for the bleach while Sanari went into the bedroom to see to her unexpected hunk of a guest. He had spread his entire body in the middle of the bed and the bottle of water was empty, the painkiller gone. He kept his eyes closed, "Do you always answer the door looking like that?" His grey eyes opened filling with warmth turned deadly sexy.

Sanari looked down at her attire and realized that she had a black bra on with her white shorts with spots of blood, blushed, and ran out of the room into hers. She pulled the blue silk shirt she was going to wear on with her sandals and changed her shorts for a black ones. She blowed-dried her hair and added a touch of red lipstick to her lips. She pulled her purse off the bed and closed the door behind her. She went to see how Fiona was coping; she was in the kitchen throwing the bloody paper towel in a trash bag to dump in the master bin on their way out.

"Give me a minute. I have some towels to add and I want to write my number on this pad." Sanari told Fiona as she took the pad and pen from the kitchen drawer and ran into the spare room where the naked American fusion lay still. Ryland opened his eyes to see his savior all dress not that she isn't beautiful to look at without clothes. As much as he's in pain and exhausted he can still appreciate beauty when he sees it.

"You look prettier without clothes." He said lightly with a faint smile on his lips. She was too fetching in her shorts and top, too sexy, yep, he's hurt, not dead.

"So, do you." She sarcastically replied.

Who's being sarcastic? Ryland wondered then he felt his naked body on the bed and pink entered his face. She noticed it.

"I've to leave. I would be back in an hour. You should rest. Here is the portable phone with my cell number. I put your wallet and cell here with the gun." She has a tinge of sadness in her voice and points to the drawer next to him.

She picked up the water bottle and took it with her leaving the room briefly and entering it again with a new bottle with a bag of potato chips. She broke the top off just in case he's unable and closed it lightly. She was well aware that he was watching her.

"I'll bring you some dinner. What do you want? Have you eaten?" She looked at him seeing the wariness in him.

"No. I'm not hungry." He said lightly and closed his eyes.

"Ok. Don't go anywhere I'll be right back." She saw a faint smile on his lips as she walked out of the room and left a light on in the hall because soon it would be dark.

She closed the door as she and Fiona walked the short distance to Fiona's car. She had very little truth to tell and less trust to give a hunk of a stranger. She felt herself being sucked into a massive psychedelic black hole with no degree of getting out.

20

"Oh, hell Sanari, I can't believe it! He just popped up, huh?" Fiona finally said something. She was quiet on the way here giving Sanari her privacy. She waited until they had placed their order for drinks and dinner with Sanari ordering take-out soup and burger for her unexpected guess.

Ryan disposed of the usual rum and coke upon a different napkin. Sanari looked at him with a "thank you, Ryan." Picking up her drink, she stopped mid-way and read the note on the napkin. *You are being followed.*

Sanari still recovering from her adventure with Ryland a moment ago automatically scanned the area to see who was watching her. She wouldn't figure out who she passed the napkin to Fiona who raised her eyebrow in wonderment. She too looked around and not spotting anyone picked French fry off her plate and nibbled on it.

Ryan had moved away to the opposite side of the bar keeping a low profile as he watched three ladies.

The hamburgers and fries were placed between them just the way they like them. The burger was cut in half and there were mayonnaise and ketchup on the side for the fries which were dipped and savored in Sanari's and Fiona's mouths.

In less than half of an hour, just when Sanari had finished telling Fiona about Ryland and halfway through their food a voice came over to them.

"Mind if I joined you? I am FBI Special Agent Olympia Van Amstel who's investigating Asa Fleischer's murder." She knew Ryan had warned them and saw both of them looking around. She waited for this particular time to move in with her questions. They had enough to drink and they should be loose to talk freely. Little did she know that she was in for a whole lot of trouble with a little bit of hell.

Sanari choked on her drink and ended with a fit of coughs. It wasn't because of who she was, it was because of who lay in her spare bedroom, two FBI agents all in a matter of an hour or two.

The light hair Caucasian man in her bedroom lying on her spear bed so sexy rushed to her thoughts along with his gunshot wound. This matter required delicacy and tack, two things that are not embedded into her persona particularly after having two rum and coke.

The sudden flounce of Fiona and the fits of coughs from Sanari didn't go unnoticed either by Olympia or Ryan. Silence prelude as both ladies bought themselves under control. The two pairs of eyes that were watching Fiona and Sanari turned toward each other in a sizzling intensified moment of pure bliss or is it agony or hell? While those two, Ryan and Olympia sized and diced each other over, Fiona and Sanari exchanged "what now" looks, and an agreement was made silently. It took Sanari several interjections between Olympia and Ryan to break the ice or warmth of intensified energy that flowed between those two and for Olympia to give them her attention. Ryan stood there observing the interaction.

"Yes, you're saying." Olympia's voice was a bit shaky.

"I was not, Sanari was." Fiona gladly and wickedly informed her. All eyes were on Sanari who was sipping her rum and coke through a straw and looked at each one, Olympia first then Ryan, reading the sexual chemistry between them. What's this Cupid at work? She put her empty glass on the countertop and turned to Olympia.

"Look the truth of the matter is, Asa was a dirty rotten scoundrel besides being an alcoholic, anorexia, obsessive-compulsive, and a chronic liar she dabbled into everything and blamed everyone for her life," Sanari informed her.

"A super-duper bitch." Olympia charmed in.

"You said it." Ryan was the only one who saw the rise of Olympia's brow as she boldly moved forward with her questions.

"Ok. Tell me what you know. I was told you three hung out."

"You were told wrong. Asa followed us everywhere." Fiona intervened speaking a little loud.

"We were stalked and she deserved what she got; one nasty

bitch off this earth. I thank the person who did it." Sanari angrily interjected.

A whistle was heard out of Olympia's as she proceeded to continue with questioning. "Is that so? You've my attention."

"Look." Sanari let out a long breath. "The super-duper bitch is also a racist and she was jealous of our relationship with Gina Razzista who is also a racist. She's an old angry lady who used to lend me books to read a very long time ago. I picked up the habit of visiting her every night. "Gina played the jealousy card to Asa because Asa is like a daughter to her who rarely visited.

Asa in turn couldn't handle it. She told her some lies about me and Gina was mean and cruel-not that's not her nature because Gina's crazy. Her husband, the preacher, raped her and used the word "fuck" or called her that. She sings whenever rape is discussed and when I used "fuck" she turned frigid. When others used it she let them off." Sanari toppled out unable to stop, however, she did and sipped on the fresh rum and coke that Ryan had put in front of her.

"Is that what you got?" Olympia asked in surprise as she thought confession was going to happen. How wrong was she? They are hiding something and giving her a whole lot of hell.

"Ryan, we need some more fries, please," Fiona mentioned to the bartender who was actively listening. It was a slow night with only the three ladies sitting at the bar and three other regulars at tables having dinner. It was six in the afternoon on a cool day.

Ryan reluctantly left and appeared before Sanari had time to breathe. In a flash, he summed up the group and he didn't miss anything, resumed the same spot he had occupied.

Olympia wondered why he was being so protective over them and whether he shared the same secret with them or a different one. She knew it had to do with Asa Fleischer. Does she really want to know about Ryan Reyes and Asa Fleischer? The song, "I learn how to spread my wings and fly" plinked in her ears for what reason she cannot fathom a guess. Could it mean that Fleischer spread her wings too far and couldn't fly? Or was it Ryan Reyes, Sanari Amani, and Fiona Blanchard who spread their winds too far and flew into the nest of Asa Fleischer? Ryan caught Olympia's face corrugated with worry for the split minute it showed up and quickly disappeared.

"What did you talk about when you were together?" Olympia's voice was choppy with agitation that went unnoticed by Fiona and Sanari, however, not by Ryan.

"She gossiped and told us everything that was going on in Sussex Place except what she was doing?" Fiona said with a sign.

"Or who she's blackmailing." Sanari finished off. "It's been weeks since she died how come you waited until we are eating to question us?" Fiona asked the Special Agent. "I've seen you before. Aren't you living in Essex Place?" Sanari a bit tipsy looked Olympia full in the eyes without blinking.

"I finally got around to you two. I'm sorry that it took this long. I had to question many people and I was waiting for the autopsy and other reports to come through before I questioned you two." She looked at Fiona as she spoke and turned to Sanari and replied to her.

"Yes, you probably have seen me before. I lived in the same place you do. I was undercover for a while and after the murder of Fleischer I came out of hiding. I am investigating her murder.

"Well, you can ask us any question another time. We're too buzzed right now." Sanari told her as Ryan poured coffee for them both.

"Oh, there's more?" Olympia asked as if she was surprised.

"Oh, there's more to tell. She can't see beyond hate. Asa the bitch got Marie to call the animal control for the wild raccoons visiting the compound. One of the animals died and when I called her she blamed Marie. I called Marie who hung up the phone. Those raccoons didn't interfere with anyone and for her to do that, was nasty.

"There's no tapestry of justice with Asa because she took people's personal tragedies as an opportunity for financial gain. She also takes the truth and commercialized or emphasized it and it sounded fake or she lies and commercialized it to make it sound like the truth. The bitch told everyone that we are her girlfriends, when my water heater got busted I asked her if I can have a shower because she lived closer to me and she replied that she had to think about it.

"I wanted to watch a show on the telly and asked her if I can and she told me that hers wasn't working. I don't have a television at that time as mine was broken. She visited everyone and no one and I mean, no one except James her lover can go visit her. She would open the door and talk to you from there."

"Oh." Olympia disappointedly worded.

"Then there was the......."

"No, Sanari what I want to know is who killed her, not this gossip stuff. God damn it, who killed the bitch?" There was no mistaking the emphasis of frustration in Olympia's voice.

Sanari drew back her shoulders and looked at her. Fiona drew in her breath and laughed. "Isn't that your bloody job? You got the nerve to ask us to do your job. You should come to join us at the pool some time. You would be surprised at what you hear. You've never known what you can pick up through the gossip." Fiona told her.

"Which pool?' Olympia asked her, looking directly at her.

"Now, now Special Agent," Fiona answered ever so sweetly. "You got the nerve to ask us to do your job." Echoing Sanari's words.

This is going to be a witch hunt, Olympia thought. Which of these witches killed the bitch is what she wanted to know, not playing some foolish tug of war with a bunch of retirees.

The take-out was placed on the counter with the bill. Ryan asked Fiona if she is sobered to drive home. "Ryan, I had one drink and a cuppa coffee. Sanari is the one drinking and boy she sure needed it. Right, Sanari?" Fiona laughed out loud hiding a secret that both Ryan and Olympia wanted to know for different reasons.

Silence followed as Sanari paid the bill with cash and left a twenty percent tip on the counter with the receipt. Ryan was watching all of them while Olympia was watching the girls. She knew they are hiding something that wasn't on the tapes.

Asa had something on Fiona, the silent one. What does Asa have on them? What could that possibly be?

21

Asa was about to open her door when a knock on the wooden frame made her jump. She took a step towards the security peephole and saw her next-door neighbor, Hank Weihert. She stepped back and opened the door, however, not before she rolled her eyes in a three sixty-degree motion.

"Hello Hank, I'm on my way out. What can I do for you?"

"Oh." Hank sounded and showed disappointment. "Can I have some sugar, please?" He shoved the cup he held in his hand towards her.

"Sure." Asa took it and walked the short distance into the kitchen, pulled the sugar out from the cupboard, and began filling his cup, giving the task all of her attention.

Hank Weihert is a thirty-five-year-old balled-headed Caucasian constructor worker, who's two hundred and fifty pounds and has a sex addiction. He lived in the same building as Asa one floor down in apartment twelve zero one with several cats. His secret is a foot fetish. He loved a manicure and pedicure on females, especially pedicures. This was the reason for being in at this time at Asa's apartment. Sanari told him the days she goes for her manicure and pedicure and he measured the time to be here every week.

He even took his days off because it turned him on, sexually. He even had invited her to watch phonograph with him just so he can ejaculate on her foot. She turned him down and told him in no uncertain terms, "It's one thing when men trampled on my feelings and it's another when they boldly asked me what you just asked. I draw the boundary line with my fingers and toes."

Does Asa have a boundary line? That would be a first. Hank wondered, puzzled. Then to his amazement, she had given him a bottle of wine a long time ago and told him where to take it. He did and he got his release on Sanari's foot! "He'd gotten me tipsy." Sanari had claimed. She told this to Fiona who was laughing hysterically when Asa usually walked into the conversation and demanded to know. They were lazing at the pool. What she didn't mention was that she told Hank the days Asa had her hands and toes done.

Asa knew that smile and the remembrance of his experience with Sanari. She figured that Sanari told him about her pedicure days. She also is well aware that his eyes are on her toes and he's thinking about a fantasy that he can use to go and jerk off. This man is sick.

"Thank you." Hank grinned at her as they walked to the door. She looked at him and shook her head.

"Not a word, Hank. Not a word out of your mouth. I don't ever want to hear you talk about sex. Every time you do I wanted to throw up."

"Damn! That woman hates sex." Hank thought.

Asa turned from him and walked away. She knew he was standing there watching her walk. He didn't hear anything she said because his thoughts and eyes were far away living in a fantasy world. She usually repeated the same thing every time he came by making an excuse about running out of sugar since that faithful day she sent him to Sanari. She smiled at the thought of sugar, he has stored in his apartment, a good twenty pounds she figured. She began to laugh at the wicked trick she used him to play on Sanari.

Asa's thoughts drifted down memory lane and recalled Sanari explaining the experience of Hank to her and Fiona; "I was a bit tipsy when he asked two questions with the first one most likely to be no and the second one a yes. The first question is "Can I jerk off on your feet? The second one was, Can I have some paper towels?

"I said no and yes and of course, he heard yes and not the no."He pulled his pants off and out fell his penis and he began to masturbate, looking at me at my feet. I had no shoes on and my toes were polished the usual red.

"I was in shock and by the time I started to protest. I moved my foot so fast he didn't know what happened and ran into the kitchen for a paper towel. I was over-shocked. I told him to leave and he was grinning.

"A week later about elevenish, he knocked on my door, and foolishly I opened the door. He pushed me aside and walked right in with a bottle of wine in his hand, apologizing for his behavior. Like a stupid fool, I forgave him and drank the wine, not realizing that he was seeking a repeated performance.

"The bastard came back a second time and when I went into the kitchen to get some glasses he was jerking off on my carpet. I ran into the kitchen again to get some paper towels just in time. He didn't ask only pulled his penis out and started again.

"I started to laugh and then I realized he was so turned on that I better get serious. I waited until he was at that point of no return then I pulled my foot deliberately away and stood up. I walked to the door and opened it. As soon as he saw the door opened he sobered up fast enough for me to kick him out and told him never to talk to me or come back or I will call the police."

What poor Asa didn't know at the time was Sanari informed Hank of the days Asa did her manicure and pedicure. This is how he kept showing up at her place for sugar. Asa being the conceited idiot thinks Hank has a crush on her. Not on her, her hands and feet!

Poor Sanari, well not poor, because Sanari didn't enjoy the experience of Hank jerking off on her foot; nonetheless she did enjoy the wine. It was her fine brand age to perfection that Asa was keeping for a special occasion. She didn't realize that was the one she had randomly picked up and handed to Hank for it was the very one Sanari was pestering her to open for she and Fiona can taste.

Hank Weihert stood at the door of Asa's apartment and sadly he looked around missing his every other week visit of sugar. Asa's dead. He has to go looking for someone new to fantasize about. He turned sadly away with his empty cup looking around him. He was about to open his door when he saw Sanari standing by the lake talking to Fiona.

Although they were on the opposite side of the lake, he knew them by sight. He wondered what they were up to and whether their toes were painted and what color. They were at The Twixt

Peach last night and he wished he could have gone and watched them. He knew he cannot go and see either one of them because they would call the police on him. He signed and walked into his apartment.

Over on the lake, where Sanari and Fiona stood, the sun was bright and not far past its apex. The glare turned the lake into a mirror making the air crisp. In three hours, it would be a cool sunny day.

A light breeze pulled tendrils of short black hair loose around Sanari's face. Fiona's teasing laughter was gone with the wind and the mist coming off the lake was evaporated by the tropical sun.

"Fi, I had to feed him last night. I cut the hamburger into small pieces and gave Ryland a little bit at a time with a spoon of vegetable soup. He was so weak that lifting the bottle of water was too much. I fed him a huge peanut butter sandwich this morning, washing it down with sweet black coffee.

"I had to roll him on his side and change the bandage on his back and then rolled him on his back to change the one in front. I went this morning and bought him some new clothes." Sanari finished with a sad feeling for the man in her apartment.

"Well, you can't do anything more. By Monday he should be able to help himself and you can go to your consulting appointment." Fiona added trying to give her friend some comfort and reassurance.

"I moved some of it, the appointments around so I can come home and check on him."

"Oh, I wished I could help you. I am working trebles for the next three days then I am off for two." Fiona told her sadly.

"That's okay Fi, think I can manage. I'll do what I can. I've to go. Got some reading to do about the case tomorrow and I want to cook some soup for Ryland and put them in containers. He can nip it in the microwave just in case I cannot make it home in time."

"Is he going to have the strength to get up and do it?" Fiona asked concerned.

"I don't know. It's not like I can ask someone to check on him. He has no choice."

"Oh, well guess you're right. See you in four days." Fiona waved and left Sanari taking the stairs to her apartment two at a time. She opened the door and walked into the kitchen to switch the washed clothes to the drier. She had bought some more towels at the dollar store to put on the bed in case Ryland's wounds bleed, it wouldn't soak into the mattress. She threw the soaked ones away as it would be too much work to wash and reuse. She took the mashed potatoes with fish stew she made before going shopping for him and nicked it in the microwave.

She put it out all on a tray, the plate of food, fork, napkin, and a bottle of water and took it into the room.

"Ryland, time to wake up." She said upon entering the room. He was asleep; she put the tray down and touched his shoulders. He opened his grey eyes and smiled at her.

"Thank you." He whispered too weak to speak much. He allowed her to stuff two pillows behind him and forked food into his mouth. He wanted to look at her, however, his energy was depleted. He was bone-tired from his twenty-four-hour surveillance and since he hadn't planned on being shot he's scraping at the bottom of his energy reserves trying to figure out how it happened. He had his eyes closed; he could barely keep them open when he felt a fork touch his lips and he automatically opened them to receive the food.

On the last swallow waiting for the fork to touch his lips and receiving none, he opened his eyes and his face cracked into a crazy grin. Her face stretched with surprise and moving with the grace of a lynx, she put the empty plate back on the tray and reached for the bottle of water with the painkillers.

Sanari studied him for a few moments before opening the bottle and moving it to his lips. She waited for him to take a few more sips before putting one of the pain killers to his lips and then the bottle of water. She repeated two more times with a cyclone of questions twilling in her thoughts.

"Ok. You can lie back down and sleep." She moved his torso forward as she pulled the two pillows from behind him. He opened his eyes and looked at her as she rested the pillow on the floor by the foot of the bed. She pulled herself straight and a short of a smile tapped onto his lips and reached his light grey eyes. She could read happiness in them.

"I'll be right outside so holler for whatever you want. I'm at your service for a long while, make the most of it Special Agent Ryland Cooper." Sanari deliberately whispered in a sexy voice with a hint of humor and sarcasm.

A gift of humor expressed by his savior is a wonderful thing to the Special Agent's ears. Expressing humor, regardless of the high pitch of sarcasm is an index of enjoyment more so with a touch of sexiness in her voice. She made his day; he wanted to heal real fast so he can get to know her. It hit him that he doesn't know her name and he was already in love with her.

22

"Watch where you're going, will you?"

Asa turned her light brown eyes to the highway for a second then back at the passenger in her car. They were headed into Tampa for an appointment with a tattoo artist. Asa had lost her eyebrow from taking excessive prescription drugs and alcohol. She wanted a permanent tattoo instead of the daily fake ones.

"Did you switch my mat?" She asked Sanari who was watching the road due to Asa's inconsistency in doing so. The woman is a wild driver with many speeding tickets, it's beyond Sanari's comprehension she has a driver's license. She pushed her foot against the imagery brake every time Asa drove too close to the car in front of them.

"No. I didn't. Why would I want to do that for?"

"To let me think that I am going crazy."

"Are you going crazy, Asa?"

"That's what you want others to think?"

Sanari caught the implication of indicting her. She secretly smiled because she did switch the map with Charles' and that was exactly her reason for doing it. She wanted Asa to think she was going crazy just as she made others feel as if they are crazy with her blackmail scheme. There were other times when she and Fiona bought her the sex toy called the "Bullet" and gave it to her on her birthday.

Asa was going out with her family for a birthday dinner celebrating her fiftieth. They told her not to open it there, as it was private knowing full well that Asa would open it to show her family what her friend gave her. Asa didn't know what it was as there was no instruction in the package when she opened it along with the other gifts she received.

She had the pink "Bullet" in her hands pushing the control and test driving it on her arm. She innocently showed it to the waitress that was passing who told the other waiters. The other diners heard the sound of the battery-operated device and were shocked at how she was maneuvering it on her arm. Apparently, her mother and her brother were as clueless as Asa, except for her father Pastor Thom.

At first, he couldn't figure out what it was and after many minutes slipped by with Asa zooming the device on her arm as if she was a little girl, he was shocked to the point he bent over with a heart attack. The man, Jon with his adult son, Ryder having dinner on the table next to the Fleischer's was laughingly observing the Bullet display and realized that Pastor Thom was in trouble.

Ryder called the ambulance as Jon pulled him off his chair and laid him on the carpet floor to rest. Asa seeing this rushed to her father's side and diagnosed his heart attack. She made him comfortable taking his vitals while James her brother comforted their mother. Pastor Thom too much in shock to speak closed his eyes and prayed for his daughter, asking for forgiveness for her innocence and damn her friends to hell.

One of the ambulance attendances that Asa knew from her days as a doctor saw the "bullet" sex toy in her hands and told her what it was; upon finding out Asa turned beet red. Her poor father died the next day and she never told anyone how or why nor did she ever tell Sanari or Fiona who found out anyway.

The waiter who served the Fleischer's is the son of one of Fiona's workmates. Sanari found out from a friend while she was visiting her in the hospital for a hysterectomy. Oh, they laughed over beers. Sanari tucked that memory away before she started to laugh hysterically. Another thought telegrammed itself through her brain when Asa and Fiona were over her apartment for cocktails and a sound surfaced as if it was her cell phone which it wasn't and it scared the hell out of Asa.

Fiona told Asa that it's how God talks to her; how he contacted people he loved. She thought it was a ghost and left. Asa never returned to Sanari's apartment again. She blocked all thoughts and focused on the road in front of them, a cute smile played havoc on her red lips.

Throughout all of this remembrance, Asa was talking and Sanari turned to look at her giving her the attention she was demanding. She tried to focus on what the conversation was about, which Asa was carrying on when she lapsed into her memory. "James put a clock in the microwave. He was so drunk. It exploded last night." Asa unaware of the memories of her begotten moments with Sanari and Fiona and continued looking at Sanari chatting.

Sanari had only come along for the ride because they want her help with an upcoming situation of Fiona's. Asa's company is a whole lot of trouble with a little bit of hell, a bloody headache. Sanari pulled the painkillers from her handbag and took them with some water.

"Got a headache?" Asa not missing anything asked.

"Yes. It's your bloody driving."

"Want to drive?"

"I'm driving back for sure. You bet on it." Sanari told her.

She, as usual, was talking about everyone and everything. Asa has to look at Sanari who hates the fact that her eyes have to leave the road every time she spoke. They were on Interstate two seventy-five west looking for the exit that would lead them to the tattoo parlor. She had told James that she was taking Candy to Tampa to visit an ailing aunt.

"Lordie Lula," flowed out of Asa's mouth every two minutes.

"Tell me again why you didn't choose a tattoo artist in Orlando."

"She was in Orlando and moved here. I already had made an appointment and paid. I don't trust the others."

"Tsk tsk."

"What?" Asa's eyes left the road again to look at her new friend.

"Oh shuts Asa, look at the bloody road."

"Huh?" Asa hit the brake and slowed down; she wouldn't run into the car in front of her. She glanced at Sanari from the corner of her eyes and saw her roll her skyway. Unknowingly, they missed the exit while still chatting about one thing or the other, well more Asa was chatting and Sanari not listening.

Today, however, Sanari wasn't within the flow of life and before either of them knew what was happening they were on the ten-mile bridge heading towards St. Petersburg. The bridge absorbed them as Sanari looked around her and then at Asa.

"We are lost, this is not the way. We missed the exit."

"Huh? What the fuck? How did that happen?

"Turn around and we can stop and ask for directions." Sanari more or less ordered her.

"I can't turn around. It's one way. We have to get to the end of the bridge and find a gas station and ask for direction." Asa said to her.

"Okay." Within the next fifteen minutes after Asa had pulled off and asked directions, they were still lost. Asa pointed out to Sanari that they missed the exit again. "Okay, pulled off the highway and stop at the gas station for direction."

"Okay. I'll call and let them know I'm late." Asa informed her.

In a few minutes, with the calls made and new directions, Sanari pointed to the road and told her to take it. Asa, a nervous wreck, worried that she will miss her appointment, went into the no-entry lane and turn right. Sanari irritated, look to see if there were any police around. Finding none she pointed to the next turn and told Asa to go there.

Asa missed the right turn that would take them back onto the highway towards the exit. "You missed it, turn there and then onto the highway," Sanari ordered her. Asa turned and both watched in shock as a huge dump trunk barreled down on them.

A thick silence waited inside as the oncoming traffic became closer to the little red car. Anxiety and frustration bottomed out as fear howled through their veins and death preceded into their thoughts. At the helm of things, Asa swung the car up on the curb and drove into someone's lawn, and kept driving.

"Where are you going?" Sanari wanted to know.

"I don't know."

"Oh, over there is the highway. That's what we want." Sanari told her as quietly as she possibly can. She's alive; her headache was worse and her nervousness was shattered.

Three lawns more and they were on the road they missed in the first place onto the highway forty-five minutes late for the appointment. After the removal of her old tattoo, Sanari took over the driving home.

Asa had a headache and besides the way she drove gave Sanari a massive one, therefore driving home would relieve her headache. Well, so she thought because the minute she pulled into Interstate four, Asa began on a non-stop talking, quite a run-on sentence.

"Do you have your cell?" Asa wanted to know.

"Yes, I have my mobile" Sanari deliberately used the British word for a portable phone to annoy her because Asa believes if people live in a country they should adopt that country's language. The next twenty minutes were addressing the very subject. Sanari couldn't care less because she was driving and had quit listening to her.

"Are we stopping for gas soon?" Asa wanted to know after her rant about foreigners.

"Yes, at the next station I'll stop for petrol." Sanari deliberately used the British word for gasoline. Asa chose to ignore her this time. She has other things that are bothering her besides the headache.

"How far is it? Do you know?"

"About forty miles." "Oh good. I'll take a nap. I got a splitting headache. Wake me up. I need to use the tinker tank."

"The what?" "The tinker tank, the toilet."

"Huh, the ladies."

"It would be dirty, Asa, very dirty." Sanari smiled because Asa is a compulsive cleaner. She had to have everything around her clean otherwise things would remind her of how dirty she is and that wouldn't work for her.

"I have to........." Sanari cut into her communication with a serious face and laughing eyes.

"Oh, I can always pull over and you can use the bushes."

"That's not funny."

"No kidding."

A few days later Asa took the car to the mechanic as one of the tires was looking funny. Bob the mechanic asked her if she hit a few curbs and to be careful as the tires are going to blow. Little does he know about their adventure? Asa went to Tampa with worn-out tires that were on the verge of blowing out to Sanari's horror when she found out from Bob at the supermarket. Bob, they all took their cars and he told Sanari because he knew she was with Asa.

Neither spoke of the incident until Asa's seven-hundred-dollar bill from the mechanic arrived. He wondered as he put four new tires on the car, aligned and fixed the damage of loose bolts and screws beneath the car what they were doing to create this mess. Crazy ass women drivers! He made good money off of them. They think that this is Mister Toad Wild Ride, idiots!

Sanari blamed Asa for trying to kill them both and Asa blamed Sanari for missing the exit and making her late for her appointment. Sanari told Asa that she was busy with the followed-up appointments.

Asa was forced to ask her brother, James, and hated Sanari for turning her down. Fiona laughed about the experience of going into a no-zone lane. Sanari wasn't and avoid Asa as much as possible, however, it seemed that Asa had plans for them both. This was a few years after Sanari met Asa and she was becoming friends with Fiona. For the next several years Asa became their tug-a-long want to befriend as if she was part of some package and using the girls as camouflage for her illegal activities.

23

"Is that all you are giving me?" Olympia demanded.

"That's all you are going to get?" Fiona festered up. "Sanari hang out with her at first and upon discovering what a bitch she is, avoided her. She planted bugs into our apartment that's how she was staking us and showed up as if we had made prior arrangements." "Bugs you don't say? How did you know?" Olympia had to ask.

"I have a brother who is an LEO and he came and visited us and found them. Since then we have been feeding her lies." Fiona confessed and then giggled.

Upon hearing her giggles, Sanari also started giggling. Surprise lit up Olympia's and Ryan's faces as they raise their heads in wonderment. Sanari pulled her wallet out of her handbag, took a few bills out, and left it on the countertop. She stood her full length and looked straight into Olympia's blue eyes.

"We bought some pornography tapes and played them for her whenever we wanted to go and do something without her. Asa loved porn, however, she hates sex." "Funny." Olympia smiled deliberately at their admission, knowing too well that it was true. She watched the tapes of erotica that was Asa's as well as listened to the taping of her wicked deeds.

"We think so." Fiona giggled and stood up adding some dollars to Sanari's stack of notes.

"Well, see ya." Smiling at Ryan, Sanari began to walk away, Fiona following her.

"Can I have your telephone numbers?" Olympia asked.

"And you called yourself FBI?" Fiona yelled out.

Ryan looking at Olympia with laughter in his eyes began to laugh, however, a chuckle came out. Hearing the chuckle, she turned to him deviously and looked straight into his eyes, "What are you looking at?"

"You, my sweet FBI lady, you." There was admiration in his gaze.

"Don't think too much it sure will give you a headache." She sarcastically threw at him. Olympia isn't used to such a direct approach. She wanted to haul her body over the bar counter and seduce him. Instead, she blushed, turned, and walked away.

"Hey lady, you owe me $2.20 for the coffee you just drank," Ryan shouted after her with laughter.

"Sue me," Olympia replied utterly blushing and walked out the door toward her car. Her cell rang as she entered her SUV and sat down in the driver's seat.

"Yes. What's up?"

"Who wants to screw you?" Randy Millisap asked.

"What? You are psychic now?"

"Naw, only a behavioral profiler? You have a Nazi living in that complex."

"What?"

"You heard me. One of the tapes had a man who had a conversation with Fleischer in one of the bugged apartments. His voice matched Interpol's. He's going under a different name, I suppose. I e-mailed you the dynamics. We want a fingerprint of his, you have to track him down where he lived."

"Just what I needed."

"Naw, you need a hunk like me in bed with you giving you a real good time."

"Come on over, my hunk."

"Oh, baby. Don't tempt me too much or I'll be on the next plane. Mmmmm, there is also a serial killer in the mix of life. There was a party and lots of people saw someone dumping something in the lake. They have photographs, go grab those will you, and check it out." It wasn't a question or a request it was an order coming through Randy from her boss, Allen Manifold.

"Yes, boss."

"One more thing, we have an undercover agent working with the DEA also. No one has heard from him in the last forty-eight hours, keep an eye out."

"That always breaks my heart?"

"Mine too." A click was heard indicating the end of the conversation.

Olympia exhaled a breath that she was holding on to when she walked out on Ryan. She took several more and bought herself under control. It's never funny when one of your own has gone missing. The anticipation is endless, especially for the family.

How long Olympia sat there she doesn't know. Thinking about her misfortunate life took up the time she had to spare from work.

Today, however, her thoughts surrounded the man at the bar, his blue eyes, and the laughter that followed her. Instinct kicked in and she knew her thoughts were dangerous.

Not a place to visit, not a healthy place to go this minute, in the middle of a murder, Nazi, and missing agent investigation. She had to stay focused as this is the assignment that would get her the raise and promotion she wanted, a desk job away from the bullets and investigation. Three cases in one place; this is big no, huge mega huge. Something fire to life inside her, something she hadn't felt in a very long time.

She's getting nowhere in Fleischer's murder. There were a number of people who wanted to kill her, who could've killed her due to opportunity and didn't, the question remain, who did? Who took the shot to her forehead? Who's trained in taking such a presided shot? Boom, that's it. She didn't know what hit her. It wasn't planned, therefore she surprised someone who carried a gun with him or her. It was a male according to ballistics.

A female doesn't carry that much punch, not even a well-trained one. She couldn't do it and she was over-trained to the point that she can fire her weapon blindfolded and hit her target. This was a man with sniper training and a military one to boot such a shot.

Ryan Reyes is military, however, nothing came back as though he was Special Forces or Black Ops. The other military officers who are retired are too old and suffering from one illness or the other. A few of the men and women have the shakes, firing a weapon to kill someone would be out of the question because they would miss the target.

All the other people checked out at Essex Place and those who walked around with concealed weapons are a citizen who defined themselves by a gun. It's the law in Florida; a permit is required, however, they are no killers; carrying a concealed weapon made them feel safe from who they are afraid of, that's all.

Who killed the bitch from hell? Irritation crossed her tired face. Added to that, she has a Nazi to catch, a serial killer, and a missing FBI agent. Hell, it's not three cases it is four. Slap her silly for miscounting. This is going over her head. She never had to work four cases at one time. Who the fuck do they think she is, superwoman!

Her first reaction was anger, however, panic stepped in. She rapidly exhaled and inhaled as anxiety took its turn in her. She felt panic and then anger again blatting in the bit of her stomach. She breathes some more and looked up at the swirling clouds waiting to cool the anger, it subsided.

Compassion overwhelmed the anger and trust took over. She pushed all of her emotions aside. No time to see them through, too much to do. "Focus, fool, focus." She scolded herself and laid her head to rest on the steering wheel. As if that was not enough, Olympia raised her head and saw Ryan taking the trash out to the side of the building. A few minutes later, the light was turned on on the floor above. She braced herself for the current of energy that zipped through her every time she saw him.

Her pulsed rose a few notches into being haywire as the intensity of the feelings between her and Ryan had grown over the weeks, spreading mixed emotions similar to molten lava in her body. She knew that she was feeling strangely transparent and showed it. He was visibly feeling it too.

Olympia was tempted to climb those stairs and find out what lies behind Ryan Reyes. She sat there debating what to do and reality hit her as a memory of past mistakes controlled her thoughts. She sat there for a second more before kicking the engine into reverse and leaving the parking lot.

Ryan heard the engine of the SUV in the distance and let out a breath. He knew she was out in the parking lot because the camera came up with her sitting there. He figured he'll give her the opportunity to come to visit with him to clarify the attraction between them. A muscle jerked in his jaw as he retrieved the memory of her touch as he gave her a cup of coffee, she did not ask for, nonetheless, he wanted to be near her to smell her morning mist of splash.

Sanari wore the same scent and he had asked her about it. His body zeal to Olympia's touch more quickly than any other female he has ever been in his life. He had removed her touch from his fingers before more sexy ideas spring forth. An erection is good enough; whenever he saw her and coming home to an empty cold bed was more than he can take this second. He certainly doesn't need any more sexual images of them together.

Ryan knew that she pulled his military records and she has a file on him. His old supervisor notified him. He was informed by the military that an investigation was ongoing. Worry still gnawed in his thoughts, although he knew what was in his file long before she entered his domain. He had forgotten the image of her that drifted through his thoughts when another came rushing out with warning bells veering him away from all train of thoughts of Olympia.

He pulled his length to his feet, opened the refrigerator, and pulled out a beer. He loosened the cork from the bottle and drank a long pull of liquid. He took a deep breath and drained the remainder. He went for another one and another before he took his clothes off and climbed into the shower. He let the hot water run over his body as he applied body wash, turning the tap to cold and letting it cool him down to the point that he was trembling.

He climbed out and toweled himself dry. He climbed into bed and pulled the quilt over his naked body. He smiled at her message when she had a dress to kill; he had deliberately undressed her and made sure that she saw him doing it. She had smiled at him and as she passed the bar with her fellow Law Enforcement Officers, she replied quietly with her eyes and body language.

"I'm not a free-range hen.....are you a free-range cock?" He burst out laughing and walked to his office looking at her through the monitor of the camera. He lay on his back looking at the ceiling worried that she would find out his secret. He was glad she didn't climb those stairs to his loft because he'll be the one to pursue her. He hoped he doesn't have to kill her too!

24

Two days have gone since Ryland Cooper stumbled into Sanari's apartment with vertigo thoughts of his attacker. He inhaled at two in the morning and felt her rhythm fill the air with a blended aroma of spices and female scent making a colorful spectrum of her presence. Each time she checked on him, bringing him food and changing the bandage, a warm chill swept through them.

This morning she filled her bathtub in her bedroom and helped him in, leaving him to tend to himself. "Bath" was all she said; he rose to her calling and was caught in the morning's mood of fresh mist.

Few words were spoken as silence teased the air between them heightening the sexual tension. He dreamt about her constantly, dreams that are locked in his thoughts and drawn out whenever she came into his room, errr....her room. The imagining fantasies also locked inside only creep out when she is out of sight.

Ryland's naked chest cushioned softly against hers as she helped him walk toward the bathtub. He only had his black briefs on. He held on to her shoulders as he lifted one leg at a time into the tub. She turned and left. He took his briefs off and sat in the warm water with only the bandage covering his wounds. He closed his eyes and laid his head back on the rim. It felt great.

He opened his eyes and looked around him taking in the body wash, toothbrush, small and large white bath towel, and clothes left in hand reach. He looked around the room and saw it painted in sky blue, very masculine with a feminine touch. A thought shoot through and he looked at the clothes as he reached for the washcloth and body wash, she went shopping for him.

A warmth as huge as the universe touched his heart and he kept it there. He smelled the scent from the body wash, a musk smell came out and he looked at the clothes and knew instantly that she washed and iron them. He had a choice of a plain white cotton shirt or a blue t-shirt that was almost identically to what she had cut off from him, except that he was polyester and hers was pure cotton with a bit of silk.

He had black briefs, blue jeans, or blue shorts to choose from; a soft sexy smile touched his lips; no one has ever done this much for him even when he had the flu. He slowly washed the dried blood off his skin enjoying the warmth of the water and letting his thought run wild with his savior whose name he still doesn't know. He didn't say much either, he hadn't the strength.

Ryland had made no move towards her even when their energy touched each other with intensity and left them hungry in the sweet bliss of silence. He can't give her anything, nonetheless, he took her touch and turned it into something, he's not afraid of the consequences. It's too late to take back their separate space. She knew it and so does he; what should he do. He wanted this thing he has with her and he wanted it to develop and work between them for a long time.

She made him feel things he had forgotten how it felt or he had never experienced. He knew what he wanted to do except he was terrified of what he might discover with her.

Yesterday when she came to change the bandages, he was thinking about her, well thinking of them standing naked staring at each other. His thoughts running from love were dangerous....... he was rethinking that again. He apparently had his hand over his heart. She had a worried expression and had asked him in a whispering voice.

"Are you alright?"

"Yes, why do you ask?" He knew a light red touched his face because he thought she read his thoughts.

"Your hand is on your heart." "Oh." He caught himself saying. He kept his hand there as she came closer to the bed. "I'm thinking that I need therapy to help me recover from my trauma. My heart beats into agreement. I've to build my immunity again to withstand your lethal charisma." She blushed a beet red and replied as swiftly.

"I see you're recovering nicely. Up and let me have a look." Moving her head to the left and back to him she gave him full eye contact.

"You're not going to put alcohol on me poor tender skin again, are you?

"Guess you've to wait and see." He enjoyed the bite of sarcasm edging in her tone.

"Would you go out with me after I am healed?" It just rolled out of his mouth unbeknown to him.

"As a date? I don't date?" came a cool reply. She was removing the bandage from the back wound and had begun cleaning and applying aloe. He was relieved because alcohol stings and he hates to have tears which he almost did the first time and hopefully the last time.

"A thank you for what you're doing for me." He was tired and his voice started strong and took a dive to a weak whisper. "Tell me you'll consider having a drink with me?" Weak voice or not he didn't give up. Where is this coming from he wished he knew.

"Your name is on the list." She had finished his back and moved to the front of him; he kept his eyes closed and leaned into the pillows.

"Wait, there's a list? Of course, there is. Can I move to the top of your list?" He couldn't help himself and a smile appeared on his lips. He knew she saw it and knew he was flirting with her.

"As for thanking me, you just did. That's good enough."

"Oh, come on now, give me a break? I just want to buy you dinner." He had barely whispered. He was ready to sleep again.

"Mmmmm, let me think about it. Go to sleep."

"Yes madam."

In the paroxysm of pleasure, he asked himself which man she left behind or is present in her life. He stopped the thought before it had finished itself. Little did he know that no matter where she went her thoughts kept colliding with the image of him, the touch of him, and the warmth in his eyes. Her voice made music to his ears, especially with her slight, very slight lisp to her twang that slid off her tongue.

The sensations felt when her olive porcelain skin touched his slightly tan one. He was no eunuch which left him with a galaxy filled with new beginnings. He used kind words of gentle seduction, from the heart to the heart, in one beat. For what it's worth, she might not want to be put in the picture that he's making of their future. He felt his heart contradicted. A tight pull that felt awful. He didn't like the accompanying sensations.

Ryland pulled the plug out from under the water and let it drain. He slowly pushed himself up and sat on the rim of the tub, took the towel, and dried himself. He proceeded to dress his aching body. He walked to the sink to brush his teeth and had a good look at his face and long hair. Something is going to have to give and walks to the shower taking her shaver and shaving foam. He walked back to the sink and made a mental note to his list of things he knew about his savior.

She hated thunderstorms. He saw her jump while she was spooning soup into his mouth and a clap of thunder rolled very loud that she spilled it on his chest. Although it was not hot, it surprised him along with the thunder rolling and her reaction; he flexed his muscles giving way to a smile on her lips. He knew he'll be flexing his muscles more often. Is she making a list of things about him? He wondered.

Ryland can sense her presence before her outline appeared through the door. She certainly is the opposite of everything he had ever encountered in females. It was worth getting shot just so he could meet her. She was a selfless and warm and very giving lady. He wondered how he came thus far in life without knowing that it was possible for him to desperately want something and have his savior return what he would be offering her.

He was unable to stem the faint hope that he had nothing for her to cling to presently. His dormant emotions aroused with passion at the first sight of this beauty that stood in front of him when he knocked on her door. The shape of his emotions and passion had given birth to the membrane of love songs and writing poems which he was never into before in his life. He has an oasis of time to woo her; he intended to do as soon as he is healthy and clean up the mess of his undercover job.

He had started a new life when asked to perform this undercover job. He had finished his report from the under-covered bank robbery. He was dressed for this job, with long hair, and a beard, and all he needed was a new name with credentials. He was asked to perform his duty by the very agency that abandoned him. Someone squealed at him and for that, he was shot. Was it an inside job? If that's the case, who is it that betrayed him?

"Ryland, are you decent?" He was jabbered out of his thoughts when Sanari bolted into the room. He met her halfway and she screamed upon seeing him. She stood staring at him and rubbing her elbow from bumping it into the door leading from her room.

She was trembling and he was lost as to what to do. No one had ever reacted to him the way she did, screaming and shock registered on her face. Ryland had cut his pigtail and trimmed the valentine sideburns and shaved the bread. Sanari absorbed his solid warmth and the trembling stopped.

"You loo....look mmmm you could've warned me." "Sorry, it's copyright," flew out of his lips. It dawned on him that he was standing in her room with only his briefs on.

"What?" She asked as puzzled summoned her face and a frown appeared.

"The look," he replied and walked past her into his room leaving her to clean his mess up which he regretted; he was too weak to do anything about it. Bathing and grooming himself took all the energy out of him. He found himself loving her more if that was possible.

Sanari cleaned her bathroom, showered, and climbed into bed. She had a long tiring day with consultation and taking care of her surprised guest. Soon she was asleep dreaming her usual dream.

Sometime in the night, Ryland pulled himself off the bed and venture towards the window that overlooked the lake. He observed the slice of moonlight blended with faint artificial lights reflected on the water and merged into his present life. The chilly wind blew off for the lake hollowed against the window; he laid his forehead against the chilly pane that sweated inside the frame.

At first, he didn't believe it, and then it happened again, a scream followed by sobbing coming from Sanari's room. He rushed for his gun under the pillow on his bed. Her room was parallel to his and he walked quickly the short distance and opened the door looking around. Finding no one he turned his attention to the shape on the bed.

Light shone from the fading moon upon the foot of her bed. He stood hearing her sobbing before he realized that Sanari was having a dream, not a nightmare. It was not the wind rushing by in the moonlight that brought tears to her eyes; it was sadness from the nightmare. What should he do? He stood there with a gun in hand deciding what to do. He knew that whenever he rode a storm out it will exhaust its fury. There lies a perfect storm. Should he comfort her? Remembering how kind she was to him, he decided that he will take his chances with this storm of fire. Ryland took the steps forward and pulled back the quilt. What he saw made him sad, very sad.

He slipped into bed with her, rolled over onto his side, and curved her in against him. He pulled her curled warm body with a cornucopia of tears into his cold one, holding her through the night.

Cold flesh has gone where no warm skin had been in a very long time for both of them. His savior was shaking the same as a leaf in a winter wind. He radiated enough heat to warm Notre Dame Cathedral in a nice cold winter from holding her. Heat penetrated through from his pores into her cells and set them on fire. Time depended on what was in them as they tapped on each other's hearts.

In dark vast space that had ignited a shower of intensified shooting sparks each time they brushed together, at the moment fused as one. She bent as a leaf, flowing in the wind against the taut masculinity of his solid frame.

The fire silently sparked in the midst of the night and they elected the flames of true love. His sudden arousal was comfortable against her backside. His erection heaved and he chuckled a low burst of husky sound that ripped through her hazy senses, evoking a shiver.

Ryland's body against hers in those first few seconds had awakened her from dormant feelings, aroused her to a yearning that she had only dreamed of. She was alive with the warm firmness of his lips in her hair. It was comforting to her; him holding her when the past intruded on her present. She had tried to conquer her storm and failed miserably.

A smile touched her lips and she relaxed her body against his cold one. Sanari inhaled deeply and felt her body temperature jump about fifty degrees warmer. With his penis nestled neatly against her backside, it made her body surge with deep emotion and euphoria at its zenith.

This expansion of his male part wedged against her suggested that he was the one dreaming about sex. The pressure was extremely prominent and her body wanted him. He heard her music and smiled.

His hands clenched in her hair then after a moment it when under her neck and she pulled his hands into her and held it toward her breast. Another reason why he came to her, sweet comfort, he needed it as much as she did on this moonlight night. It was impossible to tell where his shadow began and where hers ended. They were one; a place surfaced, shifted, and altered where silence didn't mislead and deceived them; where actions were never what they seemed to be for either of them.

Ryland found himself lost in a confusing and foreign landscape. He was a seeker without a map.

25

Fiona was in a daze trying to figure out what woke her up. She had just fallen asleep when her cell rang with Bob Marley music charming her into full awareness as her heartbeat quickened. She glanced at the bedside clock and saw it was five in the morning. Without looking to see who it was she hurryingly answered it whispering at the same time, "This better be fucking good. Hello."

"It's Sanari. I need your help. George's in a drunken splendor in jail. I was hoping you come with me to bail him out."

"Okay, pick me up in ten." As she tossed the covers off her, Fiona racked her thoughts to have a mental picture of drunken George. It took her the full ten minutes before the picture formed in her thoughts. "Oh, him!" She whispered to herself as she dressed in jeans and a white t-shirt. She stroked her lips with a light pink lipstick and combed her short bottled blond hair.

George Stanford is an all-American Caucasian eighty-three-year-old Korean veteran. He used to stand five feet ten inches, however, due to his age, he stands five feet with his shoulder slumping ten inches into his wrinkled neck. His face had seen more creative days currently crumpled with too much drinking and smoking cigarettes, however, the skin on his face is as smooth as a baby's bottom.

His grey hair receded on the top and held his tope a lighter grey than the rest of his hair that capped his crown. He has not only lost weight carrying him down to one hundred pounds; he also lost his life partner of forty-three years to cancer.

Miza was his love of all loves and he was her hero. He began drinking splendor and having sex with whoever is available. He lived in the same building apartment as Sanari two doors down, ten seventy-four.

Sanari and George became fast friends after Miza's death. Essentially, she was Miza's friend first as they would belly dance together. Sanari had begun checking in on him after the death of Miza. She had knocked on his door and upon opening. "Don't you have a boyfriend?" He asked angrily through the closed door.

"No." "Something is wrong with this country." Upon his reply, he opened the door and let her in. Sanari has gotten a tickle in visiting with George and having her afternoon tea or sometimes he would walk the two doors down and visit with her whenever she did not show up at her usual time.

After that they became friends. They spend many hours together and for all Fiona knew they still do most days when George doesn't have company. George made tea for Sanari and he would have instant coffee with vodka.

One day several weeks into the relationship she didn't show up; George had called her and wanted to know what happened. She told him that she had a cold and was in bed. He had asked if she had taken some medicine. With a reply of "no", he came over and gave her a bottle of cold medicine.

He saw her trash sitting on the door and took it out to the dumpster. He even did her groceries for her without asking for money. When he was drunk she was giving him orders to pay his bills, did the shopping for him, and fixed his meals. He let her take over and he continued to enjoy his coffee with vodka.

"George, I need some money."

"Maybe I should put you on my account?" He replied after a sip of coffee with its flavor.

"You should."

"When did we get married?" He asked upon her answer.

"When you took care of me when I was sick. Remember you bought over a bottle of expired cold medicine." It was three years expired and did nothing for her. Fiona discovered its expiration date when she bought some soup over and threw it out. "You took the trash out and did the shopping." She reminded him.

"I didn't know that feeding you was in the contract. It must be in the fine print." She shocked her shoulders at him.

"No, darlin' it was bold and beautiful. You missed it." She was used to his comedy after all that was the profession he retired from over 20 years ago. He taught her how to laugh at herself.

"When can I claim my husbandly duty?" He wickedly asked her as he took another sip of his flavored coffee.

"That's expired. You should've asked for it when you took the trash out." She kissed him and left, shaking her pretty head with a wonder of American men.

George found other friends, a belly dancer Annya, a karaoke black woman name Marla, another British comedian big fat Jack and a young man who had an eye disease of double vision.

One day on a sunny afternoon, Sanari had driven George to do some odds and end shopping. Suddenly he ordered her to pull over in a pink building on seventeen ninety-two which she obliged. It wasn't until she parked and was out of the car that she saw the store with a big bold Erotica on it.

"Oh, come on now, George you got to be kidding me."

"You've never been in one? I am entitled, Miza has been gone over two years and I could be next. Baby, you have one life to live, make the most of it. Come now. Quit being a virgin." Sanari never had been into an Erotica store, why not have the experience? Joe needed some toys to play with his women friends he had picked up during karaoke days.

He had coffee with some Korean veterans on Tuesday mornings, did some comedy twice a week, and then it was karaoke days. She wondered what karaoke entailed as she followed him into the store.

George Stanford introduced her to a smaller version of the "Bullet" and she bought the pink one for Asa's birthday present. A wicked smile tugged at her lips and soon laughter broke out.

"If I knew this was going to happen to you I would have bought you sooner." George looked at her laughing at the toys on display; she told him what she planned for Asa.

"You think it would work. That woman is a stick in the mud." George was paying his bill as he spoke. Sanari called him her "sugar daddy," however, he never bought her anything except used candles from the Thrift shops.

On one occasion, when she needed some money to fix her Jag and her check was not clear and it would take too long to reorganize her investments to get the two hundred dollars extra need to pay her mechanic, George knocked on her door and gave her the money which she deliberately paid him back in bits and pieces.

Sometimes, just for the fun, she would borrow it again and give it to him in a few days. She had the feeling he was having fun with her cat and mouse game. George and his women were something else. He often complained to her about Marla wanting his money.

"That's what happened when you pick up whore from the bars.....the places you go to." She told him. George gave her the "one life to live speech" to which she replied jokily. "Oh hell Sugar daddy, you are a bloody Eveready battery. You tired one woman out and you're not even on the pill with a four-hour erection. Don't you want a temporary fix? Hasn't your mileage run out? Your motor needs to take Viagra to restart it?" She asked him seriously.

"Sanari, I am eighty-two years old veteran, bored to death. I've to find things to do. I can only do this much." He pulled his thumb and the next finger 2 inches apart, and he continues informing her. "Read autobiography, watched TV, have coffee, and have my friends over." She got it after that and let him be, he had to errand it.

George had taken to buying Sanari Christmas gifts of cakes and tea biscuits. One Christmas she gave him his desired gift after she asked him what he wanted and he replied, "Hairy pussy." He'd loved it.

Her facial expression was shockingly surprised; she looked at him in dismay, because he loved the shocking expression on her face when he said something sexual. She turned beet red and one would think she's some kind of a virgin or something.

"What?" She ran down the stairs and then a wicked smile crossed her lips. She waited until Christmas Eve and rang his doorbell leaving a note for him. On the note, she had written:
Last Christmas I give you nothing
This Christmas I give you what you desire
She stuck the note on the door and waited for the call and when he did call she showed up at his door on Christmas day with his gift.

"Merry Christmas Sugar daddy, here's your hairy pussy." George looked at his gift in her arms. The cat purred loudly resisting the holding and jumped on him. He was the one in shock with Sanari laughing. The girl had a sense of humor. A man would be lucky to have her as his mate.

"Oops! Doggone it, Sugar Daddy. You've to run after it, you know, how you men run after hairy pussy. Don't let it get away. Hurry, atta boy, chase." Laughter broke out from her for days, particularly when she mentioned the experience to Fiona.

Sanari was snuggled next to Ryland when George the phone call came through her cell. "George, is that you?" She asked sleepily as she looked at Ryland, hoping not to wake him. He lifted his arm from her and off the bed walking to the bathroom.

"Yes. Did I wake you?" George replied with a giggle.

"No, of course not. I was up belly dancing. Where the hell's your sorry ass at this time of night?" She took a deep breath and let it out. Her voice a high pitch yelled at him. "What time is it?" She asked the air.

"In jail." "What? What the fu...?"

George cut her off. "Watch your mouth young lady. Have respect for the elderly. Will you get here and bail me out? My checkbook is on the dining room table. And Ssssanari hurry?" He stammered.

"Oh, help me!"

"What can I do?" The voice startled Sanari as she had forgotten all about Ryland. She was a bit shy although they slept together with no sex, it seems years and not three days plus one. She automatically hurried into the closet for something to wear. "I have to go pick a friend up." She exhaled breathlessly.

"In jail?" Ryland asked with a yawn.

"In jail.' She walked out buttoning her dress; she picked up the cell phone and hit two on her speed dial for Fiona. She turned and left Ryland looking after her. She was tired after the long tenuous day with difficult consultation and the other FBI agent at The Twist Peach.

Fear swept into her for the agent ever finding out about her, Fiona, and Asa dealing with the rapist. Reliving the experience of

Tampa with Asa shook her up on how reckless Asa was with people's life. She climbed in the Jag with shaky emotions after the thought of the bitch driving into oncoming traffic! It was comforting to have Ryland's arms around her holding her. He waited until he thinks she was asleep and quietly crept into her bed. She loved it when he picked her up to make space for him because she always slept in the middle of the bed. They haven't spoken to each other about the sleeping arrangement and she dreaded the day he had to leave and avoided the discussion. She was rarely home during the day; he is healing and can help himself.

When she's home, she cooked meals for the next day and writes reports before falling into bed exhausted. How can she meet someone? It felt great as if they were together for years as if they belong to each other. They belong to each other!

It was about eight in the morning before George was out of jail sitting in the back seat fast asleep. He was charged with Driving Under the Influence (DUI) and Marijuana possession. They were on the way home when Sanari asked Fiona.

"Who was the guy you were talking to?"

"Oh, he's Sergeant Blake Belington. We have a date for Friday. He'll call me tomorrow."

"Damn, she met someone on a bailed out?" Laughter broke out from them. Sanari glanced into the back seat at her drunken friend. "I really don't know what to do with him." She whispered to herself as she pulled into the driveway of their building.

"There's not much you can do. I'll get the wheelchair." Fiona told her sleepy as she let a yawn out. Since the complex is a retirement community there are wheelchairs and a sofa by the elevator for those older folks who cannot stand for a long period of time or who cannot take the stairs. George has a smile on his face as the ladies partly lift him into the chair. He couldn't keep his head up, however, he can hear. He heard their conversation in the car and grinned wider.

"Oh, for Pete's sake. Knock it off, you old grouch." Sanari told him. "I can't believe that I had to come to bail your white ass out of jail for a DUI and marijuana possession.

"What ya doin' smoking and driving under the influence?" Fiona asked him. A grin was his answer. In a few minutes, he would be in bed and he'll have time to think about his drinking splendor and his arrest. "I don't think he's in a place to answer. He can hear, can't you Georgie, you're choosing not to answer. I wonder if I sit on his lap what would he do." Fiona moved to look at his face as Sanari pushed him in the wheelchair towards his door.

A frown appeared and Fiona laughed. Sanari was opening his door with her spare keys and turned to look at him. She shocked her head and grinned at him.

"He's worried who's going to undress and put him to sleep?" Sanari said to Fiona. "Don't worry, my cutie honey bunny sugar daddy, Fiona will have that pleasure." She tugged at his cheeks as she wheeled him into his bedroom. "I'm sure shad seen better in her days. Yours are all wrinkled and old and soft and……" They lifted him from the wheeled chair and put him on his bed and pulled the covers over him.

"I know that I am allergic to all physical work." Fiona admitted and Sanari replied, "Oh hell, me too. Can you return the wheels, Fiona please?" "Sure. I wait for you downstairs." Fiona yawned and answered as she wheeled the chair out of the apartment. Sanari took the shirt, vest, and jacket off him and put him into his pajama top.

"Do this to me one more time and I am leaving you in jail." She proceeded to unbuckle his pants and pulled them down for her to put him into his pajamas. She took a deep breath and looked at him shockingly. "What the fuck?" Sanari pulled back and stood looking at her friend who had no underwear on and started to laugh.

She walked to his draw in his dresser and pulled out his briefs and tossed it to him. "When you quit grinning, you can change your bloody self." Without a second look at him, she tossed the clothing onto his bed covers and left the room shaking her head in shock at her discovery.

26

George Stanford grinned wider showing his peril white denture. He opened an eye slowly only to see her turned away from him. If they knew about his time in jail and the event that took place while he was here, they would be laughing and crying with joy. He probably will too, not now, hell, he will wait when the shock and the marijuana reared off, then he would be laughing. The grin on his face became wider and wider.

Marla didn't know that Teresa was coming over to give him a blow. Sanari had taught that he was sexually retired when he told her about Marla, Teresa, Michele, Jan, and Phyllis. Poor Sanari was in shock for weeks when he told her about his sex life. She refused to visit him. It was healthy and that was all that matters. A man at his age needs some kind of entertainment!

George had called Marla to bail him out of jail, however, she didn't answer her phone. He figured she was fucking some guy she picked up from the bar. A frown borrowed on his forehead as memories poured into his thoughts. He had gone to see his friend Annya belly dance and to sell his dead lover's costume. He was very vulnerable after Miza's death and angry that she left him all alone.

Sanari was his friend, his only friend. Miza used to belly dance and had many costumes. Annya bought them all and he took a fancy visiting her on a Sunday afternoon when she belly dance at a Mediterranean restaurant.

It gives him the pleasure of watching her as he mourned Miza. Marla was jealous of his relationship with Annya and came over to talk to him pretending to be his friend, if he was not that lonely he would not have her over; he hates her cooking. One day she invited him to karaoke. This was good for him as it opened a whole new life.

George had a physical attachment to Marla the very first time she kissed him on his lips. Then she started cooking for him and they did Karaoke shows together; he booked the shows and split the money. He wanted to spend more time with her and that was when it went bitter.

Marla started to pick up men at the clubs they did Karaoke shows and as much as it hurts, he had to let it go. One day she invited him over and this day he lost all respect for her; a whore she is at that was what he called her as he related his experience with Marla to Sanari.

Marla invited George to hr apartment. He knocked on the door and when he received no answer he turned to leave, walking to his car. George heard Marla calling him as he unlocked his car's door. He went back to the apartment and Marla invited him in. She was wearing the robe he bought her and had just finished fucking a man, who used the side door and left. He saw him walking past the window he was sitting in Marla's apartment.

He left soon after and believed what Sanari told him about her. She warned him after they bumped into each other one day on the stairs when Marla was leaving as Sanari was arriving. They talked for a while and Marla became jealous of George and Sanari's relationship.

Things went sour from then on for him and Marla. Sanari mentioned the jealousy to him and he had told her that's not so, disbelieving her. She told him that Marla is out for what she can get from him, money, and prescription pills.

George spent more money on Marla than any other woman he was seeing. He even bought her a new air conditioning system with the agreement that she repaid him. She did for a while and would manipulate him for whatever she can get from him. Unknown to Marla, George had written his will and had Sanari on all of his accounts. He had begun not to trust Marla, however, he was lonely for company and he loved singing with her.

Marla, on the other hand, stole cash he had in a draw when he was sick and she had visited him including his prescription medication, and Vicodin he had for pain. She used some and sold the rest. She blamed Sanari for the missing pills. After he healed from the cold, he realized that she was lying. Sanari was out of town with Fiona at some spa he can't remember.

Sanari had also warned him about Jack that no one wanted to be his friend and he too was jealous of their relationship. She had told him that she didn't like it when he wanted to keep hugging her and although she told him to stop, he refused plus he was a very angry man.

George admitted, lying in bed, in his drunken splendor that Sanari was right with her assumption about Marla and Jack. He had taken Jack to the Erotic shop to get a vibrator for his wife.

Jack had confessed to him that there was no sex between him and his wife, Mavis and that she controlled the money. She gave him an allowance and checked the credit card slips every week. Jack was a well-known comedian on the cruised ships for many years and Mavis is his second wife. Jack defined himself with money and comedy.

George realized that Marla wanted his money and was out to get what she can from him. He had everything he had after Miza's death; it was her idea that Sanari was a good girl and would take care of him.

Sanari didn't know that he had transferred two hundred and fifty thousand dollars in her name because he suspects Marla trying to scam him when he found her going through his document on the breakfast table.

He had a feeling that bitch Asa suspected that he had money when he bumped into her at the bank. She got a bullet in her head. George seeing the irony in the "Bullet" started to laugh and wondered why they named a sex toy "Bullet." Who thought of it?

Oh hell, what a fucking long night? What a fucking good night! He had hundreds of mileage on sex that he had accumulated over the years. The day after he first met Jan his first lover, an autumnal lever rose and he had given up on sex after he turned fifty.

Then Miza came into his life and his aging rocket ship had exactly a college lifted off, however, it survived the rigorous years periodically. A smile returned because he made progress and history whaling in the Y chromosome.

George let off the sexual steam that was building for so long. Nothing in his eighty-three years is as thrilling as a good blow job. Neeta, his part-time lover had given him a good blow, one that he would remember much later. They had been drinking heavily and then celebrated with a Bob Marley marijuana cigar. The cigar was expensive, one hundred dollars, however, it was worth every penny he paid. The lawyer he hired would be charging him four thousand dollars and according to the police officer more for the DUI classes.

The blow job was four thousand dollars plus the one hundred dollars for the Bob Marley cigar, summing it all up as the most expensive blow job he ever had in his life. Was it worth it? He wished he knew; he was too high and drunk to remember much of it except it was fun. Neeta doesn't have teeth and the blow without teeth is something to experience!

Then it was his turn to please her as she wanted to recreate a dream she had of him. They drank some more and then finished the joint. Neeta had to get home before her husband did, otherwise it would be trouble. She wanted to be tucked into bed as if she was waiting for his return whatever or wherever he's been. He said he was out with the boys drinking which meant he would return drunk. Ah, he's drunk and she's high as a kite. Ha, what a way to go, what a way to feel? George was gripping this underwear tightly, lying on his back, eyes closed and smiling. His other hand rested under his head as his thoughts drifted to taking Neeta home. He was returning to his apartment when he was pulled over, arrested, and taken to jail.

The young police found his marijuana and although he told him that it was medical, he still took him to jail. He was photographed and put into a cell with other criminals. They were all younger by well thirty or more years and they kept looking at him. They couldn't help themselves as they want to know what he did to get here. When he told them "DUI and Marijuana possession" they all laughed, giving him a high five and saying how cool he was, and disagreed with the arrest, especially upon learning his age.

"Yep, go tell that to the idiot who arrested me."

"I hear ya pops," "he should've taken you home," "yeap, taken ya home," came the various replies from the inmates. It was during this moment an African heritage correctional officer asked them to take their clothes off and put on the orange jumpsuit. Everyone began the task as the officer watched for weapons or drugs or any illegal things tumbling out of somewhere that was missed during the pat-down.

George was in his world, smiling and grinning and very much out of reality, that it took a long while before he realized the silence was in the cell. Everyone's eyes were on him as he looked around with his sleepy blue eyes.

"What the fuck you're looking at?" He wanted to know.

The other criminals picked up their clothes and ran to the further side of the cell looking and watching him in shock. The correction officer was also in a state of shock, not because of his underclothing, because of the size of his penis. The officer never knew a white man can have a larger penis than a black one.

Hell, his is small compared to this old white man's. What's size does he have? Nine inches because he is seven points five and that made him small in compassion for his old white man.

One crossed dresser quickly capitalized on the situation and approached him. "Mmm honey, you are my type .....mmm, ya wanna play after they let us outa here?" He asked as he stared into his blue eyes all the way down to his penis.

George didn't look at his admirer. He smiled and the grin disappeared when the request took charge of his brain. He tried to grasp what the silence was in honor of and why they were, all including the correctional officer, looking at him. It took him a few minutes to focus and when he did his eyes followed theirs only to discover their shocking expression was fixed on his private body.

He looked down at his penis and realized that his secret was out. He had forgotten in his blind drunken splendor that he was wearing a brassiere and panties with a ring on his erect pen.

27

Fiona and Sanari were at the pool sunbathing on a cool day; actually, they were there because it was a good place to get together for a talk. They were waiting for Asa who had worked out the details on the rapist. They decided to bring her in, otherwise, somehow, she would have followed and blackmailed them. This way she would keep her mouth shut and the secret would be safe.

Asa hated illegal business; she also hates rapists. Sanari and Fiona had talked it over a few weeks ago and decided to let Asa plan it because this way they too can have something over her and she would remain silent because she's afraid of the law and illegal activities.

Asa had called the police on George for selling prescription medication when she thought that he was involved with Michelle only to be laughed at by the police. She told them later she felt such a fool.

Fiona and Sanari laughed at drinks and dinner because they both think she's a fool and more of a paranoid "dumb fuck." They had no admiration or respect for her, however, she's good as any to help them with the rapist. Fiona wanted to let them know that the rapist called her again, a few times reminding her of his upcoming visit. A restaurant wasn't an appropriate place for discussion, too many interruptions from people they know, and noisy. They couldn't have had the conversation in any of the apartments due to Asa's bugs and potential blackmail.

They told Asa that whenever the neighbors see them going into each other place they would knock on the door and want to join in. Asa bought the lie. Well, it isn't a lie, more the truth. It came as part of the package; living for many years in a retirement community where most people are bored, lonely, and not forgetting they knew all the old folks with a handful of the new and young folks. They loved gossiping and liquor and conversation. A party is great, too.

No one would come to the pool on a cool day, even a heated pool. The old and sexually deprived men usually sit out on their porches watching the young on a sunny day. Today, they were all dressed in jeans and a long-sleeved t-shirt with coffee and vodka. The young ones are locked indoors watching television or doing something else.

Fiona was about to talk when a baby squirrel ran under Sanari's chair with the bluest eyes ever. He was wild and most playful; he wanted to play. He began playing with her shoes and upon feeling him climbing the chair onto her toes, Sanari jumped up and ran towards the pool. He followed her and without a second thought, she jumped into the warm water.

The squirrel went in and started to swim. In fright, Sanari urinated blushing with fear and embarrassment. Fiona seeing the catastrophe between Sanari and the friendly squirrel rolled back into her chair laughing extremely loud; she fell off her chair unto the concrete ground still roaring with laughter. Sanari moved closer from the middle of the pool toward the ridge where the friendly squirrel watched her. He was still a baby and had not learned to swim.

Sanari moved in closer talking to the animal. "Don't look at me with those puppy love eyes. You really had me there for a minute, you know. I was terrified, not petrified. I usually like to know a guy's intention before the pursuit begins." The squirrel turned his head in understanding and blinked his huge blue eyes at her. Fiona started to take photographs with her phone camera, added. "You never know when there is a Kodak moment. Come here Nugget." As if understanding, the squirrel turned to Fiona and began walking toward her. She named him.

"I don't believe it. You name him and he understands!" Sanari exclaimed in surprise. "I have to get out and go home to change. I am freezing." She concluded.

"I got the charm and you got the charisma." Upon hearing

Sanari's voice, Nugget ran to her and stood on the top of the pool deck, looking lovingly at her. "Oh, damn it. I am in love. You are such a cute, aren't you Nugget?" Nugget wanted to be near her, jumped into the pool, and began swimming again, however, it was too much; he turned back and took his place on the deck watching his new love, Sanari. She moved into the middle again and as fear disappeared, she swam towards the squirrel. They looked at each other for an endless second carrying on a silent conversation. It took another few minutes before Sanari climbed out of the pool on the other side.

Nugget seeing her movement anticipated her existence and ran there, awaiting her entrance. He followed Sanari to the chair and tried to climb up to where she sat on the towel as she dried herself. He climbed up surprising Sanari who suddenly jumped up and ran a few feet away looking at the critter.

Fiona began to laugh again, Nugget looking at his love with sun kisses while Sanari shook her head in wonderment.

The cold air at midnight hit Asa's hard structure into an oblivious stance. She was taking the trash to the dumpster and spotted a few neighbors standing by their cars chatting. She thought nothing of it because she already knew them and served no purpose in her life.

She was in a hurry because she was meeting Sanari and Fiona to explain her grand plan. James, her lover, and investigator of whatever she wanted to know found some interesting information.

James was a retired con artist and had the free time to wander in and out as he checked on the information of the people she passed on to him. They were friends with benefits, a fuck buddy, and someone to help her blackmail others to have money for life. It had gotten to such a definition of her character that it seemed that's all the neighbors talked about and really, she doesn't care. The tapes are hidden and as long as she has them she will be safe.

Asa's thoughts drifted to her plotting the Fait accompli for Fiona and her rapist. She smiled as she goes through thoughtfully and complimented herself on a perfect plan.

At first, she was skeptical of joining them and thought about it over a dozen times. She figured since she had nothing on either Fiona or Sanari she'll have the upper hand with her plot to frame the rapist.

She knew that Fiona still carried the experience of the rape with her. It's time she left him and the experience behind and moved into the present moment. What pain to live in and the saddest thing of all he got away with it. Well, not on her watch. She hated rapists and can plan a good plot. This is a mighty good plot. She was very proud of her piece of artwork.

The energy was strong as time grew closer for Fiona to meet with her rapist, John Miller. She loved what Asa had planned and this upcoming long weekend she had already taken off work as the front desk manager at the Cyprus Hotel on four thirty-six close to Orlando International Airport. When the rapist called, she told him where to meet her. She smiled and whispered to herself, "You're in for a surprise. You're in for a rude awakening, you had it coming." Fiona's mechanical thoughts of the rape and years of agony lingered in her life as training wheels on a bicycle which often send her into a spiral of migraines. Unlike others, who have risen above their fears with counseling and learned to ride free as the wind she had not; then there are those people like Janet Lorrison who had been helped and yet lived with the rape each day.

Others cling tenaciously to the thoughts and images of their rape and/or sexual abuse experience, wondering why they wobbled precariously from the past to the future, missing the present moment, wondering why they haven't been set free. Why do they relive the incident and kept dreaming that it'll go away come tomorrow? Tomorrow it seems never comes. Fiona is ready to say goodbye to her past and moved into the present with Blake. No more fears no more missed opportunities and no more presence of faking an orgasm. Blake is a gentle lover and she already knew their sex life will be hell on wheels. She smiled and turned on the television for company.

On the opposite side of the lake, Sanari was tossing and turning in her bed. Although it was ten-thirty in the night, she was asleep considering lately, this past two weeks her nightmare came back and kept haunting her. Fervor ran through her body as a leg was insinuated between hers, resting there exerting an arousal pressure on her.

Moments later the oily sea covered their bodies and she would surface from sleep covered in sweat. She would shower and make coffee then sit on the sofa picking into her memory to recapture the moment. Who was that man in her past that was sleeping with her? How can she ever move on from this memory that plagued her as if it's the black fever? This has been her life since seems forever.

Even when she's concentrating on capturing the loss of memory that constantly teased the edge of her thoughts, it woke her into frustration. It seemed confusing with the bits of images that kept protruding when she was under stress. Was she raped as a little girl? The dream seemed more real and ramp today that they are going to meet Fiona's rapist.

A thousand times she allowed her thoughts to tiptoe through the welter of memories and each time she came up with nothing, well scattered blurred images that made no logical sense. There are the other memories that kept echoing in the valley of what little remembrance she had of her past.

None of it made any sense, much less any logic. She felt a huge piece of her life is missing and there was no end to the rigorous images that popped up when she least expected it. There are vague images of a man who surrounded her memories and it's very clear he was into her. Was he sexually in her or was he into her as attracted? He had blinded and muddled her on some journey in the desert. Were there two men in her nightmare? If she wanted to find love such as Fiona with Blake she has to move on without the baggage of the past. It's time she kissed the nightmare she had become, say goodbye, and moved on.

On the other hand, maybe it's time she took another approach. What she cannot access from one direction she can approach in another. One thought began to formulate into another, forming solid concepts that finally made logic. She has to act upon the concept to make it a reality. It's time to be realistic and face her truth.

28

The discovery of ethnicity coinciding with worldwide society upheaval was once shone upon, is presently very common; it somewhat laid peaceful. People are people except those who lived by myths and lies are the ones who objected to the mixes of the species and have become radical fighting for separation.

Today, the rain fell leaving the air damp and moistened. The sun was setting on a cold day bearing warmth that humbled the atmosphere with a unique blend of colors. This pale sun beans through the window in a cold January afternoon to dusk Fiona fading tan features.

The sun from the window shot shades of red and orange with a fainted yellow through her golden curls and shun light gold, red and yellow colors onto her hands. She was bathed by the crisped air as the sunlight sent a crimson color to her tan cheeks. She felt the sun gossamer touch on her and stirred to let her companion know that she is vibrant. She had closed her eyes and took a deep breath to gain control of the electrifying sexual energy current that ran from her to him.

Fiona slowly opened her blue eyes and met black ones; her salad kissed by the sun had lost its attractiveness. She finished her appetizer of oysters and ran her tongue over her lips. She drank a little red wine and sat back in her chair looking away in the distance past the building that was captivated by the setting sun.

Over the music and constant chatter, in the distance, she heard a fainted cry of a burglar alarm that she knew from experience pealed loudly. Passersby would jump and back off from the naked violence of malfunctioning equipment or burglary.

Sergeant Blake Belington sat opposite Fiona basseting in the glorified energy that swirled around them. This is beyond attraction for both. He knew this, he felt this, he can touch it, he can taste it, and how he inhaled every fragment of the energy of pure love.

Yes, this is true pure unfiltered love that is running havoc in his entire body and this elegant lady sitting opposite him.

Fiona looked up at the black man sitting across from her in the restaurant and was completely lost in the energy that surged around them. She doesn't understand any of it, however, she had decided that she'll go with the flow. It felt beyond great. Is there anything beyond great? Oh, yes, beauty. She felt her limbs tremble as his sexy black eyes slid over her body in a transparent masculine appreciation.

A flame of sensations ignited in the pit of her stomach as warmth spread through her to her pelvis and wet her panties. She felt it as her whole body reacted as though he had already touched her.....in her scared sanctuary.

The ambiance between them was purely sexual and more that it seemed to be understood what their intention with each other was, that it was not causal. The first meeting was attraction and more, however, neither knew what the more was about until their first date. They had walked along the ridge of Helenville closed to the swamp drinking latte and talking. Blake didn't touch her even as he gave her the latte.

Common sense told him not to because right there and then he knew that if he did he would move in with her. He wanted her to feel what he is feeling, therefore they walked and talked. He wanted a relationship with emotional sustenance and to be the guy who would kiss her forever. He wanted her to surrender in his arm and he in hers and be the only guy to bury himself deep inside her. He wanted their emotions to guide their lovemaking to full-blown orgasms. He wanted her to want it too.

Fiona wasn't sure what to expect from Blake and decided to play it safe and hardly looked at him. She was nervous, however, as they talk about everything in life including themselves she began to see him as her beaux.

Sunlight had lit her blond hair golden bringing it to shine. Blake wanted to touch it to see whether it would warm his fingers and at that very moment, something magical happened. For a brief instant, black and blue eyes collided as a zap of magnetic energy fused between them. She sought refuge from his gaze, his in hers as they broke free.

His hair looked clean and healthy fresh from the shower. Fiona had the strong impulse to run her fingers through it, instead, she ran a hand through her hair that had clasped at the nape of her neck. Her body was bathed in a soft light diffused by the black-bellied clouds forming above threatening to rain. The sun whipped her hair that was beating against her cheeks and eyes then a flipping breeze tossed her hair away from her face.

"I like to get to know you more." She said with a twinkle that amazed Blake as much as it mystified him at first; he nodded in agreement.

"I like that too, to get to know you." Those exact thoughts she saw mirrored in his eyes and her body sundered. He watched as her blue eyes turned the shade of lighter grey from the sky's reflection. They walked and talked some more about the present life. They shared stories of their sons and daughters and grandchildren.

The sun dipped behind the clouds for a short while casting grey shadows on Helenville and slowly began to peek over the horizon. They couldn't see the sun setting from their stance, however, they felt the effect of it, the romance.

The sun was only a blush in the dawn it seems to them. In the shadow of the woods and swamp, they heard the animals cry for dinner, the birds chipped and the gators chomped on their catch. There was silence between Blake and Fiona as they listened to each other energy, making choices for a new beginning.

Blake looked at her laid back in the chair and connected his black with her blue eyes. They anchored together for a very long time without sharing thoughts or touching each other. If this is love at first well third sight it's magnificent. They had finished the appetizer when the steaks arrived. He had to look away from her to the waiter, Janet who laid the meal before them and walked away without a word. She knew that silence was a golden moment for people who found love.

They ate in silence and lingered over a dessert of blueberry pie and coffee. They needed the coffee to sober them up from the feeling of ecstasy. Blake has to drive Fiona home and only hopes she sends him away although his body is dying to make love to her. He wanted to touch her, all of her. He wanted....oh, let it go.

Not on their second date and third meeting maybe the next one, tomorrow. He thinks he's fortunate to meet someone at his age of sixty, father of two boys aged thirty and twenty-five with two grandchildren. He was looking for a mate, however, as he sat here he decided he would like to spend the rest of his life with her. Yes, he wanted to do that, spend the rest of his life with her.

In a few years, he would be retired from the police force with two incomes, one from the Air Force and the other from the police force. They can travel and live comfortably for the rest of their life. Is he planning their future together? He had gone crazy, yep really Looney.

Fiona broke eye contact as the waiter came to collect the dishes and while she spoke with Blake, she ran her eyes over his body. He is physically fit, muscular with a swarthy square-jawed face and elegantly crew cut jet-black curly hair with a white long sleeve shirt and charcoal slacks. He oozed class and all potently male, in control, not angry, elegant, and classy. She found her match and loved the chemistry they have between them.

Yes, she wanted to be touched by him, not tonight, not so soon maybe the next date. Tomorrow, if he doesn't ask her out, she will and tomorrow they will taste each other till.....his color faded. She smiled and it reached her blue eyes. Blake saw it and nodded.

"Tomorrow," was silently passed between them and acknowledged.

Yes, she can spend the rest of her life with him. The question is how do you go about keeping someone of such magnitude in your life? How can she? She had something to take care of with the girls and the sooner they get over the business she can close her past off from interrupting her present moment and her future with his gentle hunk of a man. Thoughts broke through to her consciousness with the remembrance of the weekend plan.

"Oh, no not tomorrow, I'm going away with Asa and Sanari. We're off to Clear Water. Sorry, it was planned long before I met you." She looked at him disappointed, however, he understood.

"Call me when you get back?" He smiled very sweetly at Fiona who almost fainted with joy. Well, his first thoughts when he met her were to take her to bed. It had been a long for him that he desperately desires release.

His right and left hand were getting tired. He needed a woman's touch. He has to wait another forty-eight hours or longer because he wanted Fiona forever and tonight he decided to abundant his plans of seduction.

29

Asa's bedroom was turned into Grand Central Station. The naked plan of beating rapist John Miller lay dormant at her feet. Maps were tacked over some paintings of where the event will take place.

A list of things that needed to be purchased was taped on another wall and finally what everyone's roles should be was laid on the floor below the list of things. She was sweating slightly and blamed it on the planning and the heat of the afternoon sun, regardless that it was the heart of winter.

This is Florida and sometimes January is hot when the sun came out to play. The flushed sheen on her white skin reminded her of the after-effects of being raped. She felt her body register the knowledge of being forced to shift from being happy to stone-cold to accommodate that familiar pressure in her when she realized that she was gang-raped.

Asa's inhibitions surfaced in remembrance of the five college men that held her down and took turns. Yes, she lied to Fiona and Sanari when she told them that story. It was a story she made up and wanted to believe for the last twenty-eight-plus years of her life. When a friend extended a hand to give her something she automatically took it without question. She was ganged raped, not by college men, by her father's friends who called themselves holy.

A flicker of remembrance took her back to the day her parents had a Thanksgiving party with a few close friends. She had thought that Peter was a good friend of her father's and is trustworthy. When he told her that the pill he held in his hands would keep her awake thus she can study for exams she believed him. Five of her father's dearest holy friends including two priests took turns on her sleeping body.

The pills made her powerless to fight, however, it made her conscience enough to feel the effects of the brutal entrance to her virgin body. She was only sixteen.

In the darkening sky, Asa's face particularly her eyes was full of anger, as she took the box of requirements for the upcoming journey with John Miller in the trunk of the rental vehicle. She put the memories in the past and her heart in the present. It touched her, the past of hers as if it was a tangible chill of arctic wind. She stopped; realizing she was busting with anger as the memory of emotions flooded her.

She had pulled up short in trust and her frustration turned into deep-rooted anger as she plotted revenge. This helped lessen the impact of the pain she felt after the fact of her gang rape. It had eaten at her life as a bucket of acid since she never had counseling she took up alcohol.

Pangs of fear seized as a riptide eddying around her emotions spilled forth taking her there again. She had fallen asleep and woke up early in the morning. As she left the room it hit her, what had happened. She stood still feeling the soreness between her legs and listening to the silence. She slowly opened the door and walked to her room.

The place was clean from the party. The caterers always did a good job after one of her mother's parties. Upon arriving in her room, she took her clothes off and stayed in the shower until the water turned cold. The men from then on all looked at her with smiles on their faces. She had stopped going to church much to her dismay of her parents. Whenever there was a party she would spend the night over at a girlfriend's house. She had no girlfriends, however, she had paid different girls money to spend the night. The week she turned eighteen she took her revenge and left home forever, never looking back.

Still fueled with anger she took a paralytic to standoff from the five men until she put her revenge into action. She paid someone heavily to take photographs of the men and photoshop them with porn stars, naked. She then had the photographs delivered at a particular time.

Each of the rapist's wives opened the envelope in the heart of dinner where they had all gathered to celebrate three of the children's sixteen birthdays.

This was the first time since the ganged rape that she attended the party. She was there to witness the event of her sweet revenge. She had the last laugh as she stood on the steps of the house and listened to the heated arguments. All of their children saw the photographs. Together there were enough photographs to carpet a small room.

Over the years, she had a detective trace each of them to see how they had panned out through the years. They all had less demeaning jobs, were divorced, and entangled with their family even hers. They were branded sexual abuse by the police. She had taken extra photographs of them and young girls, all photoshopped, and sent them to the police.

Fearing the police would discover the photoshopping she had posted them on the internet. A detective found them living in a different state not far from each other. They were on welfare and have addictions.

Five years later, she had confronted them. They didn't regret what they did to her and wanted to continue with what they had started. She told them what she did and laugh.

"I didn't get to tell you all what pricks you were; let it be known that you all will pay the price for raping me for the rest of your life." She laughed and watched in pleasure as they squalled in agony. There used to be gentleness in Asa, currently held toughness with a reckless streak, masked by fears and insecurities which came from being hurt excessively with the lack of love. They couldn't do anything because they would be arrested after all they were registered, sexual offenders.

Asa had told James, her lover she needed some time for herself and send him home to ponder and do what he does well, drink. She didn't want him to know of her collaboration with Fiona and Sanari because just in case things go sour she would blame them and head home.

Things wouldn't go sour because she's the planner and she's not like those two nitwit females, Sanari and Fiona. They lived a very boring life and were dumb about everything in life. She knew this because she had followed them everywhere for too long. They are into erotica more than she and James.

All Fiona thinks of is Blake and all Sanari thinks of well.....what does that iniquitous Indian Sanari think about. She talked about art, buying, and selling which she does off and on. Thinking further Asa realized that Sanari conversation had never gotten deeper and the more she thought about it the more her head ached.

Better to abandon it before she disappointed them no, she would be the one disappointed because she's truly looking forward to beating the rapist. It would help her relieve her pain from being raped. Let him pay for the others.

A smile came out of Asa, a big one spread across her face. She knew how many rapists have walked free, how many sexual abusers walked free, and how many rapes and abuse was not reported.

Fifty-four percent of rapes are not reported making that ninety-seven percent of rapists do not spend a day in jail. She had checked it out online a long time ago and then again when her plans for John Miller began to take shape.

Alone in this compound with what she knew of about one hundred men and women in their eighty who were either raped or abused or both and never reported any. She's doing this careful maneuver for them too. The justice system is not broken; it was made that way. You have to find ways to work with it or beat it. She chose to beat it since they fired her from the hospital. Someone is going to be on the receiving end of her anger. She smiled as she collected her gun and the keys to the rental car and headed for the door.

In minutes, Sanari and Fiona joined her and they were off on their journey to meet the rapist of Fiona. Asa and Sanari can feel the energy of pious rage in Fiona as they headed in the direction of Melbourne to conduct the plan.

Asa had told them to tell everyone they were heading into Clearwater if asked. Sanari knew that Asa had a kibosh in place in case Fiona became a juggernaut.

A veil of darkness protected them from being seen as well as the plan that Asa is putting into action. As they mingled with the shadows of the night, they heard the shuddering sobs being released from her throat as Fiona faced her truth. Ugly emotions welled up internally and threatened to burst through into her civilized exterior.

Sanari leaned forward from the backseat and squeezed her shoulders. She tossed her a small box of tissue and told her. "Let it out. It's human to let out the pain. It's the only way to let go and heal. John Miller had dodged the bullet and now he'll pay dearly for his crime."

Fiona attempted to gauge the level of her deep-rooted anger by peeping through the darkness of her life before and after the rape. She was living in agony and operating daily from a place of pain. The depth of her pain had made a dent in her deep-rooted anger and dizziness suddenly slammed through her as if a tidal wave had hit her. Fear whipped up in her thoughts as she focused on the view in front of her at this late hour.

Over the years, the fear had slowly become overwhelming and only permitting rage; there was no allowance for anything else. The endless sleepless nights and the void she felt within her as she deliberately bought her children into adulthood.

Tears pushed closer to the surface as her pain broke free from the shell that had enclosed her understanding. Looking back, she realized in the months that followed and the shock was buried deep within; all she had was a churning anger building into a rage that covered the love in her heart. This is the love she felt for Blake and wanted to give freely to him. He bought love out; he reached into her and pulled it to the surface and now he shall have it.

"My body has been tampered with. I'm going to kill that mother fucker." Fiona clapped a hand over her senseless runaway mouth. She didn't know that there was this much hate in her. It does not only shake her, it shocks her core. Her heart began to pound loudly and she shook her head putting her other hand over her mouth trying desperately to stop the flow of words that she had constricted for all those years.

She turned to look at Sanari and then Asa, her eyes wide and blank with surprise. Blond hair fell forward over one eyebrow covering her dark blue eyes before she removed a hand from her mouth and tuck them behind her ear.

"Consider this inflammatory rhetoric-emotion disclosure and closure all in one." Sanari comforted her. "You had the anger in you for way too long. Time to heal, Fi, time to let it all go and heal. Use this opportunity to heal and just let it be." The silence was dotted into an hour as thoughts quietly flowed for all three girls, tension build as time drew near to the meeting place. Sanari stayed tuned in to Fiona silently crying and blowing her nose occasionally.

Asa was quiet for the first time in all the years they knew her, staying focused on her driving; she drove slow and careful. She kept her eyes on the road and rarely dove over the speed limit. There was not much traffic and the drive was a constant flow all the way into Melbourne.

Sanari had anticipated that if John Miller didn't what to fight back or what if he did fight back? Men hated fighting and when they do they fight with aggression and anger. When they are confronted directly their instinct becomes hostile and they automatically become defensive; verbal assault reacted the same as physical assault-throw a punch and instinct surfaces, however, flight creatures will retreat.

Will John Miller retreat or will he fight? She refused to give him the chance to do and had agreed with Asa to drug him. She touched the syringe in her handbag that Asa had given her.

Fiona permitted all emotions to surface and let them flow with her tears.

The rage had turned to revenge anger suddenly sparked in her dark blue eyes. Intensified anger rushed to her face, and vibrated its energy down to her clenched fists traveling to her knees and settling for a minute on her toes before returning to her stomach.

Violence never took a day off from her. It had defined her life for too many years, she had forgotten how to live and had learned how to survive the rigors of years. She shifted her lifeless body and turned to the girls forcing a smile.

Trying not to hide the deep-rooted anger in her voice she

whispered, "Thanks, guys."

"We're here." Came from Asa's lips, spoke for the first time since they left Helenville. The rain was drumming hard against the windows. They had decided to go a good six hours before the appointed time. They had a stop for coffee as no one felt like eating. The sun had broken through the black belly clouds and was stepping in the coffee shop window bathing them as well as the room with a warm glow. With the evening giving over tonight the rain stopped; they all let out a much-held breath.

The three girls were waiting for him long before he arrived at the designated hour. Asa took the back behind the driver's seat as Fiona slipped in that seat indicating that she is the only one in the car. Asa had parked under a light in case John Miller was smart to check the back seat.

Asa and Sanari had crunched down in the space where feet usually rest and cover themselves with black blankets. The revenge plans had held them tighter through the fall into winter these past weeks surfaced and were about to be released.

#

Pure raw power streamed from John Miller as he stepped into the four-door black car. He didn't have to get up early, however, his internal alarm clock built on adrenaline worked as a countdown for a space shuttle launching. His usual time was after dark, nonetheless, he hadn't much sleep since he called Fiona two months ago and told her he would like to see her, to apologize for what he did to her. It worked like a charm.

Although he was told that his external picture of males changed during their transitional age which he agreed with, nonetheless his fundamental nature of lust is the same in the past as it is in the present moment.

In the part where lust captured his thoughts and made him a slave he disagreed. He never lusted after a woman he takes what he wants when he wants. He looked at his body and saw no more of a boy's structure as if he was still seventeen years old.

Dark and grotesque was his look for the night as he climbed into the car and smiled at Fiona who was driving. She flashed an angry smile and felt the rage rising from her body as his small darting eyes and ruff fuzzy hair rolled over her body with lust. She went inside her thoughts to retrieve the girl's reminder to stay cool. She groused as her mouth twisted with fury seeing the sharp blade of his face.

Although the character has a large mental capacity; it was running thin. Anger replaced the panic that had flared in her eyes, at this moment habited her personality. She added to her line of thought a character that will charm him; she flashed John a fake smile as her eyes left the road and looked at him. She turned her head towards the road before he can look into her eyes. He bought it.

Fiona pulled the car out of the park and gunned the engine towards the destination as planned. There was no traffic on the road; she deliberately drove within the thirty-five miles per hour city limit.

On the rapist's face, heavy waves of movement highlighted his triumph of blackmailing Fiona. There was no vain regret only a dark essence of fire that lit his face giving him anticipated pleasure. It ran ramp in his thoughts, particularly the coming night he would have with her.

Arrah... son of a bitch Fiona was silently expressing. Fresh intensified anger flooded through her as she felt him looking at her. Her foot hit the gas pedal and she speeds idle and went over the city limit as she continued to drive in the direction of the dark deserted area. She focused on her driving and from the corner of her eyes she saw the wide grin on his face as he stared at her.

Fiona had not recognized John. She assumed that the man she was letting in the car was him since he was the only person standing at the spot she requested. She guessed that her consciousness didn't want to recognize his face, however, her subconsciousness did. He watched her gesture and a muscle worked in his throat and twitched in his unshaven jaw; she gave no sign of disturbance.

John Miller pulled a knife out from his jacket and let the light from a street lamp deflexed on it. It spurred into Fiona's face and reflex on the back of his hand. "A little assurance to get what I want; I waited a long time for this and tonight I'm going to enjoy more." He laughed out loud, his breath inhabited by the fumes of alcohol.

Silence beholden this moment and silence reigns as Fiona kept her eyes on the road. Regardless that she could see for miles in all directions she focused her thoughts on where the wooden area ended and the flat table rock began. Her eyes were trained on the low barren rugged rock that showed the rental to an almost standstill. A few black belly clouds hugged the skyline and were reluctant to spill or say goodbye to the night.

John Miller watched Fiona with a smirk on his face. The revulsion was boiling in her and she hated to have him killed for all she has done to keep herself alive. Nope, killing was out of the question because Asa would win by blackmailing her. A bloody good beating he is going to get right where it hurts the most.

Yes, that's it... the killing was easy for him, living with impotency was painful, and not being able to be in control was pain with pleasure. Pain for him and pleasure for her and all the women he raped. John was twirling the knife in his hand smiling at her.

The energy running through him poured into the midair and made it musky with anticipation. A harsh lump of air was trapped in her lungs as she pulled the car into a spot and killed the engine.

"Tell me John Miller how many women have you raped?" The question died before it was fully born to be replaced by another. "Why did you rape me?" She turned the upper half of her body and looked fully at him.

"Aoha there, rape is a big word. I don't rape I take whenever I can."

"How many, John?" A huge wealth of emotions was hidden in those words. Fiona took a deep breath and he laughed out the reply to her question.

"I don't know. I don't keep check darling. Oh fifty, I had fun with them. It took a while to find you. Been a long time, why don't we get started." He leaned into her with the knife upon her cheek.

Fiona laughed a deliberate sexy chuckle that impacted him as surely as a bullet was straight to his penis. He was surprised at her reaction and his attraction to her after all these years. He moved uncomfortable and groaned aloud. He licked his lips showing grey teeth. He didn't know what to do. She wasn't afraid and that spoil his fun. Fear was what he jerked off on, not laughter.

Fiona's rage was building since the incident many decades ago. She was torn with hate for him as anger blazed through her, rage was instant and binging and pushed forward in the cold wall of wind. Tears trickled down her cheeks; she let them flow and didn't give them any meaning. Frightening down the panic as fear surfaced she pulled her body up quickly for her to summon the girls.

"Alright, I'd enough," Fiona yelled out, giving Asa and Sanari the clue to go with what was planned.

John was suddenly aware that a gun was at his head. He automatically lost control of the knife as another hand locked over his waist and squeezed. Fiona who was no longer held hostage by the knife opened her door and stepped out. Her knees turned to jelly; she bucked and went down the dirt road.

John was sweating and cursing profusely until he heard Asa's voice over his left ear.

"Little picker this is what you get for raping women." She stuck the needle in his neck and second he was crippled, nonetheless conscious. Sanari opened her door and went over to Fiona pulling her to her feet and walking with her to the passenger side of the car. Fiona opened the door and spit in his face.

"You're about to pay with your life for what you did to me and all those women." She told him. "And I am going to enjoy every minute of it."

Asa had joined them and with Sanari's assistant, they pulled him on the dirt road, dragging him some fifty feet from the car. The two of them had gloves on and Sanari handed a pair to Fiona. Asa pulled his pants and his shirt off him.

Fiona watched more enraged as she saw his erect penis. She turned and ran to the car for the duct tape. She cut off a piece with her teeth and wrapped it onto his penis as tightly as possible. She covered his little penis with more duct tape than she had planned. Fiona stood back admiring her work of duct tape on a penis.

Fiona kicked him several times in his penis as she released years of pent-up anger. She finally shouted out. "You mother fucker try raping someone now. That should make you impotent, rapist. I intended to kill you slowly. Duct tape is better because you'll become impotent. You hear me, you son of a bitch, you can't and wouldn't be able to ever get an erection again. You can't rape anymore." The pivotal of rage was released from Fiona. Duct tape tightly wrapped around John's penis as he lay helplessly on his back, bleeding and naked, looking at the three girls.

She had taped his penis tight, so tight that John Miller felt afraid although he couldn't feel a thing. From the way, she was talking he knew that he would be impotent.

There was fear in John Miller's eyes and John Miller had never been afraid of anything or anyone. The gamut of the actual beating depended entirely on Fiona who couldn't wait as she kicked him in his penis then his stomach working her way up to his head.

This was her day and Fiona intended to make the most of it. The minute the girls stepped back she kicked and hit him with the piece of wood she had picked up that was laying there waiting for her.

John Miller didn't feel any pain. He didn't think of the aftermath of the drug Asa gave him or what would happen after it wears off nor did he think of the weeks of enduring pain he would feel.

They were all wearing black clothing and gloves. No evidence of their DNA would be found or any evidence can be traced to them. Asa had a thorough plan. Even the car wouldn't be traced to them as it was an old model of a Toyota and common in these parts of the woods.

Fiona saw her rapist's face and thought about all those other women he raped including the other rapists who were never caught. She felt more enraged and took the same knife he held against her cheek and cut him near his penis then moved it across his cheek and down his chest. Her eyes deliberately made contact with his and saw the fear in them. A massive storm was brewing in his dirty grey eyes. She smiled.

"You go to the cops and I'll hunt your sorry ass down and kill you. Go back to your little hole and stay there till you die. Do you hear me?" Fiona yelled all she could at him. Tears ran freely and fell on John Miller's chest into the newly cut area.

John Miller couldn't move or talk because the drug temporarily crippled him; the ladies have control. The choice wasn't an option. She stomped her foot into his penis again and pivoted the knife all around it then slowly moved up to his chest and sliced it again.

Asa took the duct tape that Fiona had dropped on the ground close to John's hips. She proceeded to tear off bits with her teeth and paste in on all the hair over his body even his head. It took her a few minutes as Sanari and Fiona watched her work her way on the soon-to-be-retired rapist. "Good. That should do it." Asa stood up and admired her handy work. Sanari stepped forward and pulled one of the tapes off from his chest. She laid the typed written note on his penis and put the tape there to hold it in place.

Unknowing Asa and Fiona she had decided to call the police because Sanari knew Fiona was no killer; the note would inform the police what he had done and why revenge was taken. It read:

John Miller raped me thirty years ago. He has raped over fifty women and gotten away with it. He called me up intending to rape me again. I decided to take matters into my own hands; he cannot rape anymore. Please I beg of you to investigate and let the others know what happened to him.

Peace without vigilance, peace in the midst of a brutal storm was found in the heart of Fiona, Asa, and Sanari.

31

In the hotel lobby at five on the cool Saturday morning, Achir1Gupa was staring at the three females walking through the door from the entrance area. He knew them from somewhere, however, he cannot remember at this moment. He turned and sipped from his bottled water as his eyes followed their moments.

He couldn't sleep due to an acid problem and decided to take a walk, he didn't want to disturb his wife. They were here to attend their grandson's graduation from college. He leaned against the back of the chair and closed his eyes rattling his brain to focus and remember the three girls.

Instead, his thoughts went back to his wife, Eesha, and their nine children who are all married with children. Together they have twenty great grand and ten great, great-grandchildren. Suddenly he felt very old. He was only sixty, however, Eesha and he were married at eighteen.

They are Sikh from Punjab and were hired right out of university by an engineering company in Chicago. Eesha had risen above his rank and earned more than he did and that made the dowdy his parents paid for her worth the while considering being pregnant with their children.

Eesha didn't want a cow or any animal she wanted gold. He was angry when she asked for a gold band. His parents couldn't afford it and he had to wash dishes at various restaurants till one in the morning and be up at six in the morning to help with the house chores before going to school to help pay for the gold jewelry. He was very angry those years ago, however, not anymore. A smile tucked at the side of his lips.

He didn't want anyone else because she came from a higher tribe of people with good genes. He worked after school at age seventeen for a year before he gave his parents the money to pay off the goldsmith for the band that she wore ever since on her wrist. His parents made the formal proposal to her parents followed by a ceremony and a party in the village for others to know of their betrothal. They were attending computer engineering class when a company in Chicago hired them to pay for their education, and they moved.

For the next five years, they had five children, two were twins and the other four were his brother's children who died in a car accident with his wife. The children were bought to Chicago from the village in Punjab after they attended the funeral. They legally adopted the children who joined their family. Eesha didn't object and hired two full-time nannies with a housekeeper to help them cope with the overflow of a growing family.

Eesha was working for triple of what he made, therefore they could afford most things. At first, she would only give him a little less than what he earned consequently he wouldn't feel less manly. He found out a year later when she confessed.

At first, he had resentment for a long time. He realized that his jealousy was fruitless. It was the first time he saw and felt the love his wife had for him. There was no way they could've afforded his brother's children without the extra money she earned. He had worked it out and looked at the benefits of having a smarter wife. He understood the magnitude of Eesha, her love for him to have withheld the extra money errand.

Together, he had invested some of the money which they can enjoy. Eesha clad herself in the richness of gold twenty-four-seven, more today than before because she can afford the luxury of having many pieces of gold.

All their daughters, daughters-in-law, granddaughters, grand-daughters in-law, and great-granddaughters wear the gold jewelry she has chosen for them. She lay in bed with gold in her ear and arms even her ankles have gold. He wouldn't complain because she earned it all. He had enough problems keeping up with the children and their activities.

All the children were born here and we're fortunate that they all took in the education and weren't in trouble much. The twins, Aju and Ajin smoked marijuana while in college. When the housekeeper gave him the bag of "funny stuff" they found under the bed, they quit paying for their education.

The twins were the first shocked that under the bed was being clean; who cleans under the bed Aju had asked while Ajin wanted to know why would anyone wants to clean under the bed! The twins' allowance was withdrawn and they had to work and pay for everything. The twins are happily married with children. Aju married a Japanese girl, Ayakowhile he was holidaying in Japan when they met while walking in the park. They have twin girls. Ajin married an American girl, Alexia, and has twin boys.

Of course, his daughters were wonderful except when Sina wanted to marry the "white man," Eesha asked him if he loved her daughter and gave them her blessings, however, he flipped his lid. No, that's not going to happen in his lifetime.

In a week, all the children had moved out and found them a house and had stopped talking to him. He didn't receive any support from Eesha and eventually, he had to give in. Sina married the "white man" Lyncoln and they have a boy and a girl plus his granddaughter gave him his first great-grandson.

They had retired early. To stop the boredom, they opened a specialty Indian store in Altamonte Springs and followed by a restaurant. Eventually, they hired managers for both. They can travel the world and attend every single one of the grand and great-grandchildren' functions.

Looking back, it was all worth it. He stood proud in making the right choices and sticking through with them. They retired young and when the social security kicked in they would be receiving a high amount which he planned to use to send other children to school in India. He or Eesha doesn't feel the guilt of sending money home.

Over the years, they as well as the children and grandchildren have donated millions to send children to India to have a higher education. They have contributed to Seminole County through a homeless program and providing food for the homeless.

Four years ago, a son of a retired fireman chief died and he sold them the apartment. A revelation suddenly shook him that he rose to his feet, turning around to see if he can spot the girls. He suddenly remembered where he saw them at the monthly community meeting where Eesha and he lived. What are they doing here? This is the second set of people he saw from the Helenville compound. Eesha and he bumped into the couple who lived in building ten fourteen in apartment thirteen twenty-one that constantly worked some scam to get people money. They lived in building ten-twelve in apartment twelve seventy-three. They must find another hotel to lodge in because the whole idea of going on a vacation is not to see anyone they know. This hotel is too popular with the citizen of Sussex Place.

Achir smiled as he pushed on his two hundred and fifty pounds onto his feet and walked to the elevator. He took the elevator to his room and climbed into bed and joined his wife. Life is good mmmm, perfect.

The other couple that Achir Gupta saw was the Chilean woman who is married to a Caucasian American male. They are a well-known amount community for running one scam after another. They seemed to reveal the unseen by venturing into business with the triad structures. They fought once a week always about money. She made it quite clear that she brought in the most money and too often verbally abuse her husband who rarely can keep a job because she cannot stand being alone and he quit his job to accommodate her, to keep her company.

Lorraine is forty-eight, dark hair five feet seven inches while Bob is forty, six feet with mouth stash and graying hair. She spoke Spanish and English. She hated sex and he always wanted it. He talked little and she talked too much. She's always on the phone and he loved it because he can have quiet. She wants company and he loves being by himself. She dressed to kill and he dressed in rags.

Bob and Lorraine Phillips are as different as oil and water yet they managed to have a somewhat good marriage or they stayed together for all the wrong reasons. There's no love there. The commonality that anchored them together is what they cling to;

they knew everything and yet they know nothing. They manipulated people out of their money which is their best bet of making a living. They are involved in every scheme developed from selling vitamins to airline tickets to Zumba dancing.

Lorraine bought the apartment in this community to pull scams on the retirees. They did for a while until everyone became wise, except for Jarah Barash who rape her for thousands of dollars.

A sixty-three-year-old Jewish heritage female, Jarah Barash who is deaf, and a retired teacher for the deaf who stands four feet. Bored and with excessive salt in her body, she looked toward Bob and Lorraine for friendship and entertainment. She is lonely with no life. She lived in building ten-fifteen apartment thirteen forty-five and does not drive anymore because of unknown fear.

Jarah tagged along with Lorraine every chance she can just to have some company and something to do. No one liked her much because she is a clinger except Bob and Lorraine who tolerated her. After all, she is a contributor to one of their scam and has money. mainly, Jarah paid the Phillips for their company.

A few years ago, when Sanari had an accident, Lorraine became friends with her. She told Sanari to come walking with her and would ask her to accompany Lorraine whenever she was doing errands.

Sanari's car was total, therefore getting out was great. On one of those trips Sanari asked Lorraine if she can stop and buy a burger and Lorraine began bitching that burgers are bad for you, therefore she refused to stop; Sanari when home hungry and in pain due to her broken left hand.

After that, there was the time when she and Bob took her to listen to a presentation trying to get her to invest in the stupid vitamins scam. She refused and they decided to have her over into their apartment giving her a vitamin drink and showing her a different presentation.

She refused again and rise to leave when Bob had her cornered in the wall trying to terrorize her into investing her insurance money. It doesn't matter who it is, they are always trying to sell something that never worked. They continued to pry on the vulnerable and handicapped. They were asked by the board of Sussex place to stop, they took their business outside of the complex.

A few days ago, Lorraine was on the ramp again fighting with Bob telling him how tired she is of all of this, and the word 'fuck' was flying freely. Neighbors heard as they passed their apartment. This was the worse of the fights and as usual, when they were spotted later in the evening no one would have guessed that they had a spat so nasty.

Everything that Lorraine tried never worked out to anything while Bob cannot keep a job. He only worked when she has difficulties in paying the bills. She cannot stand it when he helped the other neighbors and would constantly call him. Jealously card is often played and for her to have sex with him she has to fight. She is turned on by having pleasure in inflicting pain on him.

Pain and pleasure are her game and his as well as they continued with scam after scam trying to rape others of their hard errand cash. Pain and pleasure speak to them loud and clear in one simple language. This is how they lived their life and would continue to do so for the rest of their lives.

Shame and disgrace followed others who lost something in their life, however, it rarely showed on the face of the Phillips'. They loved the manipulation of others and they don't realize that the relationship between them is also based on manipulation and abuse. Love is a distant friend, a concept they never heard of nor ever want to entertain.

32

The afternoon was giving way to evening, the sun was making its way west to rest for the night. Off to the east the lake emptied into the ocean and to the north, the river continued inland to a small marina where overhead a massive bridge connected the north with the south shore.

Somewhere lower down the lake came the sound of music, strange at first until she heard it for a few minutes. The music played on a reed instrument carrying rhythms that swayed sensuous sound that was more Arabian than Indian.

The lake air was crimson as the sun fell below the block of apartments over in the west. Boats, Jet Skis, and canoes skidded across the water sending it skirting to the shore, the last bit of fun before night falls on the gated retirement community. Left by the slight rain earlier, cars sliced on the wet oily road coming into the complex.

With vapor of speed and energy, the residents hoped the cars would slow down and not crash and prayed that no one with Alzheimer's is not behind the wheel. They have the darndest time in remembering that road is slippery when wet. They were the ones who made it slippery because they kept forgetting to fix the oil leaps in their car.

Sanari was standing in front of the lake, the setting sun silhouetting her defiantly flexible structure and casting white light upon the water. She was there for a long time staring into the sun-kissed cold water. She ignored the passersby and was lost in her thoughts which had drifted off into uncharted waters lingering on the tender moment of last night and the hot tide of making love with Ryland.

She had taken a sip of cocoa and rum and went to bed. In fact, it went straight to her entire body filling it with the excitement of knowing something wonderful was going to happen. It happened in the wee hours of the morning when she turned and automatically started to kiss him.

Relief had washed over her that he never made a sexual move toward her. Only someone thoroughly secure and in control of his masculinity would do what he did for her. Considering she felt his erection every time he rolled into bed and took her into his arms. The description is open for interpretation of the comfort they found in each other's arms as if they were old lovers.

Why did lady love have to ambush her and tossed her an FBI undercover agent in the shape of damaged is beyond her basic common sense? After the last few nights lying in his arms feeling secure, she shouldn't be complaining. The haunting memories of her dreams turning into nightmares made her shiver with new apprehension of the nights to come; all gone as he held her.

Bringing her nightmares into awareness every time she waited for Ryland to join her in bed, somehow had made them vanish. She climbed into bed with no fears only with warmth full of joy.

She would focus on his thumb that lay next to her breast as it ever so softly and gently caressed her nipple. She knew he was asleep from his breathing and it was so arousing. On second thought, his masculinity seems to remain intact, however, she wasn't sure about other things. She would slip out of bed and leave him there. They never speak about it even when they were together.

Neither of them wanted to spoil their shared moment of pleasure because it was fantastic. Sanari continued to live her life as normal as usual. They shared midnight walks because that was the only time Ryland would leave the apartment.

A few times they went into the twenty-four hours store for some personal items for him. They were giving each other comfort; silence was golden. They did as much as they can together, silently.

The cool wind blew into her face and traveled through her.

Memories bathed her lover in liquid fire from the aftermath of their lovemaking. Ryland turned up his collar as if he felt the stiff breeze off the ice-chunked lake.

The breath rushed out from his chest leaving rare tranquility in the toil of a sweet wake. It was dark and he waited, watching her from the window of the apartment. There was no blueprint on how to proceed with this lady who cared for him in his darkest hour.

He, Ryland was at a total loss what to do next. He had spent many days with her in his thoughts. He tucked his hands in his jeans pocket and stepped out walking toward his lover. He bowed his head down against the chilly wind from the lake and relaxed the tense muscles in his neck and shoulders.

The cool lake breeze blew in his hair and whipped his shirt around his broad torso. He focused on the caw of gulls in the distant sound of waves from the Jet Ski. The crowd noise receded to a distant place.

Ryland stood with Sanari with an invisible shaft of energy running through their body vibrating back and forth in sync with each other through the soles of his feet, connecting him to the core of the earth and all of life. She had touched the tip of the iceberg in his heart that is fully awoken against the winter landscape that did nothing to hold his attention.

Anxiety had built into fear at first, suddenly melted by the warmth of their lovemaking. Tonight, he would be slow and tantalizing and not as quick and rushed as this morning. He wasn't surprised when she kissed him; he wanted to kiss her the minute he met her; he welcomed her kiss. It felt right and they fitted well together. They were one in minutes.

In the midst of his figuring out what to do next, his penis stood strong and erected. She felt it grew and was moistened because she too was at a loss. He had moved to his right and bumped squarely into her and pulled her into his arms kissing her, he pulled her back into the front of his body holding her.

She was warm pressed upon his heated body. Sanari was relieved to have the wind touch her erasing some of his imprint of this morning that continued to this present moment. They can relax and not rush to release the sexual energy building quietly. Her hands no longer aching with the need to touch him as they lay upon his, wrapped around her waist. They watched the lake, each with their private thoughts.

The kiln of his heart had melted the chill he had towards the opposite sex. He used them to quench his iceberg heart that was long sealed away due to his undercover work as an FBI agent. He had been undercover on this job he had no time to play until last night....this morning.

The blithely of ignorance had cracked below the dangerous canvas in his psyche; he wouldn't complain. He was forced to stop and look into his dark voids of life which had grown complicated and unpleasant that he no longer wished to endure.

Thoughts joined hers as they stood side by side in utter silence reliving last night's pleasure. They hadn't spoken about their bliss nor were there a repeated performance. All day there was silence and the air was filled with the contentment of knowing what the other is feeling. It was different yet totally beautiful.

The impromptu of their lovemaking was bliss he had never experienced. Talking wouldn't have gotten them anywhere. They didn't want it. The silence that beholden them knew that their feelings for each other are true. Bliss had them sailing through the day by touching and kissing each other.

When they made eye contact a warm smile broke their lips apart, knowing and understanding what was not spoken. Lovemaking had taken them too far into love and they don't know how to get out. They didn't want to get out.

Despite everything they didn't know what was next except run; run neither of them wanted. They had done that before and it didn't work for either of them. He wanted this and he's going to make it work. Thoughts in sync and remembrance of the night they embraced surged warmer. After she kissed him, he pulled her closer. He was not asleep; He rarely did holding her close wanting her to keep him awake. He listened to her breading as he dreamed of making love to her.

He kissed her for a long while and when it became too much he undressed them still kissing her. He had lifted and placed her squarely on top of him pushing her legs apart with a knee to fall over his hips.

Sanari had ignored him and rocked away contracting her muscles, she teased him with her tongue. He couldn't take much more, he had quickly without breaking them apart turned her over and moved with her as one in the heat of a climax.

The contour of their body outlined the lake as they stood there with each other silently making choices they are about to share with each other. The change had been quick, even though it had only been three weeks.

A week that seemed years and last night had sealed their silent wish of the intensifying energy of pure true love when they had made love. Decisions made they sensed the urgency to share with each other.

"Where do we go from here, Ryland?" He was pulled out of his thoughts by her next question.

"I want to be with you. I have my undercover business to work through and who shot me. Can you wait?" He kissed her neck.

"You know I would. Will you live with me? I don't believe in marriage." Sanari had turned and faced him looking into his eyes full of the warmth of love.

"What are you doing changing the sequencing?" He looked at her surprised face.

"Huh?" She looked puzzled at him trying to understand what he was asking her. A frown tucked on above her brows.

"I am supposed to ask you that, my sweet love." Seeing her confusion, "it's a man's question to ask the question of marriage or living together."

"I'm not sure that your instruction came into my thinking when you walked inside my apartment a few weeks ago." Then she drew her head back and looked at him seriously. "Well, I'll be Ryland Cooper, how old-fashioned are you? It's the bloody twenty-first century. I'm not a traditionalist." She brushed her lips over his and looked at him smiling. He didn't contribute any more to the conversation and began caressing and taking her to a different place. Sanari was the force of nature with a pause of lady killer bee. They had gone for a midnight walk a few days prior. He had taken her hand and held it as they had begun to walk.

"I had nowhere to put my cell phone if you hold my hand."

"Oh, used the other hand."

"That one has the keys."

"Oh." He didn't want to let go of her hand. It felt good and he didn't want to answer her either because that would separate them not when he wanted her closer to him.

"I can't put it in my bra either coz I am not wearing one."

"Oh." He stopped and looked at her with anticipation and wonderment of where this conversation is going to lead. He wasn't sure because his heart began to beat faster.

"I can't put it in my panties either coz I am not wearing any." "Oh, oh....oh," he couldn't see her as it was dark and she whispered in a very soft seductive voice that took a few minutes for him to understand. His heart was beating extremely loud; he was trying to stop the loudness because he wouldn't hear her.

She stepped back a little looking up at him, her hand slipped up slowly to his shoulder as she turned into the street light. He saw her teasing smile and his heart gave a double flip and beat faster. Seeing his amusement and expression filled with warmth she lowered her head towards him.

"This feels right. You know you created it when you climbed into my bed."

"Oh, how so?" He wondered. "You didn't give me any time to think it through with you screaming and crying. Besides, I kinda needed an upgrade. My bed was cold and I was lonely." She looked at him giving him a sexy smile; he was completely lost.

"Seriously, you did right." She knew he had polished off the incident as it would not be her fault that he had come to her rescue or embarrassed her.

"I did." Oh, sweet bliss, he thought looking at her as they resumed walking. He couldn't have stumbled on any other door or custom ordered a better outcome. Karma is the bliss of heaven. If he is in heaven then he is staying. If this is the reward for all the crime-fighting he did then it was worth it, even the gunshot he is recovering from when he walked to her door.

What had begun as a tease and caught him unaware of his hidden passion had engulfed him the minute he saw her standing there in the doorway.

The wind blew a string of cold air in their direction. They clung tighter as the weight of his body covered hers from the wind. Ryland moved his arms around her waist and pulled her closer to him. He could hear the beating of her heart and was pretty sure she heard his as well as read his thoughts. He turned her around and pushed her chin with a finger up to look at him.

Black eyes met light grey ones; no words were spoken as he gently brushed her chapstick lips with his cool ones. Hands moved eagerly over the other body as though they couldn't touch enough of each other. It wasn't enough for either of them. They wanted the feeling of the pressure of lips, the touch of fingertips cascading the skin, and most of all he wanted to touch her, to caress her warm sun-beaten skin, to play with her straight silky black hair.

Desire throbbed painfully within her, longing to express her love to him. He took her hand and led her away in the darkness that had fallen upon them. He opened the door to the apartment and pulled her in, drawing her close to his body. Her head slowly fell back and his lips took her in a long passionate kiss that spelled only his love for his lover.

33

Ryan Reyes looked at the strange character that walked into his bar and took a seat at the very far corner where he wouldn't be noticed. Who the hell did the wind blow in? This man wore an old baseball cap tainted with red, is it blood? Ryan squid his eyes together to make out the spots of red on the stranger's cap; since he couldn't, he turned to the waiter and was about to ask them to check it out when she took his order and decided against it. He took the pad from the cashier and told the waitress Mayo that he'll do it.

Who is Mayo to argue? If the boss wanted to take an order let him do it, besides she knew he only did it because he wanted to make sure that the guy isn't disrespectful. As Ryan walked to the stranger's table, she looked at the stranger dressed in very faded blue jeans with a blue faded t-shirt, she felt funny, very funny sensations in her stomach. Better her boss than her; she turned to take Olympia's order.

"Hi Special Agent, ready to order?

"Oh yes, Mayo, I'll have the house salad with one of those burritos. Thank you." Olympia raised her eyes and smiled at her. She looked over Mayo's shoulders to get a glimpse of Ryan and didn't see him at his usual spot. Mayo seeing her reaction of disappointment knew of the attraction between her boss and the FBI lady.

"He's gone over there in the far corner to take that creepy guy's order. We've never seen him before and the boss usually takes orders when he has a funny feeling. Can you get his ID? There have been people missing in these parts for a while and no one knows who's doing the killing?" Mayo began to look scared and Olympia couldn't blame her.

"If you can get his fingerprints on the glass I can run it for a match on our database. I guess you've never seen him. Has he been in here before?" She knew the questions are foolish, however, she had to ask Mayo.

"Nope to both. I'll go get the prints for you and your order. Thank you."

Olympia nodded her head as Mayo left. She turned halfway and looked at Ryan and the stranger. Her heart melted at what Ryan did for his staff; such a caring person not to put his waitress through hell. She has to read his report and see if there is a clearance before she made any move toward him. She has too much at stake to screw up these cases.

She was still looking at them when Ryan turned and walk towards the bar and kitchen area, however, not before looking her way. He was caught off guard because he didn't think that he would be looking into Olympia's blue eyes. What he saw was not lust or desires for him; it was a puzzled look. He walked to her and pretended he was taking her order.

"Something wrong?" He asked her with his warm blue eyes.

"No, no, ah yes. I have a funny feeling about that stranger." She glanced at him as the feeling overtook her more than her admiration for Ryan. She glanced at her paperwork then at Ryan and back to the stranger who is drinking a huge gulp from his mug.

Ryan understanding her concern looked at her worried face. "Am I supposed to worry about him?" He asked her.

"I think that you should be concerned. Make sure that your staffs are safely home and lock your doors." She professionally warned him forgetting he usually left it open for her whenever she feels ready to climb the stairs to be with him. Ryan realized that this is the Special Agent of the FBI talking and not the lady who flirted with him, and he became serious. He too had a very funny feeling about the stranger.

"You've seen him before, haven't you?" He asked.

"Yes, I don't remember where?" Olympia said thoughtfully.

"I'm going to place this order and I'll be back to seek through your thoughts with you." With that, he turned and left. Her eyes followed him and back to the stranger. Is that blood on his cap? She wondered where the hell did I saw him? She pushed her head back and closed her eyes. She knew she was safe and knew that no one would rush her or be stupid to do anything to her under Ryan's protective eyes.

This is why she spent much time here. She felt safe and can work without looking over her shoulders. Besides, when the other law enforcement officers from the police, DEA, or Sheriff's Department have paperwork for her she rather meets her here than at her apartment. It saved them fifteen minutes off their journey and they can have something to eat too.

The Twixt Peach is known to be her office from eleven in the morning to three in the afternoon, every day.

Olympia looked at the four folders marked Fleischer, Missing Agent, Nazi, and Serial Killer. Inside Fleischer, it contained her autopsy with photographs including everyone reports that she interviewed including some of the transcripts of the tapes found.

The Missing Agent folder had a photograph before he went undercover and one of him in his undercover disguised, his aged and some of the dynamic of what he was working on which she hadn't read as yet. She had gone out looking morning, noon, and night around Helenville, even checking the swamp with no luck. He's alive her instinct told her and is in hiding, where that is, is as good a guess as hers.

On the Nazi's folder, it was empty with just hearsay and some transcript from one of Asa Fleischer's tapes of a man whose voice she hadn't recognized; she suspected that is the Nazi. She has a tail, an undercover cop on James, Asa's lover hoping he would sober up enough for questioning.

Craig James Altner was connected to the photographs that were left by the man at her door. Whether he's alive or dead, the jury is out on that one. The lab was unable to identify the man at her door.

Suddenly, Olympia turned at looked at the man behind her, way out in the corner eating his meal. She pulled the folder out and peeked into it. She pulled an old photograph of a man in a baseball cap and turned around and looked at the one the stranger is wearing. The very same except for the red dots on it, however, the photograph of CJA doesn't match the stranger at The Twixt Peach.

Olympia took her cell out and took a photograph of the stranger. She aimed the phone as if she was looking for cell lines and snapped a shot of him. She also aimed the camera at Ryan and saw him grinning. She took another and another; she has nothing to lose.

Knowing and understanding what she was doing Ryan took the plate of food from Mayo as she walked past him. He walked the few feet to Olympia's table and rested it on the only place available opposite her.

Mayo poured Ryan a cup of coffee and filled Olympia's cup. "I have the mug with his fingerprints. I told him to buy one, and get one free when I delivered his food. Sorry, your food is second. I had Ethan, the cook made his first so he can leave and I can give you the prints." A worried frown etched her brows together.

Before Olympia can reply Ryan said, "Put it in my office on my desk." Mayo nodded and left. Olympia moved the folders to the side of the table and Ryan lifted the plate to her side. She picked up her knife and fork and proceeded to eat. Ryan understanding that she is trying to be professional looked at her forking food into her mouth. He turned away and looked out the window before this thought turned sexual. He broke the silence.

"Do you recognize him?" He asked her and she looked at him chewing on her food. He smiled and nodded. "He acts as if this is the normal thing as if he does it every day. He's oblivious to the blood on his cap. Or he knows and defines himself by it or daring you to do something about it."

"I know. See if you can boot him out. I don't want to talk about him while he's here." Olympia suggested forking more food into her mouth thus that anyone observing them would see that she was starved and needed to eat. Ryan pulled himself up and went to the register and wrote up the stranger's bill and took it to his table.

"That's for you when you're done eating. Let me know when you're ready. I'm sitting right over there with the Agent from the FBI." Ryan gave him an eye contract which the stranger refused to accommodate. He continued absorbing his food and even took a sip of his beer before Ryan finished and walked back to Olympia's table.

She had finished eating and was having coffee. She had never eaten this fast or it was a long time since she ate that fast. She pulled a folder way down from the bulging files stacked upon each other on the table. They looked as a broken column from an ancient ruin, each stacked at different heights and getting worse each day that Asa Fleischer's murder goes unsolved.

As Ryan sat on the opposite side of her, she opened the file on the missing agent and showed it to him. "Have you ever seen him before?" He looked at the long hair bearded man and said, "yes, he was here a few times for chicken curry and basmati rice. It's been a while, a few weeks, I think that I've last seen him. I can show you the security tape." He looked at her lifting a brow.

"Give it to me. He's an undercover agent missing. The tapes are evidence, my only hope of ever finding him. How about hearing any rumors about Nazis?" She concluded by putting the photo of Ryland Cooper into the correct folder.

"Wow, you're busy, in Helenville? No." He shook his head and bluntly asked her, "anything on Asa?" He looked at her directly in her eyes as she glanced up surprised. Olympia's instinct kicked in and she wondered why the interest in Asa.

"A lot of what and who she is. No, no leads on the killer." She watched for any signs of any changed behavior even the coloring of his skin. Damn, she wasn't disappointed more relieved.

A thought slides into the other silent ones, why does Ryan Reyes have to do with Fleischer's dead? A huge rumble slithered over her instinct.

Ryan and Olympia looked at the stranger standing a few feet from them. He lifted his cap and looked directly at the Special Agent and nodded at Ryan. He headed a few feet to the door and left.

The thing about all of this was Craig Peter Altner stood outside the building looking in from behind smiling. She got the message, "catch me if you can." He had left the money for the meal and the two pints of beer on the table because he doesn't take orders much less followed them.

There are nobodies, therefore there is no evidence to attach him to any killings. He didn't take pictures as stupid as his uncle did...oh, he doesn't want to think about it. He was horrible at what he did to those poor women.

He got into his truck and drove the distance to Sussex Place. He was getting restless due to the FBI investing that woman with the bullet in her head. He had to settle for a cat, a blond and white stray cat that came to his door and he let her in.

The cat jumped into his bed and found the fetal hollow of his body. Her legs twitched as she herded sheep in her sleep. She lay tucked in the safety in his arms as he stabbed her to death the next morning. He did feed her before her untimely death.

No one will ever commit him because he knew the answers to all the trick questions they are going to ask. He watched enough TV to know them well. Now to that woman who took photographs of the lake a few nights ago. He has to find her.

Lorraine Phillips has a photograph of him taking the bodies in the trash bags to the lake. She and Bob were returning home from the community social party when the photograph was snapped with her new digital camera of the lake. She took one because the flash only went off once.

Craig had recognized her voice when she loudly told her husband that she had "gotten a good shot of the lake." Craig realized that she probably didn't even know what she took because it has been several weeks ago and not a word to him. He guessed that she didn't look at the camera again. He wanted that photo and he intended to get it one way or the other.

Time to kill again. He can feel the urgency of his hunger building in his groin and felt it in his heart. He smiled; time to kill.

34

The call came in when Olympia was having a steak with baked potatoes and broccoli. The beer sat half marked in the mug as she stepped away from her food, keeping an eye on it, she backed into the wall away from the customers at The Twixt Peach.

"Amstel. I can't talk."

"Listen, I'm sure you can do it." The voice of the FBI technician rang in her ear. Randy Pillsworth was a retired hacker that the FBI caught hacking into the military and made a deal with him. Since his first hobby was hacking, he took pride in that everything can be hacked. He took his job seriously. Working for the FBI made it legal.

What the FBI didn't know was he had wanted to get caught because he was tired of looking over his shoulders; he had no friends. This way he was paid a decent salary, he has friends and doesn't look over his shoulders, anymore. Yep, he did good by tricking the FBI to catch him. The job doesn't get the girls because he has to keep his mouth shut on the job which is described as a technician.

Anyone wanted something on the net and in cyberspace, Randy is the man; he can get it. His mother is happy for someone who is twenty-five without a college degree and making not a lot of money, however enough to pay his and his mother's bill and entertained a few girls.

Randy Pillsworth is rich.

"Ryan Reyes," Randy whispered very softly in her ear that Olympia's eyes followed the owner behind the bar and pushed the cell closer to her ear as the beat in her heart picked up speed.

"Yes." She pushed in a professional voice to disguise her interest.

"He's thirty-nine, honorary discard seal. He's been in the military for twenty-plus years before some Afghani militant with a roadside rage turned over the transport. He went backpacking around the world for a while after discharge.

One of his fellow seals lived close and together they bought the Twist and modeled the old house into a bar below and he lived above. His friend owned a garage a mile from there. He's as clean as a whistle."

"But?" Olympia wanted to know more, she knew there are no "Buts" with Randy.

"You got to be kidding me?" He yelled in her ear; that was the moment she pulled it from her ear and knew Ryan saw it too. He has been keeping an eye on her discretely and boldly showed it since the day he sat down when Altner was here caring less who saw his interest in the Special Agent.

"Thanks, Randy." He didn't bother to respond because she knew better besides she just insulted him. When he reported hacking into a place it is direct and precise information that is in that report. There are no "buts" and she's going to pay for that dearly. What can I do to make her pay? Oh, let his mother wins a cruise to the Caribbean; that would settle the insult. With that, he sent her a nice short e-mail with the detail and a huge smile settled on Randy Pillsworth's lips for the rest of the day.

She's never surprised that Randy knew her location. The cell gave that away. He knew she would only be eating in this type of bar because of her job and keeping an eye on Ryan. She wanted more from him and didn't get it, she has to go hunting. Olympia returned to her meal and began to formulate a plan for surveillance of Ryan Reyes. The minute she put the phone down and began to finish her meal it rang again.

"Ikin has something on the Nazi. He's on his way to the Peach." Captain Frost informed her. "Call me when you have more time, after dinner. I'm sending you logistics on other things. The toxicology came back on that Fleischer woman. She was loaded with both alcohol and prescription drugs."

Ryan knew instantly that the call was from her headquarters and it was about him. He caught her eyes looking at him behind the bar and pretended that he was looking for something. He kept his eyes on her the moment she walked through his bar the very first-day watching Sanari and Fiona. He knew she was new around here.

He had her fingerprints on the beer mug checked out the first time she came in by an old friend who worked in Law Enforcement as an undercover agent. Olympia is as clean as a whistle, well except for the covered-up story when she was shot. A tall tail she told and gotten away with it. He put some more emphasis on the glass he was wiping and must have rubbed it too many times.

"Keep that up and you are going to break it," Mayo warned him with a smile that she knew what he was thinking. He put the glass on the rack with the others.

A woman would do that to you, make you forget about what you're doing, or repeat the same thing over and over again. Oops.... thinking about the devil. Asa was the devil Olympia is the sexy thing he ever saw and smooth as silk. Is she wearing silk? Silk suits her.

Ryan raised his light blue eyes slowly and looked at her with his best seductive smile. Damn it! She's not looking. She was sitting in the corner where the stranger was sitting hoping to pick up something from the energy she had told him about last week. She had moved there ten minutes after he left and ordered him to put a reserved sign there subsequently no one can contaminate his karma.

A police officer who he saw in here before came through the door and nodded at him and Ryan moved his head and eyes in the direction of the Special Agent. The police followed his lead and walk towards Olympia and sat down.

Mayo saw that and soon delivered free coffee to the deputy. The deputy had opened the folder as she was pouring the coffee for him and give it to Olympia, who took it and was looking at it when Mayo intervened.

"Oh... him, he comes in here every Saturday night with his wife and Mrs. Gray for super." She told them and walked away.

After the deputy, left Ryan joined her. She told him who they were looking for and he raised an eyebrow in puzzlement. Then he remembered their conversation about a Nazi; his memory traveled back to his instinct warning him of danger. He had printed his photo along with his wife, Mr. and Mrs. Gray with another man.

He walked to his office and pulled out this miscellaneous file on odd people that made his instinct kick in. He looked through all twenty photographs and his notes on them.

He pulled the one on Asa and shred it. No need to give her more than she needed. She's dead and gone. Whatever works, he would oblige Olympia; her command is his wish; no how does it go.... her wish is his command. Get a grip, will you?

Ryan walked to the bar and picked up the same glass and then remembering that he wiped the glass, he picked a different one, put it under the tap, and let the water soak it. He took the tap off and moved into a position where he can look at the whole bar including the Special Agent.

The Special Agent walked towards him. "I was thinking about you." He whispered ever so sweet putting the glass on the rack behind him and looking at her seductively. "Hacking into my perceived identity gave me permission to be bolder and decisive than I ever was in my life with a female." He wanted to tell her, however, he reframed from it. He wanted her to come to him; he had since changed his thought about chasing her. Chasing is for those who date and play dangerous games.

"Yep, right. Tell me how long you knew Fleischer, Blanchard, and Amani?"

"Who?" Ryan frowned at her in wonderment.

"I am not playing games, Ryan."

"Neither am I. I didn't sleep with none of them." He raised his eyebrow and peaked into her face seeing the seriousness in her expression. "You think it makes a rat's ass worth of a difference to me what precinct of Law Enforcement you call home?" He asked her, showing no fear and not a bit of desire he had felt earlier. He was cold and serious as she was; she never saw him this stern and Olympia didn't like it. She hoped she never had to see that side of him again!

She thrust her body forward and brushed the back of his hand with her fingertips. Against the countertop, his fingers closed into small drumming fists.

Olympia came silently and violently turned to face him contacting his eyes. She wanted to envelop him in her arms and kissed him senselessly and rested her aching body against his, touching and kissing him everywhere.

Instead, she noticed that depending upon his mood, his eyes changed color as if it was crystals in a kaleidoscope. It was dark blue with anger. Ryan Reyes is hiding something and she wanted to know what. The direct approach, oh, who's she fooling. She wanted it out the way so she can have the freedom to make love to him. What is he hiding? Who is he protecting?

Hearing her whisper his name, no not whispered, saying it made him lose control, except she didn't know that he did. Her touch on his hand continued to linger with aftershock from the contact and played havoc with his emotions.

Ryan wanted to kiss her and make love to her right here in his bar on the very counter where her fingers are touching the top of his index finger. His Seal training came in right about now. He inhaled without letting her know he did.

"I'm not overwhelmed by your questions. My brain goes faster than speedy Gonzalez. Sorry, I can't help you. I don't play games either unless it is strip poker." He smiled a sexy smile that warmed her heart.

Olympia blushes a deep pink and then red. She had no choice because it bought back memories; she was thinking of getting naked with him. Ryan saw the memory flash and didn't like it. He regretted saying it. "Who are you talking about?" He was wondering if that memory was him or someone else.

"Those two girls and the dead one? You know the one with the bullet in her forehead." He has evaded the query, however, and put the hacking of his information on hold. He decided to assist her with the investigation.

"Oh, you mean Asa," pointing a finger to the middle of his forehead. "Fi and San. I don't know their last name. We're all on the first name here." He informed her.

"Oh, of course, you are." She belted out sarcastically.

"Fi and San about ten years and Asa about half that. Asa followed them here. That woman has a nasty name around town. Everyone got something nasty to say about her."

"Guess you heard it all here."

"Nope, you got it all wrong." Ryan returned sarcastically with a bold lie.

"Anything you want to tell me." Olympia took some bills out from her wallet and lay them on the bar counter. She had left a tip for the waitress and deliberately came to pay Ryan personally. He knew it too and liked it, particularly that she felt the same about him as he did with her.

"Nope. Everything said under the influence is strictly confidential." He grinned at her. She grinned back and made a contract with her blue to his blue eyes, cool with warmth flooding the dark blue into a lighter shade of blue.

He pushed the folder with his notes towards her without breaking eye contact. She took it without breaking her eye contact, still serious. Her blue eyes said something; something a whole lot different than serious.

How in bloody hell can she ever be serious with his hunk of a man. Something in his eyes she couldn't name and couldn't walk away from, making him more attractive. She did, however, today maybe not tomorrow. It's getting harder leaving him.

Olympia had no urge to punch the accelerator of her vehicle to a high which she should do and turned the case over to another agent. She opened the folder he gave her and looked at the photographs.

Who was Ryan collecting them for? She was well aware of the security camera in and around his place and before she asked him he had mentioned that he used the same tape over and over again. So, he had printed these before the tape-recorded the images.

Emotions of something came over her and prevent her from driving out of town. Besides, she lived here. Much was said in that split less than a minute of contact. They both knew it; it was only a matter of time.

35

A month after John Miller's confrontation, the girls returned to their normal lives waiting for any trace of evidence leading to them. Asa assured them that none would ever be found because there was no evidence. She was extremely careful with her plan and knew how to scrutinize everything and eliminate the competition as well as evidence.

She assured the girls that John Miller will never mention the incident because he was afraid of Fiona. She made a bet with them for beers that nothing will ever happen to any of them.

This is where Asa, Sanari, and Fiona were found on a late Saturday night, sitting at the swamp with a cooler of three brands of beers, one for each of them. Ominous shapes blended in with the landscape of the marsh as the occupants hunched and waited for one of them to toss them their meal. The bayou has an aura of danger and the smell of death.

Very few people, if none at all, ventured near the swamp much less sit and have beers. They were all alone except for the wildlife that inhabited the swamp. They were on their fifth bottle when Fiona spoke. "Thanks for the support. I am so over my past. I couldn't have done it without you two."

"You're welcome." Asa and Sanari replied simultaneously.

"I checked for the aftermath and found that when the police found him they took him to the hospital. They ran a check on him and found that there were assault charges filed and were dropped. One was for rape. He wouldn't tell them anything and when the police asked John if he wanted to file charges he said no. The police let it be. He's back at his home living in his trailer." Asa concluded proud of her handy job, hoping the girl would invite her as they did today and she doesn't have to follow them around.

"How do you know this? How did you plan it so well, Asa?" Sanari asked her as she drank her beer.

"I don't care how you did it. I'm only glad you did." Fiona told her.

"I do. I wanna know coz girlfriend, you plan it as if you were a Law Enforcement knowing all about DNA and evidence."

"I've something to tell you and I hope you two would not........"

"I know it; you're some kinda cop or something," Sanari interjected.

"Yes, I'm an undercover FBI agent."

"Grrr." It left Fiona's mouth dry, what a lie, this bitch is telling.

Sanari belted out a choking spell as the beer ran into her nose while taking a sip from her bottle of beer as Asa let the information out.

"Are you alright?" Asa asked smiling proudly.

"Where the fuck does that leave us?" Sanari asked with the understanding that they both knew she was referring to the John Miller incident. Sanari saw how delusional Asa is and wondered when did she begin to be delusional? Everyone knew she was a doctor.

"I'm in this as much as you are, there is nothing to worry about. I can lose my job." Asa assured them.

"Why are you undercover?" Fiona asked her to play along with her fantasy.

"Don't....I had enough." Sanari began to say and was stopped by Asa who had her hands in the air as she too reached for another beer.

"Don't you want to hear the rest?" Disappointment showed on her face.

"Tell me when I'm sober," Sanari concluded assuring Asa that her secret was safe. Asa would never tell them that she had saved a police officer's life or she still had a contact at the hospital when she called over at Melbourne Hospital to find out about John Miller. She let them believe the lie because they owe her, big!

Fiona pushed herself to her feet and seeing a deer standing a few feet away she walked over holding the beer bottle to him while talking. The deer drank it all. "You sure know how to take care of a lot of things, Asa."

"I am glad you can." Sanari charmed in and stood to her feet and walked toward the deer. The deer stood looking at Sanari and as she approached opened his mouth and received the content of the bottle. In a few short minutes, Asa joined them; they were all drunk including the deer. That was three years ago.

Fiona and Sanari sat drinking beers and remembering the one moment when it was worth knowing Asa. They were quiet; nurturing the thoughts that flowed through memories of their best friend and a worse living nightmare. She was a whole lot of trouble and a little bit of hell tucked into one small body.

The two girls went for the fourth beer, nibbling on chips and salsa. The sun dipped behind the light grey clouds casting dark shadows on them as the sun's rays wavered to the end of the day. The night slowly tumbled in and the moon shone its light on the two girls whose thoughts lingered in the past.

"Who do you think killed her, Fi?" Sanari had some sadness in her voice. She plugged a chip with heavy salsa in her mouth.

"I wished I knew. I was scared that Blake would find out. When Asa was good and ready to blackmail me, I would lose him." Fiona let out a long heavy breath that she didn't know she still kept inside of her tucked away neatly.

"I am grateful that she's dead," Sanari said quietly and took a big gulp of her bottle of beer.

"Me too." Fiona signed as a thought popped up. "Do you see how she twirled her thumbs one over the other and keep circling them over and over?"

"Yes." A long silence followed before Fiona's train of thought was expressed. "It shows how she kept her control."

"What happens when the thumbs get tired? She moved them the other way, reverse?"

"Sanari!" Fiona yelled out loud and started to laugh.

"How're you and Blake doing? Coming into your third anniversary?

"Yep, no complaints Sanari. I loved him very much and the kids, as well as the grands do too. Even his kids and grands are ok with us."

"Him moving in this past year was good for both of you, huh?

"Yep, in six months Blake will retire and we've plans to travel. I'm quitting my job. We've already worked out the dynamics and come next month we'll be debt-free and hell I'm free for life." She started to laugh. Upon hearing laughter, a black bore came grunting making an oinking sound breaking the conversation to a halt. Oupgna the wild boar, they usually fed with all the leftovers and scraps of food. She's used to the girls' laughter or the sound of their voices.

She knew it was safe and called to her children and grand pigmies to come for dinner. About twenty bores came to the fencing and gorged on the food set out for them and were watched by their admirers.

There was once when Sanari spikes the food with rum and fed it to them. Not forgetting the bacon, she fed them for a week, and then there was her spicy food. They were grunting for a week and they had to give them bland food for a long time. Oupgna would smell the food before eating it and finally, she trusted them again.

"How are you and Mr. FBI? Fiona turned to ask the questions.

"Oh, great. We're talking a lot and making plans for the future. Most of it depends on Ryland's job. He had not called in, he's missing. Someone in his department leaked his undercover. He's quiet about it and waiting for someone to find him. He only comes out at night." Sanari picked a pebble off the ground and threw it in the swamp. Oupgna and her family had finished dinner and left the premises.

"Isn't he bored?

"If he is he didn't say. I am teaching him how to cook my food and he teaches me his steak and potatoes stuff. Ryland has been reading my collection of books and he does the cleaning and laundry.

Oh, Fiona, it's great coming home to a wonderful man, a meal, and a house that smells of morning mist. I loved cuddling in his arms." Sanari's eyes lit up and a smile was stuck on her lips. Fiona couldn't see either, however, she doesn't need to; she felt it and knew of nature from her own experience.

"Have you told him about your nightmares and history?" "No." Sanari inhaled deeply before belting out an answer.

"Do it soon, hon, don't wait too long. You've found love for the first time in your life. Don't screw it up. Don't let the past tamper with your present. You deserved to be happy. Get it out once and for all. Take it from me, I know, I know about this Sanari.

"The first few times Blake and I made love I was scared and it took about five times down the line for me to let the control go and enjoyed his lovemaking. I know that's not the case with you.

"The longer you hold on to the past it has a funny way of creeping into the lovemaking and making it sour. Promise me you'll tell him soon, Sanari, promise me!" Fiona had raised her voice a bit too loud for Sanari's comfort.

"I promise I'll do it very soon. I promise, Fi." She said quietly in barely a whisper because she knew what her friend said had some truth to it. Fear entered her and she knew that she didn't want to lose Ryland.

"Good. Do you think that Ryan and Olympia are lovers?" Fiona changes the subject and asked a question at the same time absolutely happy that her friend would take her advice. They don't usually give out any advice to others only share their struggles and difficulties and of course happiness. She had moved beyond happiness and enjoying the bliss of joy. Sanari will bet too the moment she let Ryland into her past.

"I think there's something there for sure. I think Olympia's job is keeping her from being involved. I told Ryland about Asa and that Olympia is investigating her case. He knew of Olympia, however, he said he never met her. They worked in different cities and the department until this moment in time. I have a funny feeling whoever killed Asa did such a darn good job that Olympia isn't going to find any evidence." She told her friend finishing the last beer.

"I agree. He knew what he was doing." Fiona added tossing down the last drop of her beer into her mouth.

"He?" Sanari asked with a frown.

"Only a trained person with a lot of physical strength did it. No one around her, the women don't have that precision. It has to be a military man Blake says. He heard the other officers talking about it and he agreed with them. A man with long-range skills that can do it with his eyes closed."

"Well, I'll be. Ryland said the very thing. He asked who I know with military skills. I told him half the damn compound is military more men than women." "So much for that. Asa didn't know who she was fucking with. Probably didn't bargain on getting killed either? Of course not!" Fiona answered her question.

"She was asking for trouble anyway." Sanari comforted her friend.

"Yes, she was. She was a whole lot of trouble and a little tipsy bitsy bit of hell." Fiona laughed and Sanari joined her adding, "Tipsy bitsy bit is an understatement, Fi, the bitch was a whole lot of trouble and a little bit of HELL!"

#

Everything was going to plan, it would be a fun night; a night both he and Fiona would remember. The very first time they made love he felt her tension and he romanced her more, slowly Fiona relaxed with him. It was their third anniversary and he wanted to do something neither of them had ever done before. He had planned it very carefully. He had borrowed the boat from his fellow military comrade Ryan Reyes who owed The Twixt Peach.

All the retired seals had contributed to the boat. Ryan eventually bought them out and owned them. The Seals of the Sea was the boat's name and was parked on a ramped-off from a retired Korean veteran Bill Morning's dock in Cocoa Beach. It was private and Bill wasn't there to greet them because he was visiting his son, Bill junior, and family on the U.S Virgin Island.

It was smooth sailing as Blake smiled at Fiona, who stood looking over the side of the boat as they took off for the unknown destination. The deep blue sea on a moonlight night was all around them.

It was a windy night when they arrived on the docks. Blake had taken the cooler with the wine, cheese, and assorted sandwiches. He had thought about everything through and through, double-checking his plans for the extraordinary night. It had to be special to remember their life together in the years to come.

Beautiful memories they would've together as they sit in the rocking chairs old and gray. He had a feeling something in her past had her uptight those first few times they were together. He wanted to let her know that their lovemaking is compatible, therefore their relationship has developed into lasting love.

When he had picked Fiona up in the late afternoon and given

her a kiss that promised not to be disappointed with the upcoming events. His thumb had trailed close to her opened lips when he had wished her "Happy third Anniversary." She had tasted sexy that it took all of him to control himself from not taking her right there. He couldn't get enough of her. He ran his hand along her legs feeling the slight tremor of her body; she pulled him closer to her.

He smiled and told her to be patient. He loved the chills that he provoked whenever he touched her. She does the same for him and more, much more. They had driven mostly in silence, chatting here and there about nonchalant topics. They talked about the latest developments in the children and grands. The sexual tension building between them heightened the prospect of a wonderful night. He pulled the boat alongside the dock and turned the engine off.

Blake threw the rope with its knot to one of the planks, secured it, and stepped out extending one hand to Fiona. She took it and watched while Blake pulled the Seal of the Sea closer to the plank as his muscles contracted. She observed his muscles resisting the pull of the boat on the waves. She moved in closer to him to hold the boat as he tied the rope tighter to the plank.

The waves were pulling the boat and pushing her against him. The wind whipped her dress wildly over her head. She felt a cold draft cover her body before Blake's hand was on her thigh running up to her waist.

The sun was sloping quickly behind the horizon leaving a color view for Blake as he stood only a few seconds watching his lady love trying to control her dress.

A smile touched his lips, he had let go of the rope and pulled her against him. She let the dress go as she felt warmth run through her body at the slightest touch from him. He pulled her up to her feet as her knee buckled.

With her back to his front, Fiona laid her head on his shoulders and her hands anchored on both sides of his thighs. Blake was wearing shorts and she felt the hair on his thighs sending electric waves of heat through her entire body. She felt him, his erection on her backside as he kissed her neck.

Oh, oh, oh, my, my, my, she thought. He bent his head and brushed his lips on the other side of her neck. He was waiting for her reaction to his erection when he didn't receive any from her, he turned her around and moved her hips to his from side to side purposely watching her. Her head shot up instantly and her soft blue eyes popped wider at the same time her mouth fell open.

She moistened her lips and kissed her lover letting her tongue mate with his; his hand found her core. Blake pulled her into his chest and laid his checks against her as their bodies together danced to the invincible music of the disappearing sun.

Blake turned Fiona around and danced to the beat of the tossing water with the wild wind becoming wilder. Every moment of their bodies was in sync with the wind. Beneath them, the dock rose and fell from the relentless pressure of the waves that were stirred from the wind. The shadows of the tree above swayed in the wild wind against the moonlight and night sky, bending and dancing in their wiliness to play music for the lovers.

The wind pushed against them and Fiona shivered by his touch. He let her go as his hand ran up her thighs and she moved her hands to his shoulders and joined them behind his neck. The other of his hand went to her back where it collided with her skin and the other pulled her bare hips into his anatomy.

In the moon's light, Fiona felt his other hand on her waist holding her steady as her dress flew over her head. The wild wind had access to her thighs and hips as she stood almost naked on the swaying dock. The light from the moon emphasized her no bra status and the gloss of her red lace panties.

She clutched distinctly frozen into immobility as his fingers stroked the skin at the edge of her panties then slowly beneath her. There was no resistance as she welcomed his fingers when they slipped between her parted thighs. She felt his hand move down her thighs and over her backside under her warmth moving the lace panties away from her skin.

Fingers were inside sliding in and out, up and down against the inner sanction wall of her g-spot. She let out different sounds of music that sang with pleasure as her head went back trying to pick up a rhythm that was harmonized with Blake's.

In the heat of the moment, Blake was harder and more aroused as Fiona was dripping with sexiness. She felt him pushing against the hollow of her rim of fire where his fingers played new music to her ears. His fingers slid lightly back and forth drawing passion and more sexiness from her.

His thumb found her outer core and traced circles amount it through the lace of her panties and then dove under the lace to touch her delicacy, again! She obediently began the delicious climb toward release.

"Oh, Blake!" Fiona wanted all the pleasure he gave her with every cell of her heart. He left the involuntary pleasure of her body against his fingers and thumb as they worked in unison to give her the double pleasure she so craved. His thumb slipped away and replaced it with the heel of his hand as he pressed against her; his fingers performed magic in her. She felt herself in his grip between fingers and palm as he rocked her with a rhythm of double orgasms.

Blake looked at Fiona and frown with a smile. She doesn't know half of what's to come and he'll deliver. She's an earthquake with a volcano and tidal wave all rolled into one. Some and more with a cocktail that tasted divine. He raised his lips and pulled her to his to taste her, to assure her that this is only the beginning.

"I want to make love to you Fiona. I want to taste you in my mouth right now, right here on the dock." He whispered deep into her ear so the wind that roared would not carry it through the trees. The wind blew her short golden curls into a wild mess. He tangled his fingers in her blond hair and she ached closer crawling into his arms.

"No kidding, really, ya think," she managed silently to herself. The words were drowned in her thoughts as she let out sounds deep from her that let him know she wanted the very thing. Her hand fisted into the ends of his hair and tugged as she nipped on his lower lip tempting him to take her right here, daring him.

Blake abruptly removed his fingers from inside of her and lifted her off her feet. Fiona clung to him from his sudden movement and from the feeling of being drunk. She lay back against his arm enjoying the feeling of arousal, the warmth, and the strength of his hand. Pleasure lifted her eyes as he watched her, laying her down on the dock.

Absorbed by what he saw, Blake gazed for a few seconds before he sank to his knees in front of her. His head below her was shut out by the sudden heat of his mouth enclosing her. She clutched at his head for support. He pulled her panties so smoothly from the warmth of her body and found her center with his mouth. He traced and circled her core as she lifted her pelvic to him.

She pushed against him with a body that was wild with sensations from the day she met him. The wind tore the passionate music from her opened mouth taking it to join the music of the trees.

It blew her melody against the heated heaving body of his tongue rocking her core into an intimacy of rhythm that matched his body. His fingers were against her inner core inescapably pushing her legs further apart as his tongue against her took access to her core.

Sensations upon sexual sensations flowed from her essentials as Blake's tongue pulled in the endless flow of her liquid honey. She felt the sweetness in every nerve cell that ran layers of ripples in her stomach and breast. The honey poured endlessly enclosing her thoughts with the lightness of sensual sensations.

"Blake, Blake, Oh Blake!" She was all his and he can do whatever he wanted with her. She never had this much pleasure in all of her life. In a few wild exotic moments of pure bliss, the pleasure turned to powerful sexual energy that built at rapid speed. He was enjoying watching her lose control again.

Blake's body lit up and he moved his hand in response to whatever he was feeling. He pulled his clothes off while she was climaxing in his mouth and waited for that particular moment when she inhaled. He quickly and gently dove into her. Feeling him in her, Fiona moved her legs over his back and pulled him into her. He bit into her neck with his sound of music as he reached his first to her third, the peak of exotic release.

37

"There are five maintenance crews that take care of everything here and I mean everything here. The big fat one is Bill, the one with the waistline over the stomach; he doesn't do much and he was arrested for selling marijuana. He's best friends with the manager John, the gaunt man over there with the square shoulder, rounded tummy, and round horn-rim glasses.

The short one is a Native American of the Blackfoot tribe name Wayne while the other one next to him is the all-American male that loved to give service to the elderly women." Fiona concluded.

"The blonde one is a gigolo." Olympia had to ask and she was not mistaken.

"Yes, he has a price. Everyone loves him."

"Charming guy?"

"Exactly." Fiona looked at the lake. She was explaining the complex to Olympia who walked up to her while she was feeding the fish, duck, turtle, and other inhabitants of the lake a week after her third anniversary. It was a cool late November morning. The sun had broken through the horizon a few hours earlier.

The first rays painted the lake with a bright yellow light that bounced off of Fiona's blond hair. The teasing laughter that was with her was gone, evaporated as if the morning mist before the tropical sun dried it. Her eyes were alert as Olympia approached her. She walked with the agent and sat on the grass by the walkway.

It was early for anyone to be out. The residents are probably doing something or the other before they came out of hiding to socialize or gossip.

Olympia was also questioning Fiona about Asa and their relationship. Everything in this place is informal. She had to go through a whole lot of hell for a little bit of information. She had notes tacked on the wall of the various people who wanted to eliminate Asa Fleischer's murder.

Olympia turned her attention to the figure of Fiona who was pointing in the direction of the pool where children were playing and swimming. On this cool morning, the sun in full heat kept the two ladies warm.

"The pool is heated and that is Mama Bear from Puerto Rico with her daughters. The two oldest one is for different men. One lived with her and the other with her father. The other four including the baby are for the present husband who's a pilot for some airlines. They collected money from the government for the children and traveled all over the world. Her children are the best-behaved kids around here."

"Tell me all you know about Asa, everything, Fiona." She gave her eye contact that basely said don't mess with me.

"She fuck with everyone around here, blackmail whatever she can dig upon them. She knew where to find us, me, and Sanari, and followed us everywhere. I am sorry she had to die like that; no one deserved it. Asa had to push someone into a rage to get that bullet in her. She was a neatnik with subtleties ancillary beneath the surface of whatever she put herself to do.

"Asa fooled everyone with her neat petite delicate frame. Her cleverness provided something more to her main function. At first, she fooled everyone then the blackmail began." Fiona paused and took a deep breath.

"She mistook and used others' outrage and urgency for efficiency and conviction to her advantage. She thought she was generating pungent perfume when she could not love and the reason for her depression, guilt, and shame all in one. Her definition of love is the reason why she was depressed, she couldn't love herself; she wasn't enough. Her rebellion is the state she was moving through which for me is a high indication that she doesn't know how to process life as it has been offered to her.

"When people don't have enough adequate information to work through traumatic and abusive situations, they define life through it and hide it somehow. They cannot adjust to the trauma and abuse and they rebel against it. While they are doing that they inhale fear along with oxygen. Asa was fastidious, very." She looked at Olympia and gave her a thin smile with sad blue eyes.

"Really?" Olympia asked, her smile widening because that was her thought on Asa Fleischer.

"You should talk to Sanari she has her doctorate in giving advice." Fiona grinned at the Special Agent.

"I plan on it." Olympia attempted to rise when Fiona laid her hand on her arm keeping her anchored. "You don't want to hear about the rest of what I have to say?" She gave her the saddest puppy lot of disappointment.

"Ok. I guess it wouldn't hurt." Olympia grinned realizing that she liked Fiona. She gave her eyes a three-sixty-degree turn.

"Anna Fairmont is the African American disabled retired social worker who had an affair with the preacher, Alan Parsley. Everyone that slept with Anna has to leave money. She's jealous and spiteful and flows with the back-stabbing bitches of Essex Place. She doesn't like Asa and Asa was racist against Blacks. They made her uncomfortable." Fiona informed her.

"What, a prostitute?" Olympia asked in shock. She shouldn't be considering her job. Sussex Place has just about everything in here, a little of this and a little of that: A little bit of hell and a whole lot of trouble. She shook her head.

A loud noise drew their attention to the parking lot where a U-Haul truck was exiting toward the entrance. The driver raised a gloved hand in a wave to Fiona who nodded and smiled in acknowledgment.

"Who was that?" "That was Ty, an honorary discharged marine who was once Sanari's lover. They broke up several months ago." Fiona refused to give out more information about her friend. The agent didn't need to know that the Marine killed an Afghani family and that was when Sanari's nightmare began plus when he asked her to marry him she told him that she doesn't believe in marriage.

Sanari saw his anger and didn't want to live with it. She told him she wanted to live with him not his rage. He didn't understand the difference between the two.

"Why?" Olympia had to know about the broken relationship.

"Oh, it ran its course. Ty had some serious issues from the war that tampered with the relationship. They were two limited people who met that were bound to result in a fracture disaster." Those were Sanari's words. In the reality, in the rim of things, Ty faced all of his demons during the relationship and stirred the demons from hell in Sanari.

"That would do it. Why are you telling me about these people? What do they have to do with Asa Fleischer's murder?"

"Have you found the murder weapon and the place where she was killed?"

"No."

"Why not asked the maintenance crews? Be careful with the management coz they are liars and have a conspiracy going on about something or the other with Asa. See what Mama Bear can tell you. She speaks both Spanish and English and is up at all different times of the night. You would want to talk to the Japanese couple Takehiko and Kaori Izumi too because they were friends with Asa. We all shopped that their market.

"Trace and Damien are gay couples who are our friends. We hang out together often. They knew Asa from the hospital where she worked as a doctor and knew the truth as to why she was fired. She and Trace did some surgeries together. There was that Brazilian stripper Soba who slept with Charles and left suddenly because of mold in the apartment she was renting.

"The Russian Anya who disappeared and slept with Julian Matera who's from Venezuela, separated from his wife, however, he still lives in the same apartment. They all hang out with Asa from time to time." Fiona took a deep breath.

"It's a felony to lie to a Federal agent. What's your give with Fleischer?" Finally, Olympia was doing her job.

"How did you come to live here?" Fiona was dying to know, therefore she had to ask the question.

"After my injury and I couldn't be in the field anymore, I bought this apartment from a friend whose grandfather died several years before retiring. The boss found out and tore the retirement paper up and asked me to find out about the Nazis who are living here. He's wanted for war crimes."

"Have you...." Fiona began to ask and was interrupted by Sanari who had walked in quietly and joined them. "You must be talking about the couple in building ten seventeen apartment fourteen zero two, old Mr. and Mrs. Bishop who lived across from Mrs. Gray." Sanari contributed to the conversation, hovering over the two as the sun hid in the clouds above them.

"What?" Olympia asked.

"How did you know that?" Fiona wanted to know.

"Because I went in there a few times asking for a donation for the food bank. They have a whole bunch of Nazi stuff in the guest room. They've three bedrooms. The grandchildren stayed in the other one. I know all this because one day when I went for the donation, the door was open and I stuck my nose into it. Mr. Gray saw me and saw the shock on my face. That's how the fucking bastard started pinching my backside every chance he got. It was kinda blackmailed, I guess. Mind you, he donated money too. The price I paid for my curious nose." Sanari finished and let out a breath.

"Thank you. I'll take it from here." Olympia revealed. "Nothing on the Fleischer woman?" She had to ask.

"Nothing much. We didn't like her and just played along after we discovered the bug. My brother, Roland found the bugs after I asked him how someone can know all of the time where Sanari and I were going. I told him Asa is always there. He visited and found the bugs. He checked her out and told us her story plus to be careful." Fiona informed her.

"I need the name of your brother and where he worked." "Ok. Anything else? I've to go." Fiona reached for her cell phone and gave her the number. "Everyone wanted to kill her. No one had the strength or guts to do it."

"Yeap, Mr. and Mrs. Bishop will be arrested for the war crimes. Diego the drug lord that lived in your building was arrested last week." Olympia informed them.

"Thank you." Fiona rise to her feet and so did Olympia. Sanari had remained standing. She had come to collect Fiona.

"I still have to question you, Sanari," Olympia told her. "You are the last one before I make my report. It's been almost four months and no evidence on Fleischer, the truth is I'm tired of it. I don't think I'll ever know the killer. I'm going to close the case as unsolved due to lack of evidence."

"Come talk to me over the weekend, we've to run. You know where I live." Sanari gave Olympia a very friendly smile.

"Thank you," Olympia said with a sad smile. They were nice girls and she would have liked to be their friend. Maybe the Gods would smile on her this time.

Fiona and Sanari walked a few feet to Fiona's building. Blake and Ryland were cooking dinner for them and they had to go shopping for the necessary ingredients.

Olympia headed in the direction of the office hoping to catch the maintenance crew, the characters that made this place exclusive from the rest of the other retirement complex.

38

Settling into her seat Olympia turned the volume higher and pressed play on the remote control of her DVD player. She had in one day interviewed all the people Fiona had mentioned to her and came up with more of a mess than anything else.

They all knew of Asa and had a motive to kill her except none killed her or admitted to killing her. They were all at a party of someone or the other and had photographs to prove it. She took their entire camera and sent it off to Randy. She had enough of it all.

She found out that Clarke Brissel had an affair with Asa or she had it with him. He knew about James, however, what James couldn't give Asa he did. They were regular lovers about twice a week she would visit him. When Clarke's blue eyes met Asa's sparkling brown ones he was frozen in time.

A magical moment took place as energy filled the space between them. How long they were looking into each other eyes he didn't know, except that his heart melted from cold to warm. Opposite attracts, go figure Olympia thought.

Clarke asked Asa out on the spot and was shocked when she asked him for his number and dialed it from her cell. When his cell rang he didn't reach for it. A voice had drawn this attention to the path leading out to the door from the market where they met.

Asa turned, smiled, and ordered him to call her in "24 hours." He did ten minutes later as he climbed into his truck, giving her direction to his apartment, ten minutes from where she lived. Clarke Brissel, fifty-six the all-American male jammed shut his mouth and smiled all the way home.

There are two different types of men, those who are dishonest and others who are honest. A smile appeared on Olympia's lips as her thoughts drifted to the sexy bartender at The Twist Peach. She didn't want to think of those two types of men in the same category.

Olympia had made a habit of going in there for a drink or a meal and ended up using the place as her office. She is addicted to Ryan and knew it would not be long before she was joining him in bed.

She laid her head on the back of the chair indulging in some fantasy images of undressing Ryan Reyes's tan body. She really can't take this anymore and decided that her professionalism and these cases will have to come second while she quenched her thirst for him. She took a sip off from her beer in a mug and popped Carmel popcorn into her mouth.

In a flash of a second, she choked, not because she missed the entrance or chewed too quickly; it was because of what was playing on the DVD of Asa Fleischer. She ignored the wetness on her t-shirt from the beer that tumbled from her mouth and ran down to her black panties. She was intruded by the sound and noise that came from Asa Fleischer and James Asher.

"Oh yes, oh yes, James."Asa answer with the warmth of an iced mocha. "Push it harder, harder. Oh yes, hit me, hit me." Asa was saying to James Asher who had Asa on her breast and face while he jammed his penis into her from the back. He smacked her on her protruding cheek as he moved in and out of her.

Adrenaline pooled from inside of him. James was waiting for a chance to fuel his next move of anger from him. He was waiting all week for this, the only day he can fuck her all he wanted. Once a week they made sex an adventure and he look forward to it. He's taping it unknown to her. "Like this baby," James asked breathlessly smacking her on her backside check.

"Oh yes, no harder, harder James. Make me proud. Be the wild boar I know you are."

With no more encouragement, James Asher pulled out his Viagra penis, smacked Asa's backside hard, and pushed right into her as hard as he can as holding her steady by her hips. He repeated the maneuver of his sexual play over and over again. Sweat was pouring out from all corners of his body.

Asa Fleischer and her lover used sex to be the aftermath of their anger to make it more passionate except that it doesn't create passion only more anger. Neither of them had an orgasm as Asher ejaculated in her. Asa collapsed from exhaustion.

Olympia watched the separation and the wide space between them. There was no intimacy as the DVD turned fuzzy. She turned it off and sat there in silence, and furious. Sex isn't the aftermath of anything. What they were doing was using sex to make it exciting, as well as releasing their anger. No one can measure pain against another person. Pain is personal and it's how you work it through not deal with it. Sex was a temporary fix.

The whole incident sent a massive wave of rage coursing through her blood. The pain and pleasure of the human species run havoc into the sex making it erotica and not exotic.

Erotica is pain while exotic is pleasure and romance is the cutting age for sex. How easily the human species confused the two and defined their lives by it? Placing pain to sexual habits formed dangerous attachments. Naming helped understand the attachment as well as the people association with sex. Insane with pain, she can feel the violence in their thoughts during the sexual acts.

Anger wasn't what she entertained when Olympia was tired and furious. Anger and sex wasn't a combination she cared for and never will. Ah, there is no comparison between those two and her.

Special Agent Olympia Van Amstel is trained and experienced with this type of sexual format due to her work once a sexual abusers' investigator. The work she did had a higher purpose; she fought, argued, and missed family occasions even missed important dates all in favor of rushing to have the career she longed to experience. How much more tapes she has to go through? She counted ten. She had only sent the ones she had a review to Randy and since she decided to close the case she had to look at them all. Tonight, was that night and already she was sick to her stomach.

She is an experienced investigator, nonetheless, her personal opinions are her own and they aren't for public display. The line between right and wrong often is very blurred for those people who have pain and seek pleasure even when war and violence are an everyday occurrence. Her life is too short to stress herself with people who don't deserve to be an issue in life.

She pushed another DVD into the player and saw something different. It was another one with Fleischer and Asher; was it the third or fourth. How much more of this she has to take and see; six to go? What did she do to be torture like this?

Bullet or no bullet to her head, Fleischer was a nasty business who never lie only avoiding the truth. Women, on the other hand, don't lie; they don't tell the truth.

Two different species of females, then the others that are the same as Asa are Kryptonite to the ones who are honest. She wanted the truth, regardless of the consequences. She had stopped being an embarrassment to sexual confusion a long time ago.

For this couple, it had fixed their story as well as fit their truth. It doesn't matter what trauma people experienced there are choices, always choices. It's called morality and truth.

The things the human species do to avoid and suppressed physical pain is to create mental annoy, emotional distress, and verbal abuse. Thinking and feeling negative is merely inadequate information that had process the traumatic experience incorrectly. The avoidance of pain only created more pain.

Olympia's thoughts refused to telegraph a different message of Asa Fleischer and James Asher. Much can be told about people's behavior.

She knew the truth of them both. She had interviewed James Asher soon after removing the tapes from his apartment and freezing the money that was deposited from Fleischer. He still believed that the money will be returned to him one day. James can believe what he wanted, however, that money will be returned to the people she blackmail and if they aren't alive then it goes to their children or grandchildren unquestionably not James Asher. She still has to listen to the audiotapes to hear what it would deliver, probably more back mail.

Olympia did not doubt that he didn't kill his lover because

he's a spineless bastard, who believed like his lover that the world owned them. They are merely collecting their dues; dues that they and many others had come to believed the world and its people must pay one way or the other for their painful past and traumatic experiences.

Asa Fleischer lived by those beliefs. She lit and played with fire; she deserved what came to her. Case closed.

Olympia had never made that assumption nor does she judge anyone on why they do what they do. She collected the evidence and let the courts decided upon the crimes committed. She moved on to the next case. Today, however, she made the judgment call and felt the tension rise in her. The person who pulled the trigger has her admiration.

The tension in her body was being released as she finished her beer. The sexual encounter of the third kind that she just saw was a toxin, poison that has killed millions of people who wanted to stay alive. It was sort of a new fang and abseiling for those who don't know the pleasure of living life.

She pushed another tape in and watched it including the last one. On number seven, she made coffee and had nachos to munch on. She couldn't fast forward anything because she wanted to know what information passed between those two. She had to watch them, all listening and collecting evidence.

It was two in the morning and Olympia stepped out onto the patio and looked at the quiet lake. She wondered what lurked beneath the waters and promised to look at all the photographs Randy send her on the night of the party to see what she can come up with in connection with the serial killer.

She walked to her laptop that was sitting on the breakfast table and open it to write her report on Asa Fleischer's murder. It was another four hours before Olympia hit save and send it off to Randy.

She stood up and rubbed her shoulders tired and ready for bed.

The wave of toxic came crashing from her and she ran into the bathroom tasting the beer she drank running from her into the toilet.

She jumped into the shower and scrubbed herself with avocado scrub, shampooing and conditioning her hair. She had it cut short to her shoulder from the usual long length before she came home from The Twist Peach last night.

One came down two or was it three more cases to go was the last thought that drifted through her before she fell into a long-overdue sleep.

The moon stood still for a second before moving on to what it does best; shone its light guiding earthlings to see where they are going and what they are doing. Don't blame the moon when a dry white or a black belly cloud moved in front and covered its light. The only illumination was a little stream of moonlight that played through the window of Olympia's bedroom.

As beautiful dawn broke, other earthlings' sounds came forth as the moon resplendent disappeared and the sun broke through the horizon. If the weather knew what the earthlings' tresses can do during its light, it would stop particularly on the little hill at the tip of Essex Place in the retirement community of Helen Ville where Craig Peter Altner prowled. He was hiding in a boat that was dock below the boardwalk waiting for the Special Agent to go to bed because he wanted to take a ride and sit on his graveyard of young beautiful people.

Craig Altner's irritation flamed from anger to rage and felt his traitorous body respond to killing her. These are stifling times, at if he wanted to keep his graveyard safe he cannot and would not kill an FBI Special Agent. He does not kill innocent people or those who would bring attention to him.

Anger, desperate, and misery he pondered on staying where he was until she goes to bed.

What the fuck did she do staying up late? Craig's anger simmered far too close to the surface most of the night as he kept watch on Olympia's apartment. He couldn't fathom why of all the nights she was the only person in Sussex Place that was up till dawn. He hauled himself from hiding and headed home before the other residents awaken. What he didn't know or bargain for was that others were up.

"Hey, did you see a blond and white cat around here? She ran out……" Hank Weihert was asking Craig Altner who look at him, shook his head in a "no" and continued walking. Hank liked to think his cat was an adventurous troublemaker and continued calling quietly for him.

If Hank knew that Craig had killed his cat, Spitfire two weeks ago to quench his thirst for killing, in desperation, he probably would beat the living daylight out of him. Hank was bald head as Craig was, however, he was stocking with fat and worked out at the gym over at Universal Studio.

Hank goes to that particular gym to pick women up and bring them back to his place. Hank's a sex addict. The only movies Hank looked at are all erotica and he rarely sees the same woman more than three or four times due to boredom and goes prowling for more for another sex fix.

He tried to seduce Asa, Fiona, and Sanari which didn't pawn out too much except trying to jerk off on Sanari's manicured foot. The girls had sent him to another woman who they said was a friend of theirs and needed a Friday night date.

They had told him that he was expected when he agreed to go on his first blind date. He took the day off from work. He was all dress up in his best jeans and white polyester shirt with flowers when he rang the doorbell at seven in the evening with a smile on his face ready to seduce. An old lady opened the door with sparkling blue eyes when she saw him.

"Oh, good you're on time and you bought flowers. I like a gentleman. I like you." She said to him.

Hank smiled and replied, "thank………."

"Oh, Phil he's a hunk." She interrupted him and had turned to speak to someone in the room, probably her husband Hank thought. She lifted her arms out for the flowers and he gave them to her. He stood at the door waiting for her to fetch his date. He couldn't see much inside as the door was three quarter closed, however, what he saw was a living room filled with much stuff that he felt a headache coming on; he turned his back to the door looking around Essex Place waiting, waiting for his date to walk through the door.

A few minutes the old lady, Milli appeared and said over her shoulders before pulling the door close. "Put those in water Phil and don't wait up for me."

Hank wanted to die when she took his arm and said to him smilingly, "It's such a pleasure to have a handsome man escort me to the Bingo game at the Club House. They don't make them like you anymore." She proceeded to walk and Hank had no choice; he moved his legs with hers taking a small step. He opened the door and took her around the corner to the game room. He had no time to be mad with those girls because granny started to tell him that she used to be a hooker than a madam for all her young life. He heard the stories for an hour as they sat in his truck parked at the entrance of the building. The game started at eight.

As if that was unbearable he found out that Phil who she kept including in the conversation was her husband.

"Was?" Hank asked frowning.

"Yes, dear. He died twenty years ago with a heart attack. His thing was in me." Seeing her escort's face, she smile and tapped his arm. "I've always included him in all the conversation. It's good for his soul."

That did it for him. He wanted out. He was thinking about how he could get out of it because that was more important than being mad at Asa, Fiona, and Sanari. He realized that he couldn't because the place was packed with old ladies fifteen minutes before the hour. He was the only man there. The attention he received was unbelievable.

At the end of game four, he won; they crowd around him. He was confused that he looked at them too. Before he knew what was happening his shirt was ripped, no torn from his body. His one and the only white polyester shirt was gone, made history by a bunch of old ladies in their eighties.

They started to clap and chant "dance, dance, dance" to him and then he got it; he understood as they stepped back and sat in chairs making a circle around him.

Someone put some very loud disco music on and his hips unknowingly to him began to move. Slowly and very slowly he removed his clothes even his boxers. The old ladies clapped and chanted for him; he thought that the police would be here. When he took his blind date home she kissed him on his lips at the door and sweetly said to him.

"Thank you for giving me such a good time." Closed the door in his face; he walked back to his truck. As he sat there in awe he turned to look at the building shaking his head in disbelief. He saw an envelope sitting on the seat that this date left five minutes ago. He picked up and opened the envelope only to see money, one hundred dollars after another; he counted twenty. Inside he found a card with a large letter written "THANK YOU, HANK."

"Eureka." Hank smiled a wider smile and all the anger he felt towards Asa, Fiona and Sanari disappeared. Two days later he heard that his date died, followed by three others who were there on that bingo night. He sat at the funeral of them all happy to know that he has given them some little happiness.

Hank danced for the other old ladies once a month. He was well paid.

He was heading towards his building when he saw Mr. Bishop a strange potbelly man with a head too large for his neck. He wears a toupee that doesn't fit well with his balding hair.

"Good morning." Hank smiled forcefully showing a missing tooth. Mr. Bishop nodded a slight nod to the stranger, showing his pot belly due to the white shirt being too small for his torso. His belly hanging out a bit too much for his taste, though he's sure Mrs. Bishop would like it probably to fall over him; such an idiot she is at times.

Mrs. Bishop unknowingly to Mr. Bishop loved Hank. She used Mr. Bishop's hard errand cash that he received selling Nazi memorabilia he collected from his days when his great-grandfather was with Hitler and what he bought and sold in his years as an art dealer to see Hank dance naked.

Mr. Bishop wanted to know what's he doing up this early on a Sunday morning when most people sleep in? He stopped and turned around to look at Hank who felt as if he's being watched, had stopped walking and turned around looking at Mr. Bishop.

Hank spotted Mr. Bishop looking at him ways down the path. He made eye contact from the distance and grinned at him with one toothless. A wider grin played on his lips as several thoughts floated around other thoughts, however, one came out more than the others, a wicked one.

Hank Weihert pulled his pants down and showed Mr. Bishop his "Willy Wonka" and as if that wasn't enough he turned and bowed his waist and showed him his erected penis. Take that to Mrs. Bishop, you perverted old man, thought Hank. Go tell your wife you saw my "Willy Wonka."

Mr. Bishop was embarrassed that he turned and ran down the path hearing Hank's laughter following him. He was confused about what took place and ran from it; he ran straight into Charles Callahan who held him at arms' length with a "whoa." Mr. Bishop looked up still in confusion and embarrassment; he saw who smacked into him ready to let his anger out.

Charles saw the whole show between Hank and him from the broad walk on the lake and deliberately chose this moment in time to have a laugh at someone else as well as have something else to talk about besides politics and his mother.

Charles did exactly what Hank did, grinned and as the grin became wider so did the shock on Mr. Bishop's face, who recognized it immediately and pushed Charles away from him, and continued running. He didn't want a repeat performance. Charles was laughing and watched Mr. Bishop covered his ears and kept running almost stumping and falling. Charles's face became serious for a split second, only for a split second. Upon seeing Mr. Bishop straightened and did some fast walking for his age, started laughing again, louder than it would travel towards Mr. Bishop.

Losing sight of Mr. Bishop as he rounded the corner of a building, Charles stopped laughing and turned up the stair towards his apartment. He had just come from his aliening and senile mother who lived two buildings from him. He made her breakfast and turned the TV on for her. He had gotten a call from her this morning at five because the TV wouldn't work. "It's broken Charles pumpkin. I want a new one. Come and take me to get a new TV." "Give me five minutes." He had strolled out of bed wondering what to do with his mother. It seemed cruel to put her in a retirement home since his father died six months ago. Plus, that would eat up all of her money and who would pay his mortgage as he can't find work. His stupid sister would get a fit because she has been taking money out of the account for herself as well.

Charles Callahan was out the door and ran into his Father Parsley who used to live above him. They stared at each other and although they were headed in the same path they turned and went in the opposite direction, neither wanted to think of the other.

Alan Parsley was watching through his window across the lake when he stopped Sanari from feeding the ducks. He thought what a fine woman and if he could get his hands on her, he would show her what a wild man he was in bed.

For a hundred and ninety-five pounds standing five feet eight inches, he was surprised to inherited building ten thirteen in apartment thirteen zero five from Mrs. Tonnalli, a ninety-six-year-old Caucasian widow who attended church every day. He guessed she was bored and has nothing to do since her husband Phil died some six years ago. They left the bulk of their money to the grandchildren and the apartment to him with a "thank you" card. Alan Parsley is a preacher.

He's not a faithful preacher by any standard; he never was and he never claimed to be one that is, a preacher. People asked him to be one and that's how he became one. He found out it is an easy way to make a living. People of all ethnicities gave him money to preach the gospel.

Alan Parsley preached and what Alan Parsley did, no one cared because everyone says, "Praised the Lord" whenever Alan Parsley read a verse or quotation from the bible. Why? He once asked and the reply was that "Them preachers all cheat or they like young boys. If you cheat we know you ain't no preacher. You still sound good to me." Well, Thelma Williams told him. Thelma Williams spoke for the people. Alan Parsley cheated and the people turned a "blinded eye" and forgave him.

He married Thelma Williams who also cheat and had him believe that Theo is his son. Alan Parsley knew this from day one because Alan Parsley cannot have children due to some kind of dysfunction he had from birth. He let it be and treated Theo as if he was his flesh and blood.

Alan Parsley doesn't care because Alan Parsley lived for two things; money and sex. Never mind Alan Parsley promised Thelma Williams that he wouldn't cheat on her; he just is a bit more discrete than he was before their marriage. Thelma Williams thought she gave him what he wanted in bed and he would be happy. Her mother who was a hooker told Thelma Williams, "give a man a blow and he'll give you anything. The pig will stay with you." Yes, this is true, however, as Thelma Williams found out "she ain't staying faithful, blows or no blow;" she cheated on Alan Parsley, who was yet again unfaithful to Thelma Williams who he called his "turnip" why? He doesn't know why. His turnip has a sexy figure, particularly after the tummy tuck she had after giving birth. He gave her all the money she can spend and that woman can spend, for her and everyone else she fancied.

"Oh Lord, help me." Alan Parsley is well aware of how many times the Botox face woman cheated on him. Why the fuck can she leave him, particularly when she confronted him about cheating, he can't understand? He's forty-five and she thinks she's twenty-five years of age. If she thinks she can file for divorce and get all the money, she's wrong.

Alan Parsley arrived home and spaced the floor in his living room trying to be one step ahead of his turnip. She can't use his STD against him because he never told her that he had crap. After the pregnancy, he always used a condom with her and every woman he has sex with in the last twenty-five years. He bought the condom wholesale and by the boxes; he'll never run out. Never know when opportunities strike.

Turnip does nothing for anyone especially him. He had once sexually experienced with a white male hooker when he was sixteen years of age. This was how he contacted craps. If she filed for divorce there isn't much she'll get because for one thing, he kept all the receipts on every penny she spent; the second thing he hid was his money in the Barbados bank he opened the day they accepted him as a preacher.

Money started to roll in. He went there a long time ago with some other college friends for fun when they turned eighteen because they can drink all the rum at eighteen. He drank all the rum he possibly can without getting alcohol poising like those white boys; his blood was good, and he drank.

He visited Barbados again as he told everyone he needed a vacation before he started to preach, a weekend away was great. They all chipped in and paid for it. He spent four days there. He opened his account and drank all the Mount Gay and Cockspur rum he can and slept with all the hookers he could with the little money he had left from the drinking. He rarely visited the place again because he doesn't want anyone to know about his money. He had a way of getting money into that bank without a trace. Offshore banking is the best.

Tired of thinking, Alan Parsley plugged his headphone of iPod into his ears and began doing some serious jig on his polished wood floors. Less than ten minutes later, the wood gave way and Alan Parsley found himself flying down through the floor yelling "Hallayula" right into the neighbor downstairs Charles Callahan's lap.

Charles Callahan was sitting on his sofa watching pornography with one hand on his gun and the other masturbating his penis. Upon the intrusion, both their faces registered shock. Alan Parsley is a Democrat. Charles Callahan is a Republican.

Ryan Ryes didn't expect to see Olympia appear at midnight. He didn't see her today at her usual time; she didn't have lunch or dinner and figured that she was working on one of the four cases she was investigating. He missed her. He consoled himself that there's tomorrow.

He had closed the Twist Peach and was walking up the stairs to his apartment when his instinct kicked in. He reached behind his back under his t-shirt for his gun. He relaxed his hold when he inhaled her scent, a wicked scent of lilac. A smile reached his lips, touched his eyes, and warmed his heart.

As he entered his domain, he felt immediately the frisson of passion that stirred in both of their eyes. She was sitting pretty on the sofa looking at the door he just entered. She was wearing not the usual professional stacks and shirt, instead of a purple flower dress that fell on her muscled thighs.

The dress rode high on those firmed legs as her nipples crest against the soft fabric letting him be aware of how aroused she is, ready for them to mate. A pulse jumped excitedly in her throat as her chest rose and fell quickly. The apex of her legs amplified her core.

At this stage, she wouldn't be requiring major cosmetic work nor any major surgery for that matter; she is already fine-tuned to perform and perform her will because he was waiting for her since he saw her. She was giving him the killer ache for ravishing her at this moment, however, this ache will fade after making love to her.

Dear Lord, what he's looking at this late hour is a sensual nemesis and he loved all of her, already. He was waiting for her for many weeks before she walked into his life. She was beginning to undress or tease him that she was making no mistake as to why she was here. He doesn't care. Tonight, belong to him-both of them.

"I had a long difficult day. I threw up due to something I saw. I slept all day and I came over tonight. I was planning on tomorrow night. I need comfort tonight. Can you give me that?" Olympia finished the startled Ryan and let out a breath she was holding since she decided to see him. Her tone had an edge of annoyance to her explanation. She needed something from him. With the surge of blood pouring into his manhood he headed in the opposite direction.

"Hang on to that thought and yes, I can give you comfort." He replied as he walked into his room. He started across the floor to the designated area with a walk that could have gotten him arrested for attempted seduction-maybe not, he was flammable. He was dressed in a white t-shirt and blue jeans that were tailored to fix his structure. He oozed power plus elegance and class. She found her match. He returned without a shirt.

"Olympia and more, lots more." He smiled and disappeared again.

"I would like a preview please?" She asked him seriously.

"No preview." He said with a wide grin as he stepped into the shower.

"I love seeing the preview. I know what's being offered is to my liking." She said disappointedly pouting her lower lip in a teasing fashion. Little did he know that she was trembling more than a leaf on a tree on a windy day. Olympia didn't blink when he first walked away and was standing still looking at the space when he returned with no shirt, filling the space with his male structure. She was still there looking at the very space when he appeared again all naked under a towel and tan all over, in her view.

Waiting for the finale after meeting him would be worthwhile. The air rippled between them smiling of freshness from Ryan's quick shower and her lilac mixing was the aphrodisiac they needed for the romance that will be flourishing between them.

"Olympia, you asked for it." He dropped the towel. The Full Monty was released to a dance yet to be discovered. Ryan was muscular throughout his physique with a tawny suntan that highlighted his square-jawed face and showed elegantly crew-cut light brown hair with sexist soft blue eyes.

She was going to undress and slyly said to the man in the wet birth suit. "Aren't you going to turn around?" She asked and sat down before her knee gave out. They looked at each other for a while until Ryan covered the space between them and stood right in front of her, very, very close that her mouth was right in front of his manhood.

It drew every nuance of emotions from her, giving way to the passion that hung tight between them. She inhaled and let her tongue out, slowly and ever so lightly running it up and down his shaft. His body swelled more towards her mouth, to a hardness that made her tremble with fervor.

This man must have radar because she had been throbbing with passion, designed to mate with him. She realized that she had been subconsciously searching for him all of her life. She grazed at the edge of the skin of his manhood with her teeth and used her tongue to flow with an upward stroke.

"Hello handsome, what mischief were you up to today?" She asked about his erection as her tongue did an intake to an unknown territory under his scrotum. She lifted herself from the sofa onto her knees and was quickly pulled to her feet by Ryan.

"Waiting for a beautiful girl to make love to him." Laughter broke out from Olympia.

"Oh, Ryan." He covered her with his body putting one hand against her back, he twined the other into the curtain of her hair as his lips captured her mouth. He kissed her putting all the weeks of waiting and longing into the kiss telling her how much he wanted her in his life. Olympia received the message and couldn't tell him hers because he had kissed her breathless. She broke her lips away from him breathing hard as he encircled her waist and pulled her against his wet naked body.

"I want to slowly undress you. I need to touch you and kiss you everywhere. Mostly, I want to watch you come alive when I'm inside you." Ryan leaned down to catch her lower lip between his teeth and lifted her into his strong tan arms.

He raised his head and their eyes connected with mutual

understanding. He lifted her to his body not breaking their eyes' connection. He moved with grace as he entered the room he just left. He laid her upon his made bed, on top of his black and white bedspread, and watched her for a long while.

Upon making the decision that he wanted her as naked as he is, he leaned into her and kissed her while removing her clothes, just one piece. He soon discovered she had neither a bra nor panties on.

Her hands found his wet hair behind his neck as her tongue sought his lips. As they mated, lifting the band of sexual tension that was built since the day they met many weeks ago when his blue eyes met her blue eyes.

Presently, both in the naked, Ryan turned on his back and lift Olympia right onto his erection, and guided it slowly into her. They felt the slick velvety tip of his engorged erection make contact with soft feminine sexuality; they trembled with passion.

She took all of him and leaned forward, blowing lightly into his ear, laughing. Her head fell back and he handheld her hips in place making her motionless for a bit……… enjoying her wrapped in the throes of his excitement.

A moment of stillness was required as they enjoyed the sensations that erupted from the penetration. He took her with all dazzling speed yet with gentleness and unspeakable pleasure. Satisfied, he began to move her hips with a natural rhythm that she picked up and swayed with him.

He used his erection to feed the ache inside her, to coax and tease her with intense sensations. "I want to do it all over again and again for the rest of my life." He felt her tremble and turned to nip her into a long searching kiss.

"Until you become me and I become you, one." He kissed her neck and kissed a path to a nipple and took it in his mouth. The sound she released seduced him more and told him he had accomplished what he had set out to do. He wanted her to want him as much as he wanted her. The response from his body was one with her lithe curves, bending together to enhance what they are already feeling.

It was some seven hours later in the morning when Ryan rolled onto his side and fell to the floor. His body hit wood as he rolled onto his back. It took him a moment as confusion played a rolled in the frowned as he looked around.

"What the fuck?" He uttered as he sat up and rubbed the painful area on his head. He pushed himself up and rubbed his backside trying to figure out how the hell he ended up on the hardwood floor. He looked at his bed and saw Olympia had pushed him out; he had rolled over to give her space. He looked at her in his bed and realized that she was on her stomach in the middle of his bed. He's going to have to get a bigger bed tomorrow, mmmm, today as he glanced at the clock on the bedside table.

Ryan climbed into the bed squeezing his body in the little space she left. He felt his thigh pushed against hers and he gained exquisite pleasure. He pushed her legs apart and let himself in from behind. He heard her make a wonderful sound and went ahead with his maneuvering of their body as one. They exploded as if they were the display of the Fourth of July fireworks; that made a rare attendance, however, accidentally touched off prematurely.

The two of them as one in the first light of dawn with their glittering skin as ripe golden oranges from the sunlight as the sun broke over the horizon. Through the window, they heard the first stirrings of the morning creatures singing to their rhythm making the love fruitful and beyond beautiful.

"Did you sleep well?" Ryan leaned over her and kissed her between her breasts.

"Yes." She took hold of his hair and pushed his head back to kiss him passionately on his lips.

"Do you have something you want to share, spill it?" Olympia thought about the question for a split second. "I thought I did last night on several occasions and this minute." She smiled sexily at him as she laid her head to rest on the pillow.

He picked himself off from her and stood up. "Going to open the bar and get us some coffee. Don't go anywhere." He spoke in a firm soft whisper.

"I have to get to work." She informed him.

"Take the day off." He ordered and was gone for ten minutes returning with coffee. Bringing coffee for her after they made love was romantic and intimate. She was in the same position naked on the bed with no covering as he handed her the coffee. She took a few sips from the cup. She loved him with her in bed as he slipped coffee from his mug.

"Who's going to run the bar?" She wanted to know.

"I have Billy, who took over for me when I need a day off." He lay next to her in his full clothing. Realizing this, he stood up and took it off and fill the space next to her, taking her hand into his, he kissed it.

"You're spending the day?" A brow flew up over his left eye on his handsome face. The sound of his tone filled with promising splendor. It was more an order than a question or a request.

"Yes." "How did you get here? I didn't see your car?" Ryan asked her as he took a sip of black coffee from his mug.

"I took a taxi. Your door was open."

"Oh. I left it open for you. I didn't know when. All I know was that I was wishing and hoping."

"Wish no more. I want the same things as you do and much, much more." His eyes sparkled with mischief and he grinned, wide.

41

It was the beginning of December with Christmas being a few weeks away, the maintenance crew was busy with various repairs including adding lights in trees for the upcoming events held at the Club House. The sun was up keeping the cold winter days out from Helenville.

The residents were occupied with a gift list and family visiting. It was a busy time for the residents. As usual, the inhabitants sat out at the pool wrapped in coats, blankets, and various warming clothing. The latte and cocoa were spiked with an enormous amount of alcohol as they chat about everything and nothing.

The thing about this is, as much as it was social it was over the rim with gossip. Many residents of Essex Place had Alzheimer's and were senile. They wouldn't remember the conversation in s few hours much less the next day.

"The leak doctor visited eight-six-year-old Mrs. Footingdale again. That's the third time in one week considering that building was recently re-plumed."

"Really?"

"Yep, sir. Three different ones to booth until maintenance went in and told her that there are no leaking problems and to stop calling the plumbers. You know what she told him the cute one, "I have the leak problem. I was wondering why they keep checking the pipes." There was a silence because the people that were sitting listening didn't know whether to laugh because they too have the same problem.

"What happened?" Mr. Moore asked.

"He told her to call her Medical doctor and not the Leak Doctor, he made the call for her and the appointment. He also notified her son."

The buzz began again after a few "ohs," "poor thing," good for her," and a few more other comments. It was the same every day all year round at every pool with the young and old. Some of them laughed, some were rude, and some were serious with some even falling asleep.

"They're no good lawyers or judges in this country, all they ever do is manipulate."

"You know that Home Depot is a rip-off. They charge you two dollars even when you paid in full before the due date. I don't shop there anymore. I go to Lowes.

"Ya don't say."

"I do say."

"People kept telling us that America has a variety. I don't see it like that. I see more of the same thing. Variety means an abundance of other country products, not the same thing made in the USA. Besides most of the food product is synthetic and not real." "Monsanto food, GMO-Genetic Modified Food, not good for you, and Obama and Bono from U2 just signed to feed Africa with it; it gives you cancer and other health problems. His body can't process it.

"The thing is, they don't eat it, why sell it……such hypocrites. I don't support Obama anymore especially when he sends those drones to kill innocent people. I forgot which country and the whole affair of Benghazi. I told my grandson not to listen to Bono music anymore and he told his friends and they have all boycotted him.

"I agreed. They say you can get rich here. All I see is if you rip or rape someone off their money or through exploitation you'll get rich. I made my money in my country and retired here."

"Why did you do that?" Fiona asked him.

"No one knows that I have lots of money here. Well, you know now. In my country, everybody comes begging and I got tired of giving."

"Sears, you say. I quit buying from them when they sold my credit for my water heater to a foreign company and they pulled back the date one day and charged me fifty dollars in a late fee."

"Did anyone know that the Sheriff's a crook? His deputy planned drugs in my cousin Juan's car because he was bad-mouthing him. The Sheriff beats his wife and when she called 911 they send deputies to his house.

Juan saw the whole thing and when he started talking, the sheriff ordered the deputy on Juan. The minute Juan got bail he left and we don't know where he is.' Juanita finished.

"I heard that and the reports disappeared from all of the 911 called."

"How ya hear child." An elderly female asked.

"I can't tell you. It's true what she's saying plus the Sheriff's department has a whore... a hoe that fucked her way up to the top. She had an affair with the Sherriff when he was married to his first wife and she slept with lots of the other deputies. If anyone messed with her she goes straight to the Sheriff and the person gets in trouble." Sanari added what she knew to be true.

"Did she mess with you?" "Yes, she did. The bitch, hoe verbally abused me a few times and I wrote to the Captain complementing everyone except her. She was furious. All the kids knew she was a hoe. They were the ones who told me. I don't work with her anymore." Sanari told them.

"Oh, come on. Abuse is a big word. She probably was expressing her freedom of speech."

"You don't say. Don't become confused between freedom of speech and abuse. There's a broad line between expressing your right to speak and verbally degrading someone in anger. Two different things altogether, people don't know the difference, especially women." Sanari explained to them.

The silence was only for a few seconds before the topic was changed. This is why it's so beautiful. Everyone can express their feelings without being trampled on at this moment since Asa and Gina are dead.

"We'll never win the war on terror not when we're part of it." This was noted by veterans nodding in full agreement.

"I was watching Sex in the City and I can't figure out what's so sexy about those women. There's no chemistry. It's a stupid show and that Mr. Big treating her as if she was trash." A teenage girl with long black hair climbed out of the pool to talk to elderly Mrs. Panndi.

"She's trash to sleep with a married man. Most of them look anorexic and the story is stupid. Good for you child."

"A gun only stopped the issues; it doesn't find a solution to the conflict of interest. Banning the gun is not the solution."

"I don't care. We should've tighter laws on guns. People aren't qualified to carry one." Sanari said to Joe who defined himself along with Edmond and Charles by the gun and walked around with concealed weapons.

"I went shopping and everything is either made in polyester even the designers' clothes. Emporio Armani uses polyester with his clothes. It's cheap fabric and he charged lots of money. Where's silk and cotton? If you look at Hollywood they have the designers' clothes with those trays hanging behind them and the fabric is cheap stuff. The clothes control them and they cannot control the clothes."

"I wouldn't buy a Hyundai if it's the last car standing. The way I look at it is when they first came out they were unreliable cars. I got ripped off with mine and the dealer was mean and cruel. The company was no different because for making a lemon there was no refund and I lost. The cars suck."

"You know that Bin Laden was in Pakistan all this time and Bush knew. You know that he knew that 9/11 was going to happen and he let it. How come he's not charged with war crimes? Bush and Cheney destroy two countries for greed and money and the towers were strapped with an explosive that's why it came down."

"Love affair of conspiracy is what they are doing over at the cove and conspiracy led to fraud and fraud my dears are a felony and a felony is well over 10 or more years in jail."

"I love the American spirit. I don't like American life or politic."

"How so?"

"Is that so?"

"Yes, just so."

"What is the American Spirit?"

"The caring and sharing and the helping hand of people here."

"American life?" Asked all American Iraqi veterans. All the people sitting by the pool were silent; browns went up in wonderment as they await the explanation of American life. All the Americans were listening because a foreigner was talking.

"The exploitation of others, materialistic life's not for me. I like the fact that when you need help you can rely on your worst enemy to help me. You can't find that anywhere in the world."

"Really?" Another female questioned.

"Yes, and you know what? People who are exploiting others with materialistic things, mostly money, come here and live and do the same thing. America created the needs of other countries in the world by being destructive with wars and they can't, wouldn't, or afford to deliver what's needed or promised to the people of the countries, that's why many countries hate America. They don't know the difference between the people and the country."

"That's true. You should see the mess in Iraq and Afghanistan we made there. They don't want you people to know. Most of it is buried that's why you civilians are naïve and the world hated us." "Oh." Came from another elderly lady whose expression is in confusion due to dementia.

"Who exploited who?" A young man wanted to know.

"Look at all those so-called singers, who sing about erotica and make millions. That's self-exploitation because if they can sing they wouldn't have to recreate themselves or sing about the dark side of sex."

"That's true. They carried deep-rooted anger. They always have to generate drama to sell their songs. Look and see how fast they died out. They aren't singers, they are entertainers." Sanari acknowledged the talker and the conversation went on for the next few hours until the sunset and the old-timers left. The young remained for another few hours.

The Sussex Place is a firestorm of gossip and opinions that either embarrassed or uplifted the listeners. This is the pleasure of living in a retirement community. Olympia's brain was turning into scrambled eggs with all of this and no answers to her questions which were custom made, for the answers that were ignored beat against her brain giving way to a migraine.

Not one of them ever mentioned Asa Fleischer as if she never even existed!

Calculated thoughts with computer-generated opinions for brains are what these people are in connection with Fleischer. Everyone has an opinion and they have a right to express it, however, are their opinions based on facts or myths or lies or deceits? What are their true opinions based on? How are they processing life, on culture, religion, or evidence?

"Did you hear about the black preacher falling through the floor on the white man's lap?" So, said the neighbor who goes to Allan Parsley's church.

"How do you know this?" her friend asked.

"I know this because I was ear-dropping."

"You don't say. Tell me more." An eyebrow raised and body language spelled "Gossip."

Fiona whispered to Olympia that she and Sanari were in the dressing room over by the mall trying on clothes when they overheard the conversation carried on by Anna Fairmont and some unknown females. After standing in the dress-room listening to the story told by Anna they left the store without buying anything. The mood for shopping was over as they begin to laugh with tears running down their faces. The images between Alan Parsley and Charles Callahan were the laugh of all laughs in the retirement community.

The girls sat dried faces sipping lattes and munching on shortbread biscuits, chocolate chip cookies, and a blueberry muffin. With serious faces, they leaned into the arms of the chair looking around them to see what was going on, and acknowledged anyone they know is listening. The silence was to allow them to catch their breath after laughing at Parsley's and Callahan's incident.

They saw Mrs. Bishop, Craig Altner, and the Guptas who all acknowledged each other with a nod. The girls turned their backs to the crowd and do their usual thing. They do what they usually do when they are together; they gossip and catch up on the latest in each other lives.

Today, they included Olympia and the whole residents of Sussex Place, well just the regulars who usually joined them on a nice evening at the pool for drinks and snacks.

"You charge by the hour for this golden advice." Olympia sarcastically asked them. Sanari and Fiona looked at each other thinking that Olympia has a dried sense of humor. Someone else continued the story of the preacher and all ears were tuned in even Sanari and Fiona who knew about the incident.

Olympia turned her eyes skyways she didn't care a hoot, however, she listened; something she's good at, well trained, listening is a quality of hers and she is excellent at it. Crimes are solved by listening, too many crimes. Let things be the way it is Olympia thought; it's Utopia here in Sussex Place.

#

Who killed Fleischer? Where's the missing agent? Is there a serial killer living here? The Nazi was the easiest of these cases. Olympia had gotten a court order for surveillance on Mr. and Mrs. Bishop waiting for a slight mistake and they'll be arrested. As much as she closed Asa Fleischer's case, it still haunted her.

The serial killer continues to be unidentified, however, surveillance is on the nephew, Craig Peter Altner.

There are no more leads on the missing agent except that he used to go to The Twixt Peach. A smile appeared on Olympia's lips as thoughts of her and Ryan together. She gave the images attention and then she tucked them away; they would not intervene with her work.

A great part of her job is to put the evidence together and think them through or talk them over with the partner or team. She has neither of those at this present moment, therefore her thoughts will have to be her partner and team. She's going to have to let go of Fleischer's case and let it be, at least today.

Those were the questions pondering in Special Agent Olympia Van Amstel's thoughts for the last two weeks. She had coffee with Sanari a week ago over at the Twixt Peach and noticed the extra food she carried out, why, for who? Nothing seemed to pan off to anything much less answering those questions. The residents dodged her whenever they see her and as soon as she approached them they asked for their lawyer.

Christmas is in two days and then the New Year. Life seemed to travel in slow motion since she and Ryan became a couple. They had to keep their love affair quiet until she solved all of the cases.

It's unethical and unprofessional of her to be involved with anyone who lived in the vicinity of these cases or who is acquainted with the people that are suspects. He understood and supported her thoroughly. She has to ride out the storm of what the information created. What did it create nothing? Frustration lingered on her forehead of Olympia. As if sensing it her paces became hastened and she rubbed her forehead. The gossips at the pool a few days ago were nothing to do with the cases she was working on.

Was that the norm or were they talking about experiences because she was there? One thing was for sure, she was able to observe them all together, the Republicans, the Democrats, and a few Liberals all in trivialized conversation bored and lonely.

The whole crux of the matter seemed pointless. As the hours dragged on and the weeks passed, no one knew where the scene of the crime was only that Fleischer was discovered by two hunters in the swamp.

This was merely a very small part of the whole of Asa Fleischer; the part that she chose to display was blackmail while the killer is still at large, unknown to all. To fix a faux pas of this magnitude murder, missing agent, and serial killer, oh yes, the Nazi would require an army. For Pete's sake, she is the lone army!

"Time to visit Armani," Olympia spoke to herself. She had meant some weeks ago before she closed the Fleischer case and forgotten all about it. The coffee at the Twixt Peach was inconclusive due to the takeout food Sanari seems to always have with her when she leaves a restaurant or the Twixt Peach.

Who is the extra food for? Since Fleischer's case is closed well, unsolved due to no clues, curiosity was thawing at her. In the endless conversation with the locals, she had picked up something about where Sanari, Fiona, and Asa had ever visited Melbourne again. The questions she sensed were deliberately ignored by Sanari and Fiona when they were at the pool.

Sanari paid an elderly a compliment and everyone ran with it drawing laughter and more laughter, evading the questions.

Fiona's skin color changed from a reddish tan to white, however, no one noticed except Olympia. If anyone had asked Olympia about the change in Fiona's skin color, she would've guessed it was the compliment of the cold weather. She knew that no one ever mentioned Asa's name and referred to her as that girl or the other girl.

The question concerned Fiona, Sanari, and Fleischer being in Melbourne together, and if they did what were they doing there? Olympia was still mumbling over the whole mess of gossipmongers when she arrived and knocked on the door of Sanari's. Randy promised to send the photographs from the camera in about two hours and she would be busy sorting out that mess and adding time and date to everyone who couldn't have killed Fleischer.

Maybe if luck has it she can identify the serial killer. If Lady Luck permitted it, that is, and knowing her luck probably wouldn't do, not in her favor.

Shock ran through her when a man opened the door with no shirt and his hand behind her back. Boom! She could have been shot! Getting old and careless, Olympia scolded herself. She recognized him as much as he acknowledged her, otherwise, he wouldn't have opened the door. He knew who she was before he spoke she said seriously in her FBI-trained voice.

"Don't shoot. I'm going for my gun and offload it." She didn't let go of the eye contact and neither of them blinked as she reached for her gun and slowly removed it from the holster. She pulled the cartridges out and returned the empty gun to her holster. She kept the cartridges in her hand.

"May I come in, Lost Under Cover Special Agent of the FBI?" She asked calmly. "I was getting ready to send the SWAT team to search the whole God damn compound for you." Ryland nodded and moved aside to let her in, removing his hand from his back. He walked to the chair where he had left his t-shirt and quickly pulled it over his head.

"Have a seat Amstel." He gestured to the sofa as he took the opposite one from her.

"I would be damn. Every agent in the area is looking for you. I recognized you from the photo your boss sent out. I never thought that you would be lodging with Amani." Ryland was silent for a long while as he tried to figure if he can trust her in telling her his truth. Why he's hiding from all of them. Olympia understanding the silence waited a few minutes before saying, "I smell something fishy. Does Amani...."

"Keep her out of this." Ryland's voice was stern as he stopped her. He frowned and making a decision he continued. "Someone shot me. The bullet grazed my side and went into Diego's cousin. I guessed the shooter saw me running for a safer cover and this time I got it in my side. It went right through. I ran out of there as a bat out of hell. I ran all the way here thinking that this was my father's old friend's place and found Sanari." "Why did you not contact your handler?" "She's dead. I was undercover for two years tracking the kingpin here. I bumped into Ryan Reyes at the Twixt Peach. We are retired Seals and he put me on to Diego who is the middle man in Florida."

"Where were you shot?" Hearing the mention of Ryan made her heart rate climb and she knew right there that she loved him. She kept her cool and showed professionalism, cold emotionless eyes.

"Behind the Peach in the woods, that's where all the business took place. No, no one heard, and if they did they would ignore it because there were hunters in the woods. I think someone in the Bureau is in on it. They recognized me and tried to eliminate me."

"Maybe it was your partner, the handler."

"I think you're right about that. She had someone in the Bureau as her partner."

"Wow, that's big, who?"

Ryland shook his head gesturing, "I don't know. I've been here holding up for weeks trying to figure it out and I've nothing." He told her in frustration and let out a long breath, a breath of weeks in hibernation only going out for a walk with Sanari, long after sunset, or to the shops in the next county for necessity.

He had been using her money promising to pay her back as soon as he returned to work. She nodded understanding and paid for everything without questioning him. He doesn't have any identification either and the fake one he had was lost in the wood running for his life.

"I'll see what I can find out." Olympia was waiting for approval. She saw his frustration and understood the dilemma of who to trust. "Why me?"

"I knew Massy. I had worked a case with him a long time before you came into the picture. He showed me a photograph of you. I recognized you the minute I peeked at you and decided to trust you a few minutes ago." Ryland told her.

"Oh!" Was all that Olympia managed, the past still haunted her.

"For what it's worth, he was separated from his wife a long time before you. They lived in the same house because of the children, money, and his job."

"Oh."

Ryan let her ponder on that for a few minutes. He laid his head back on the sofa trying to figure what he should do now that his cover is blown. Olympia was also in silence trying to do the same when she remembered why she was there.

As if reading her thoughts, Ryland lifted his head. "Sanari isn't the killer."

"What...huh....who?"

Before she could finish, he interjected, "The owner of The Twixt Peach, Ryan Reyes." Seeing the shock on her face, it hit him that Special Agent of the FBI Olympia Van Amstel was sexually involved with his fellow Seal. No, wait she's in love with him.

"Oh, what a mess!" Ryland said out loud to the air. He stood up and started to space on the wooden floor.

Seeing Amstel's color on her skin stopped and looked at her. He had a deep need to comfort her. "That Fleisher woman was hell on wheels, let it go. He had reasons to shoot her, you either asked him or close the case. If you love him let it go. We get one shot at love, take it. You'll never find the weapon or the scene of the crime, not even I know where it is. We never had this conversation." He was in love with Sanari, who was he to tell her the truth. He was in the wood waiting for Diego when he saw Ryan put a bullet into a woman's forehead. It was after he came to live with Sanari that he found out who she was and have no remorse about Ryan taking the shot at her. He's not about to tell Olympia anything else.

Ryland wouldn't pull out secrets and share them with her either. He never asked and doesn't want to know. What he does know is that Ryan wouldn't have killed her unless he had damn good reasons. Those reasons he doesn't care to ponder on either. He has to figure out what to do with his mess and doesn't have Sanari involved.

Olympia rose on her feet, pulled her gun from the holster, loaded it with the cartridge, and returned it to the holster. She was shaking violently. She needed to get a drink; no, she wanted to get drunk. She needed to be alone, to figure out what to do.

Ryland was sitting only for a split minute and quickly rise to his feet when the door opened and Sanari walked in with a beautiful smile on her face. Seeing them both, a frown appeared and a surprising look followed by shock replaced the beautiful smile.

Olympia walked through the door and left in a hurry. Sanari's eyes followed her down the hall to the stairways. No elevator for the Special Agent today. She turned to Ryland and said, "You can go too."

Ryland walked through the door and followed his fellow special agent's footsteps. He turned when he heard the door softly shut and retracted his footsteps. He tried the doorknob, found it lock, and rang the doorbell.

The door opened immediately. As he stood silhouetted in the doorway, he looked at her and saw from Sanari's expression that her thoughts had slipped into an alternate universe, fear trumped in her eyes. He didn't like it one bit. His heart twitched and missed a few beats. He knew that he'll never leave her. Never!

He walked in, took Sanari's hands, and pulled her to sit on the sofa with him. He felt the warmth of Olympia where he sat. He looked at Sanari, "I'm only going to say this once, once Sanari, listen, please." He took a finger and put it under her chin and gently ever so gently turned her face to meet his eyes. He waited until she slowly and fearfully raised her eyes to his and as she did so her lips parted. He lost his speech and wanted to kiss her.

Ryland leaned in and kissed her. All that came out of his mouth was "I love you." He kissed her deeply with passion, pulling her upon him. She felt his arousal and responded in kind, returning silent answers to his questions. He smoothed her fears away. "I don't ever want to leave you," Ryland told her breathlessly as they surfaced for air. "I wanted to stay with you for the rest of my life. I have a job that got me into a heap of trouble with a traitor and I've to figure it out. It scares me to know that you can get hurt."

She had waited all her life for that special someone to walk through the doorway of her heart and leave his indelible mark on her. It happened to her with Ryland; he managed to do that-leave his incredible mark on her.

Sanari thought it was very romantic of him to have painted her toes with the red nail polish the day she squeezed her fingers in the car door. He had seen her doing it with pain in her eyes and took the nail polish from her and finished the job. She had returned in kind by shaving him and cutting his hair into a crew cut. There was an intimacy between them. She had fallen in love with him all those moons ago.

"You're the pill for my nightmares, Ryland. Because of you, I sleep soundly. You're building into an addiction. I've no use for the real thing. I've no more nightmares." Ryland's eyes lit up upon hearing her words and smiled. He pulled her to him and gave her a kiss of pleasure.

"Why the nightmares?" He asked. The question of the nightmares bought memories of restless nights that had somehow assumed an identity of its own, more of life of its own, giving her fears.

Those memories kicked out others because as soon as she was awake the conditioning of the images and the infliction of fear coupled with her past biased her view of the new day.

Sanari's past is about to become part of the present. Will her past survive this relationship with Ryland? The nightmares were a mass larger than the sum of the two of them combined that vibrated in her, suspending her breath as they hovered and waited for her scream each night followed by tears.

She pulled away from him and rested her head on his shoulders. "I too have secrets and I'm ready to let you in on them. It doesn't mean that you've to tell me yours. I trust you one hundred percent and more if that's possible." She moved her head and kissed the side ridge of his chin.

"Thank you."

"I was born in Afghanistan to a family who's Sunni Muslims. I found out that my father is...was a terrorist when I was eight. As soon as I turned thirteen I ran away from them when they visit Turkmenistan in Tajikistan. I met a man and his family there. They were more than one family; I knew I would be safe.

"I promise to marry his son if he took me to New Deli with his family. I didn't marry the son and left as soon as we reached New Deli. I worked in a factory that makes saris and saved my money. I caught a refugee boat that was supposed to be heading to England.

"The boat sank and those who survived were picked up by a fishing boat from somewhere in the Ocean. I don't know who or what country. I don't remember. An American submarine picked us up from the ocean because the boat sank. We were dehydrated and sick from floating on debris for weeks. I woke up in a hospital in Hawaii.

"I was in and out of consciousness and don't remember how I got here. I know this because they told me. I don't remember much except a lot of people were poking at my body. I told them I was from Jordan and my name is Sanari Amani.

"My real name is Bibi Uzra Farfanzi. I told them that I was an orphan and my papers went with the boat. I am a product of that outcome; in reality, I got stuck in this country by default."

"It's nice to know what your default setting is." Ryland had to say something. He wanted to comfort her, to chase away the ghost that still haunted her. What would have happened if he didn't spend the nights with her; he has to travel for his job? Would her nightmares surface again? "Are you still living in your past? What would happen if I have to return to work and can't spend the nights with you?" He had to ask her; he wanted to know because this can make or break the relationship they have with each other. Sanari's past is either stronger than their love or their love is stronger than her past.

"Huh? What are you thinking?"

Ryland had one weapon against her past ghosts, no ghosts only reality. Ryland's intelligence was not stripped. The one characteristic that would override her past ghosts would be his love for her. He was prepared to do battle to give their love a chance to grow stronger. His love for her was much stronger than those past bloody ghosts. "I don't want part of you permanently trapped in the past haunted by old ghosts."

"That could tear our relationship apart?" She finished his thought.

"With your vision and memory being a tricky thing, have you ever thought or had help from a psychologist?" "No, I was afraid that they would report me and my citizenship would be revoked.

Fear kept my mouth shut, not even Fi knows. Yes, you're the first. As much as I love you, I trust you with all of my heart. The past had to be over and I should be done with it. I agree. You know, the side effect of a psychologist? "First, they labeled you, then they branded you and then they crucify you. They don't care about your innocent or fears." Sanari's voice sizzled in anticipation of what he was going to say next to her.

Before Ryland had time to process the rejection of his idea of a psychologist, she invaded his thoughts with more memories as fear echoed in the valley of remembrance. Intensified sensations pooled together and skipped along her vein dancing upon her nerves as the memories of her nightmare surged into her vision focusing on her conscience.

"The nightmare is a mystery because the images were vague and blurred. They surfaced in my dreams. Two men were in bed with me and one of them trying to have sex; he put his hand between my legs as to spread them. I would walk up screaming. I don't know whether I saw this happen with another girl or it did happen to me."

"Tell me all of it, what happened from your first memory till this moment." She saw the pleading in his eyes and heard it in his voice, Sanari couldn't fathom what Ryland was getting at because to tell him everything could ruin the relationship and she doesn't want to do that to them.

"You want me to resurrect the past everything from my first kiss to my first sexual experience and I'm not supposed to get angry? How's that going to solve the nightmares? I already told you, that you are the pill for my nightmare. I asked you to leave and you said no, what gives?" She had moved away a few inches looking at him. Seeing his silent question, she answered, "no, I was not raped. I was a virgin with my first love." Ryland rolled her statement in his thoughts. He moved for the first time and put a figure over her opened lips. "Shhh, you don't have to tell me about your lovers. I don't want to know.

"Your past is over and I hope the nightmares never come back. I think it's about the doctors poking over you in the hospital. Since you had fears and with being unconscious you became confused. I understand if you want to know. I don't."

She has gotten through to him as she intended, what is he complaining about? The confusion came into the conversation and marked her features. He's gentle and smooth while she's a bit rough, nevertheless, the fire of love between them is the lusciousness of a tropical paradise that made his heart spark better than moonshine.

Relieved flowed into her being and seeing this he pulled her to sit upon him. Sanari pretending to feel his erection jumped on her feet. "Is he always standing tall?" Looking at the area of his prized jewel, Ryland grinned.

Blushing to a deep red, Ryland reached for her and pulled her to sit on him. He was not "standing tall" when she mentioned it; he's now. Focusing he kissed the curve on her neck where shoulders met. "I have to figure out some stuff on my job situation. Amstel knows we are going to figure out who shot me. It was inside one of our people who knew about me being undercover. I don't know where this is going to take me. What I do know is that I don't ever want to lose you." Upon realizing that she took him in, paid for everything, and trusted him more than anyone plus he loved her more than ever, if that's possible. Warmth poured out of him and he kissed her.

This kiss was of love, his love for her, and she welcomed it. She felt the intense warmth of love burning and tingling in every fiber of her being.

Sanari responded by removing the t-shirt and unbuttoning his jeans, he caught her and lowered it off from him, and help her with his briefs. He removed her dress over her head and kissed her again on her neck the very spot he did before the undressing.

His hands were at her hips as panties were pulled away from her body down her thighs to ankles in one swift movement. There was no bra; yep Sanari was braless.

Ryland looked at her and let his tongue travel where it willed, very freely with gentleness, it made a map to her spiritual heart in the center of her breast, and then he took a nipple. As Sanari belled out some out-of-tune sounds he pulled her to sit on him. She took all of him into her and began to fine-tune the music she was making on him; with him in her.

The intrusion was absorbed by the intense physical pleasure of his possession in her body with the urgent of an unruly sweetness that tantalized tingling sensations.

Ryland seemed to have pleasure in doing the teasing. She slides her fingers through his head and felt the fine texture of his low-cut hair between her fingers. She tore at his mount and withered under the warmth pressure of his mouth as he rode with her. The gentleness of his lips caressed her thighs and the tuning of her music became intensified.

"I missed you." He said against her neck. That was the loving thing he ever revealed considering she had only been gone an hour with Fiona for a drink and they haven't been apart much since they met.

Ryland lowered his mouth to hers to taste her exoticness. He rocked her hips to ride his erection while his mouth explored her ears and neck then her breast, occasionally retrieving to the warmth of her lips tasting her sensuous aroma, and yet again to her neck traveling to her nipples.

Sanari's music was louder than any other music to his ear. He picked up the pace and she began to be more expressive. He stopped kissing her and watched her enjoying herself. She twisted around to break his grip on her hips only succeeding in driving his erecting deeper. She bellowed out a tune indication of an orgasm. Her hair fell forward, breathing suspended just for a few seconds.

He couldn't drag himself out of her body. He had a plan for the next round of lovemaking. Step two meant staying buried inside of her until she came again.......with him. He gripped her thighs and lifted her on him and slowly lowered both into a sitting position on the wooden floor. He lay on his back and rolled over trapping her beneath him never breaking them apart. Her hips sank to the floor and he thrust into her to make his point.

One hot stoke that made every muscle in their body clench tight. His eyes moved from her eyes to a part of her lips in a kiss of love. This is his turn to make music; his tone softened and his eyes burned with passion of love for her. His breath became uneven and her gaze lingered on his spasmodic jerking of a pulse in his jaw.

She expended her right finger to touch it and climax again, only a fracture of an inch when he pulled out and pushed into her. Her hands fell instead onto his neck and she glanced into his eyes, searching for in return his time to sexually express himself.

Ryland stopped and watched her waiting for her to join him. She lifted a finger and stroked his lean cheek and run it along his jawline. He reached for her finger and pulled it into his mouth. His hand went under her back and anchored her shoulders close to his body.

He held her there against his tense muscle and she sensed as well as felt his masculinity. He wanted her to feel all of him. He wanted her to receive the same awareness he felt for her. He lowered his lips to touch her parted ones.

A kiss of true love was expressed. His tongue moved against the side of her neck and she quivered passionately. Her legs came up a bit further on his waist and rest there. He moved his tongue to the middle space between her breasts and worked both nibbles. He heard her music and he deliberately stopped and replaced it with his thumbs rubbing and outlining her breast.

He gazed at the nipples with his teeth, a little enough to have her moving to his beat. This was sensuously and tremulously passionate giving into the foreplay. He pulled out, his eyes never leaving hers.

She gasped as she felt the hardening of his manhood against her stomach. She felt her sexuality leave her and slowly slid through to the floor. They breathe quickly, shallowly, and unsteadily, endeavoring with success to embrace what was happening between them. Their senses were very much alive titillated into awareness as he began to move in her and she with him.

This was the first time he has ever given this much pleasure to a woman; she was not a woman, she was a confident lady-lady who enjoyed the simplest pleasure of life and him.

"I love you, Ryland Cooper." She whispered in his ear with the musical intonation of her voice. Ryland lost control and released her as she loudly came with him. He felt her huge explosion of feelings running through her and she felt him too.

44

The spotlight lit up the stage forming a circle around the five feet seven inches man. His gun was evidence that he was looking for someone who appeared from behind him in hand cups, dressed in a three-piece suit and a top hat. The audience thought it was real at first until the owner of the little club announced, "Please give a warm welcome to Korean veteran and comedian George Stanford."

Craig James Altner knew his time would be over soon. He moved from behind the bar in the comedy club through the outer door to the back of the club. He climbed into his truck and drove as if his life depended on it. His life depended on it. He didn't leave because of the comedian he left because he spotted that FBI girl walking in from the side door looking at him.

He had worked for the club off and on for two months looking for a pick-up because he had to abandon his last victim. The stupid Asa girl had to go and get shot and the FBI is out looking for the place where she was killed. They were all over the complex. He hadn't a chance to kill again because she was always everywhere every time he went out to hunt fresh blood. He's getting antsy and having an anxiety attack.

The comedian told his audience that he almost lost his manhood on a drain pipe while with his present lover and said that she lost her to society. A little laugher broke loose and George Stanford continued. "Why is it I have a feeling that my precious crown jewels aren't getting the respect they deserve? I don't use those blue pills. I see nobody has changed." The comedian says. "Oh yes, she has," pointing to Sanari. I've gotten younger to her older." The audience laughed and looked at his admirer.

"Is that plastic surgery I see on your face?" He pointed to Fiona.

"Is that the nerd talking?" He pointed to a friend.

"No," came a reply. "The ex-lover."

"You sleep with her?"

"We all slept with her and half the campus." The replies were fixed by friends and the audience thought it was real and the laughter broke all barriers. Who broke the sound barrier? George Stanford did. This very night was the night that George Stanford broke the sound barrier of every earpiece in the audience.

Special Agent Olympia Van Amstel flashed her badge and saw when Craig James Altner made him existed. She wasn't concerned about him anymore and knew it would be soon before she appended him.

After looking through thousands of photographs with the help of Sanari and Fiona she was able to collect enough evidence to get the Judge to issued two court orders, one for the lake and the other for his apartment.

Nothing would stand up in court unless she can link the images of someone dumping black trash bags into the lake to the serial killer Craig James Altner. She wanted to catch him red-handed in the act, however, that would be difficult because he just ran from her and that meant he's on the alert of her. She wasn't concern about him.

Olympia was looking for Sanari and Fiona. She needed a girls' company and advice. She had let the girl watched the Nazi being handcuffed along with his wife at one in the morning when Sussex Place was asleep. She and Sanari and Fiona had become friends when she sought their help a week ago in sorting out the photographs. It took four days of constant work in labeling and categorizing all of them. Finally, late on the last day, they found what Olympia called evidence for the serial killer. The last case to close before she asked for some long overdue leave.

Before that Olympia had to work through Asa's murderer and the only way she knew how was by avoidance. The man she loved killed Asa Fleischer and she had to come to grips with it. What to do? It took her a week of silence and pretending to work, showing up everywhere for no one suspected what she knew and avoiding the Twixt Peach, Ryan more particularly.

With nothing to do she pulled the bug tapes with the names Asa, Fiona, and Sanari from hiding. They amounted to the others that she stole from James. She had removed this one for no particular reason, just a hunch, and send the others for analysis. The taping was lousy and only a few minutes were taped before it went dead. John Miller's name was mentioned and the sound of a body dragged and Fiona yelling.

"Tell me John Miller how many women have you raped?"

"Aoha there, rape is a big word. I don't rape I take whenever I can."

"How many John?" "I don't know. I don't keep check, darling. Oh fifty, I had fun with them. It took a while to find you. Been a long time, why don't we get started."

"Alright, I had enough," Fiona yelled out.

Somehow Asa Fleischer mugged the wire she was wearing and the rest of what took place that night was fuzzy. She couldn't even guess who else was there and Fiona's voice was not recognizable since Fleischer was the one taping the events. Special Agent Olympia Van Amstel assumed that it was Asa with John Miller.

She had Randy checked out John Miller and found out that he had several investigations on sexual assault. He was never charged nor was Fiona's name ever mentioned with the females that lodged complaints.

Maybe he raped Fleischer and Fiona and Sanari helped her. Who the fuck knows and who the fucked cared? Fleischer and Miller were bad news.

For the next two weeks, she placed John Miller under surveillance in his state with the local law enforcement and found nothing. Although her instinct told her that Fiona and Sanari were there too, was this was their secret? She deliberately left them out of the picture and destroy Fiona's voice on the tape. Why bother, she has a bigger fish to fry....Ryan Reyes.

A seed with a wise concept collided with an errant thought began to form a plan of action. It had somehow taken root in the back of her brains-a conceivable thought so undignified that she laughed out loud at the absurdity. She's watching comedy and no one would suspect what she's thinking.

Sometimes, in life, something must be destroyed for something to be created. The thought had no business or reason being there. Still, it remained there and fear died a quick death. Panic surged as she tried to return to consciousness.

It didn't happen. Logic took over. Ryan's behavior doesn't fit the profile of a murderer. Brilliance doesn't act as a murderer because it carried a different behavior, Olympia rationed with her heart. The fire of love instantly flared into life illuminating his sharply etched profile into her thoughts and the love they shared. They had operated on different planes in different worlds with different yet similar codes of conduct that were not remotely close to matching up with each other.

Opposite attracts. She had been conditioned to balance evidence to a rational logical conclusion with the evidence matching the crime.

"How?" She needed to know.

"Why?" She wanted to ask.

Forging no language in managing the conflict of interest, the silent dialogue continued making logic to her confused torn one. The perennial existential challenges of living without love delivered a host of new questions to accompany the planted seed, growing into a hunger for excellence.

Olympia willed her thoughts into silence, nonetheless as she discarded the seed of one thought, another surfaced and the inert thought faded away; a more logical one sweep through the crack of her common sense. The thoughts began spinning, rolling out a whole new concept. She had been here before, she knew it; she felt it.

"Grrr." Beyond the edge of logic and the Eureka moment laid anxiety. In addition to falling in love and anxiety, anger grew because she knew from the experience of violent situations that this would no doubt cause an avalanche of flashbacks to the previous time when she was shot by her lover's wife.

"I'm not the problem nor am I the conflict of interest; I am the solution; the conflict of interest is true love." Mystical views of cherished moments spent with the man who loved captured her heart was permanently itched in her memories and suddenly came the whole picture of what needed to be done for her to live with him.

Olympia felt the fullness in her life came from the things that were not experienced. She desperately sought to know the things she never experienced and Ryan's love for her was one thing she dreadfully pursued to know the full extent of it all. Lost in a private sea of despair that pinched her out of the cranny in which she hid, she boldly ventured into more lies and deception to preserve what she desperately seeks.

"Everyone thinks that I am a dorky little old fool, I beg to differ." A wide smile tucked upon her lips as sensations engulfed her as if they were the waves of the ocean. The coincidence was one thing and this seed was too much. The realization of her thoughts slammed into her.

Calm had abandoned her in favor of grinding panic. Panic took hold forcing her to return to reality and her oath of truth. Heated passion matching every bit of the intensity that radiated from Ryan to her took over and panic vanished. Tired thoughts don't operate at maximum efficiency and they would eventually fade as if it was ancient ink. It was ancient ink, the story that she wrote on Fleischer and her murderer. Together they were polar ice caps that melted with one smile and put hell to shame.

"Was that a load question?" The reply came from a loaded question.

"Honestly" Olympia whispered silently to herself in the dark corner that inhabited her frame. "It wasn't a question; it was a statement, a mere thought that formulated into a question.

Would the appropriate people buy it? The lonely world slapped her as she assessed not being able to live with Ryan. What prize would she pay to have him touch her? She killed the question.

"Things only mean what value is placed or given to them." She stilled her thought and entered the rim of conscience. She worked the thoughts around in her brain. The love Ryan has for her and she for him helped her. He put words to her thoughts that she had difficulty expressing. He helped her gave a thought form, a structure and made them concrete.

The trauma of her life especially the affair and telling her parents who abandoned her, not so much over the affair; over the fact that she lied in the report to cover herself. Her parents being retired law enforcement themselves couldn't live with the truth, therefore they told her not to return to their home, the home she grew up in. This was twice, first her real parents putting her up for adoption and then her adopted parents.

This was the reason she worked hard in the bureau, to find her DNA parents and when she did, they told her they didn't want her to be part of their life. They had moved on to different life partners with a family of their own. She was in history. Olympia shivered in simmering anger and pain fed the face of her rage. Rejection seems to be the main course in her life.

Reality checked in as she realized that she has chosen men who would reject her. Having the pain in the relationship meant that she was suffering from being rejected by both her parents. Ryan was the first who didn't reject her. He had told her he loved her.

Olympia had look at him with confusion and frustration that was bordered on fear. He loved her. His confession didn't help the anger that was slowly building into a rage inside her. What was she supposed to say when she didn't know that strange emotion called true love? Even now, she was driven with a huge red blanket with the heat of rage.

She taunted the rage turning it towards both sets of parents with scorn that mocked her features. The fury had flushed out the truth when true love comes calling and causing every cell in her body to work as one and every bud to bloom in her heart. The anger faded into pure dismay within her.

On the heels of dismay was something that quickly approached the release of years living life and making decisions in anger. The reality of her truth tightened the knot in her stomach, more fierily than ever.

Hearing the anger in her silent voice and tasting it on her tongue gave her a visual of something nasty and made her pushed away from the thoughts of panic, hate, and death.

She had twisted towards Ryan with emotion brimming in her wide blue eyes and his gaze caught her off guard. It was filled with warmth as he came into his own with her. He filled her with love and she felt something happened between them as if he had planted his seed in her in the middle of the night, and tasted as the hundred and fifty proof rum she once had years ago in Barbados.

She was scared of his admission that she shoved it aside. Olympia ran her hands on her stomach and rested it there for a very long moment. She wanted to embrace life, be spontaneous, and liberated. She has it because it's easier to receive love than gave it; should it ever appeared and touch her heart. It did for the first time she met Ryan Reyes.

Loving a person and being in love with them are different emotions. She was happy that she found out and not died not knowing; not knowing would have been horrible.

In her final report, she stated that Asa Fleischer found out about John Miller who raped women and tried to blackmail him. He put the bullet in her forehead. She had thought it through and knowing what to say or write and to who is part of the whole; knowing when to say or write is the second part and the final is knowing how to say or write it for maximum effect. She can do this. She had done this before. She will write an additional report in the morning stating that she uncovered new evidence based on a tape from Fleischer's collection indicting Miller.

A woman can become passionate about reading profit and loss manuals especially when she compared love to true love. What is profit and loss, the pain and pleasure with love as a gained asset of pleasure with true love? Steve Jobs had come of age early, breading fiery air of the very business he would later dominate in this world. She's Steve Jobs. She can work out the emotions churning inside of her. She can take a deep breath and move on with her life. She had done it before she reminded her brain. It's time for her to program a new program with new reliable data into her hogwash brains; this came to fruition with the awesome power of love, once again.

The antidote of love and faking reports to save herself; it became her poison, intoxicated by Ryan's compliments and his love for her. It was different with the affair she realized at this moment and all her other affairs. She had chosen those men; she hadn't chosen Ryan. It just happened. She was the hungry wolf in search of the next territory, except no more running because she had found her territory.

Olympia couldn't understand the emotion on Ryan's face when he whispered one day in the middle of orgasm that he loved her. When he had expressed it; it took a while for her to wrongly identify it as shame and she never replied nor acknowledged it. Instead, she ignored it.

"We've learned much of how others treated us from how we treated ourselves. I didn't see it then, I do now." She whispered in the dark then looked to see if anyone heard her. They didn't as they were too taken in with the comedian.

A few weeks later, John Miller was arrested and charged with the murder of Asa Fleischer. He was scared and fragile, he figured that he would be safer in prison for murder than hanging around waiting for those other two whores, meaning Fiona and Sanari to come again and vandalized him. They killed that woman and somehow they are going to kill him.

Craig James Altner the serial killer case is left. That'll be swift, quick, and very soon. Olympia's breathe a sigh of relief of cleaning up a huge mess in Sussex Place, this retirement place she had come to love.

The night she had sought the girls' advice was because she had a decision to make, should she stay with Ryan or leave. She had seen traits in Ryan that she had possessed had buried due to her affair and job. He had bought them to the surface sharing them with her, pulling her out of emotional hiding.

"I'm high on knowledge and chase it until my brain backfired. I'm acting upon things I know and not the evidence that's presented to me. I can't do that, otherwise, I'll lose the only man I truly love." She whispered in the dark club as she had waited for the show to be over.

She had left the club without the girls' advice. The spectacular and mesmerizing cascade of love is beautiful in the day and spectacular in the moonlight. Decision made she drove home to write her report and ponder over her choices.

The DNA of any vehicle is the VIN number. What's the DNA for love; covering up a murder witnessed by an FBI agent? I can't match up what I think with what I feel; there are entirely two different things. She once had her personal life presented with a professional conflict of interest and was shot for it.

Here she is again with the same dilemma, a personal conflict of interest, her heart with professional conflict of interest, her lover murdering "the devil." This little misdemeanor isn't punishable by a mere slap of a fine for a thousand dollars; it's prison time.

Olympia knew she's trying to hold on to the energy that will eventually move to a different something or it can become intense with guilt. She had to let everything go because she was afraid to let it stay. She's not ready for intensity in her life yet she desperately sought it out, the intensity of true love.

She's the queen of the FBI presently. She brought to justice a Nazi war criminal, a rapist, well to the FBI a killer of a doctor and soon a serial killer. No one would question her motives only she would know the truth. Can she live with it?

45

The house with the bar was situated away from the copse of trees and from the forest that surrounded it. The old building was plain and wooden with a barren parking lot that was as rough as a dirt road.

The woods were some thirty feet away with an abundance of wild habitats and fifty feet from the swamp at Essex Place. They roamed the woods freely and hid from their predators.

The wild animals that took refuge there have two types of predators to worry about; their kind and the human species. The wild boys go hunting here for whatever is in season and sell the skin of their catch to the highest bidder for shoes and bags.

Gunshots can be heard at all times of day and night. No one bothered to keep tabs on the hunters because they usually disappeared before Law Enforcement arrived.

Today, the wind chill was below forty outside and pounded the window with its hounding, penetrating the ears of the compound and who lodged there. A breeze kicked up the chatter of the regulars, a crackled above the music as if they were the buss of a gas stove.

The cold air of winter poured from the northern ocean closing most restaurants and bars, at present flew its wind into the Twixt Peach. The fireplace lit and the last ray of the dying sun picked out the purple high lights in the blond waitress's hair that was ruffled by the cold breeze when she ventured for wood outside.

The man behind the bar was ready for a break. The waitress with the high lights, Melly came forward with a question and received "Not now," from the bartender. He had learned to use warmth and compassion with difficult characters, however, today he was far more it.

The reply was cold as a cucumber as the wind outside. He was sweating up a storm. He walked outside leaving Melly to manage the bar. He strolled along soaking up the feel of the place.

Dressed in the usual jean and matching jerkin that was opened to his waist, one hand resting on his stomach while the other hand behind his head; he stood there in the cold afternoon wind as his thoughts ran havoc all over the place. He looked relaxed and visibly comfortable, however, he was far from it.

There's something there that forced the water to flow this way, to blow the wind here. This was where his journey had bought him from the fleabag motels on the outskirt of various towns. He had seemed to live on the edge of the world certainly on the edge of any reality; he had ever really known. The past was over as a Navy Seal as he looked back bleakly into his past. Only fate can come up with such a self-serving twist on such a hideous cliché of his life.

Olympia had not been here in a month. Christmas came and gone with him becoming drunk on the newest day of the year, all alone. Dismay spread through him as the meaning sunk in. He had nurtured a seed in her the last time they spend together.

Ryan didn't pause to investigate the real cause of his dismay over the weeks, however, today it hit him hard. He had been selfish in planting his seed in her and only cared about the notorious gambler he was in suggesting himself a husband for Olympia and a father for their innocent charge.

Sailing in an arc in a cold breeze toward him was a leaf from the forest floor. Ryan Reyes stood tall on the stairs to his apartment. He paused for a long few minutes with his head tilted to catch any sounds that were brought in by the wind. He knew how to keep his attention on what was near as well as in the distance.

It's a wonder the trouble he has gotten himself into when he let his fears and hormones do his thinking. The fear of Asa coming at him that warm night was hell. She had followed him into the wooded area. He was in the process of taking his t-shirt off when she faced him off with a proposition.

"Wanna fuck?"

"Yes."

"Me, too. I want it hard and good, a good hard fuck."

"I can do that." His thoughts caught on the erotica thinking full of what he can do with her. He'll see where she's going with this before he stopped her. Making her lose her emotional balance might help him keep his intact. He found out as she slowly moved in for the kill and he realized that her "hard" to his was on different levels. He sensed trouble, danger.

Ryan was standing shirtless about thirty feet in front of her. He was waiting for her to undress when misunderstanding charge as weapons stepped into his vision.

Asa shock the living daylights of him when she said, "Go on hit me. That's what men do when they can't solve their problems any other way. You got my permission to hit me hard, real hard." She slowly maneuvered toward him. She had picked up a pick of wood and was going at him, gun in one hand and wood in the other. "I want you to hit me with this. I want to feel the pain and pleasure at the same time." She pointed the gun at him. "Do it." She ordered him. "Do it now.

I dare you."

"No, I wouldn't do that. I'm not into S & M." He proudly told her, too proudly because Asa heard rejection and didn't like it.

"Oh, come now, be a man, a real man, and hit me." She begged and challenged him at the same time.

"What about that you don't get?" He spoke out of anger and not out of love. Pain and pleasure mixture, he's not into as the tension exploded into anger between them. The surge of emotion fuel his limps when some unnamed emotion constricted his heart. He knew what fear looked like, what it smells like, and how it sound, even tasted, nevertheless what's happening here between them is the opposite; more of attack and defend.

He watched every word he whispered and kept his boiling anger tamped down; she cannot feed on it as if she's a vampire. She's a fucking vampire; she's out for blood in a different way. Ryan's cold eyes hinted at the rage bubbling just under the surface, it turned dark blue.

Asa had begun advancing towards him with the wood in hand

daring him to take her up on her offer. In his haste of understanding what she was saying saw the wood flying in the air coming towards him; he moved in panic or was it his training to defend.

Ryan pulled his gun that was stuck behind in his jeans in the middle of his lower back and fired the bullet into her forehead. He had fired the single shot that killed Asa Fleischer!

He took his clothes off and lifted her and drew her into the stream, removing all evidence that would implicate him. He walked to his apartment naked in the middle of the night. He knew he wouldn't be seen because today was Tuesday and the Twixt Peach was closed. He prayed for rain.

On the twisted side of his other predicament, his hormones were working overtime, screwing with his decision of planting his seed in Olympia when they were making progress in the relationships. He never fell so much love for women and fear of losing her at the same time.

The epithet of every soldiers' life that seen war; a whole lot of hell with a little bit of trouble. He put his emotion on ice relaxing for a second, the moment he chose to do this with the last woman he fucked a long time ago, long before he bought his place. He had given up on love and family, the very thing he desperately wanted in his life.

Ryan wanted Olympia with no emotional attachment. Personal feelings didn't figure into the equation of his life. He climaxed inside of her many times, always using a condom even although she told him that she was active on birth control. He had told her that condom was ninety-eight percent effective. He was more careful than ever. He realized that he wanted more of her the day they came together as one. It happened on the third night she came over always at midnight. He felt something inside him rattled his feelings and couldn't understand the emotion.

The tresses of Olympia's new look, that of a lady, an FBI that wore lace under her stiff jeans. He wanted desperately to just teach and impress her of what a good lover he knew he was, regardless of what the last woman yelled to him before she took off with a younger man. He tried to impress her with his ersatz formula, one skilled and failed at some level before he realized that he was impressed with hers; she matched him perfectly.

The irony of it all was with his proving and her needing, she was the one who taught him that there's more to sex each time they made love. His fucking had turned into making love unknowingly to him.

The simplest gratification of his senses with hers was no longer quenching of sexual thirst; it had turned into an exercise of two caring people that experienced something unique when they came together as one.

This was a spiritual thing that fed his hunger and made him desperate for more from her, he planted his seed in her. He had told her that she doesn't need birth control because he would always wear a condom; he lied. He had never experienced this kind of release of love with anyone. He found it in her arms!

Ryan had decided what the conflict was and operating from desperation to keep her here, he made love to her when she was deep in sleep. She responded with vapor, not realizing that he didn't use a condom. This was his solution; his selection was made and the quest began. He knew she was pregnant because her cycle shifted.

What he didn't know was why she no longer visited him. He was too scared to go to her. He knew she knew of the pregnancy. She had to; he'll have to wait it out until she made her choice either to arrest him or let him go.

Quantum probabilities argued against a fixed future; it argued for something even more complicated with a future that contained all probabilities of the two of them in which they had to steer their course of the relationship or she had to make a decision. He had to do everything; he knew how to bring about a particular outcome that would keep him to her. He went ahead and fixed one for them without asking her. He made her pregnant.

One minute he was cursing through life doing great then with no warning he had to go and fall in love. Someone had gotten to him and took up residency in his brain. Walking on the path of love, he had covered much distance of what he wanted more so when this digital self-collided with his true self, he realized that he wanted to get married and settled with Olympia as a family.

He had once a long time ago envisioned or rather had a vision with him and a female looking as beautiful as Olympia. He had lain that thought to rest and sucked the vortex of his premonition and bought it to life.

Reality painted him a nasty picture based on truth and he had to face the outcome of the relationship after he confessed to her. Olympia stirred his emotions into an unpleasant mess and she doesn't love him as he loved her. He knew this because she never once told him that she loved him. His heart had an illusion that she had loved him. Perhaps without this exorcism, the relationship will never be all that he wanted; he knew that was not the truth because he had drunk in her trust the day they met.

Only after meeting several pockets of resistance did he gave in to his feelings for her and admitted that it was more than lust. She too needed to adjust to the spreading pleasure of him stretching her night after night. He never made love to someone many times in the night's solace. He realized that they never made love in the day, a few times in the early hours of the morning when Olympia overslept. She usually is gone well before four in the morning.

Ryan smiled at her teasing, "I'm not sure about the kisses or the touching. Can I run it past you one more time? I can make you mine, on my conclusion or detection of whether I like to be touched and kissed?" She had made love to him and he loved it.

It was a tumultuous release of their body as one floated free and weightless on the land of exotic liberation. Olympia's touching and kissing had promised relief in a fashion that he had learned to trust and love. His gaze had collided with hers for an intensifying moment. He held it there for as long as he can, however, and not as long as he wanted to because her cell rang.

This is exactly what he didn't bargain for because as soon as he looked at her he gave in; he looked at her anyway. He didn't want to risk breaking the fragile spell his thoughts had walked, had woven with keeping her to him forever.

The stoic moment passed and her cycle changed. He had noticed and wondered whether she did too. He came to life since he met her with a different perspective. New thinness was with him. This was overwhelmed by the fury burning in him. The impact burned along the same path of longing for Olympia.

Fiery sensations burned through his cold skin, burning into him for the very first time since he quit hiding and hoping that she would come to him. He had faced the truth since they met; they were completely one.

Jealousy crept into his feelings and he let out a deep long breath. He wanted her to think of him as a warm-hearted lover not as a cold-blooded scum bag. Jealousy wasn't a feeling he was used to especially of her job. He swallowed a dose of it as he retreated into his broken heart. What has he done to warrant this jealousy? He asked himself in disgust.

The best times were the times spend with her, talking about what they wanted to do, skydiving, sailing, and hiking were three things that came out of the revelation. They had mentioned they wanted to do not together just wanted to do. He had hoped they would do it together. Every day was a brand-new day to be delighted with each other. When their eyes met he was zapped by true love, something he never felt before until he met Olympia.

"Your love, Olympia is the breath in my heart." He sadly whispered to the darkness of the cold wind. He climbed the stairs and decided he was going to put that in a note and send it to his lover.

As he entered his domain and sniffed her scent several avalanches of thought sailed through him. He had misunderstood when they parted, of the pregnancy not realizing that she could've aborted the baby. He didn't ask her, therefore she doesn't have to ask him. Maybe she didn't know and she knew of his other secret; he killed Asa.

On the note of this revelation, he felt shattered in every cell in his body.

46

Olympia drove and left the county behind her leaving the sunset sky that was milking the color of shell pink on a cold winter day in Florida, creating an avalanche of distraction. Blackbirds were spotted flying over her head and she silently told them to go away and that she was not dead yet.

In her review mirror, she pondered for a split second wondering if the Gods would magnanimity bestowed gifts upon her. She needed two about this minute; one that Ryan doesn't reject her when she goes to see him and the report stick for closing the case on Asa Fleischer. The arrest was made of Miller and the trial was in full force. She doesn't need any of the past coming and haunting her in the future.

If the weather knew what stress had done to her she'll be in sync with life. The endless web of existence she was surviving in came into full view and she realized that she wanted to live life without the fear of loving someone. Her internal alert rose to the next echelon giving her wobbly knees. Her breath caught somewhere between her lungs and her throat, her heartbeats quickened. She pushed on the pedal and pick up speed.

Let the police try giving her a ticket. Who in their crazy mind would want to give a very angry confused FBI special agent a ticket? She drove faster before her asteroids of emotions kicked in again; in this off-the-killer moment when nothing worked for her. Self-pity is in sync as she sympathized with the old Olympia who had set herself up to fail at love. Neptune seemed to dip its toes in the Cancerian ocean and thrust her to seek refuge in her own company as Olympia pulled on her deep reservoir of strength.

She needed time to sought thoughts through, regardless that

she had made a decision last night at the comedy club. She didn't talk to Fiona and Sanari; she walked out before the show was over. She was too vulnerable to talk to anyone besides the least people knew they better for her plan to work.

Instead, she lay in bed awaiting a surge of energy to propel her out. It took its time; she sobbed all the way through her four cups of coffee and a very hot shower. Whatever baggage of emotions she had been holding on to broke free from its cell and the veil of darkness was gone.

The dark storm clouds that were on the horizon are no more. A new chance of life and love shone through from the day she had sought temporary respite from the summer heat hiding out with a cold heart, dusk at Sussex Place had cool her thoughts and jolted her into reality.

This is an American standoff as she put her personal and professional life in perspective. She had done that with her last affair because she didn't have time to think things through. There were two others at the scene of the crime, always. Those were devastating intensity or more insanity to come up with a plan in a few minutes.

The clandestine approach of her character has taken a toll on her mental capability. Each time she came to the surface for air the sheer force of life just engulfed her again. She always wondered whether her lonely heart ever bloomed into a garden of love. It did and now suspense and romance collided, where mystery and uncertainty intertwined and smash together with romance.

Love has a prenuptial twist to it; true love doesn't, it's built on trust. Passion should be at its zenith, wild and non-consuming, not primitive and pre-historical.

"My point exactly," Olympia spoke out loud above the roar of other cars trying to pass her. She was comparing her past lovers with Ryan. She didn't want to think of those men in the same thought as Ryan. Ryan stood above them all because he loved her. They didn't and never would because they were like her, hunting for love.

Yes, she can live with the rigging of the story covering Ryan for murdering Asa. From the evidence, she gathered Asa Fleischer was a whole lot of trouble and a little bit of hell rolled into one big anorexia alcoholic blunder. Everyone was her entertainment.

Ryan had moved smoothly to her motion and he had swum in her ocean of love. Isn't an improvement from love to true love on the automatic apology route? She was applying psychology with men as her target practice.

Ryan was far too close for her peace and he was her beacon in the night, in the darkest of hours. A current of sensations knocked her senses into submission to the slight mention of his name. Thinking of the mystique of Ryan Reyes sent a wave of ecstasy through her.

"I like the spirited creature you are Olympia, the wildcat in you is an awesome quality."

"I like the creature with lots of talents, the more he has the more you know he will be creative in all aspects of life particularly in making love to me." She had replied to his vacuous phase of calling her a wild cat.

Two days after they met she wanted to ask him some questions and had to admit there was something there about him. She was in a panic attack as she lifted her cell phone to call him. She closed it trying to understand the sensations that poured out from her and at the same time controlling them. She had space for an unknown length of time before giving up.

Why was it difficult to make a simple business phone call? She had picked the cell phone up and closed it a dozen times; because the receiver of the call is someone she has a sexual awareness for and he doesn't know about her feelings for him, She does know his feelings for her. She's mentally, verbally, emotionally, and physically aware of him. Every time she thought of him or see his smile she became sexually aware of every core, every fiber of her body.

She was lost for words and was surprised when he warned Fiona that they were followed. She saw him wrote the note. She had hoped that he wasn't aware of the excitement in her voice. She couldn't think; she Olympia with controlled emotions cannot think and tremble with vapor thoughts.

Panic turned into anxiety and her muscles in her abdomen contracted with a spasm of tightness. She bent over holding her stomach because she found it difficult to breathe.

It took a few minutes for her stomach to calm down after counseling herself that it was only a "business call." She opened the cell phone and punched in his number and couldn't do it. She stared at the "on" button for a while before closing the phone. Instead, she drove to the Twixt Peach and sat away from view. She would leave with the same fantasy of him....of them each day.

The broad classically mounded lips swooped onto her pink ones as soon as the business conversation came to an end. His spontaneity told her he too felt the tension that surged each time they are together. Lips opened in sensual welcome as his hands found her waist pulling her closer to him for a long sensuous kiss. She shivered again her pulses raced as her body responded to the feeling of those hard hands holding her against him.

Olympia would leave it there because anymore thinking would drive her crazy with desires. She was known to leave her investigation and drove home to release the sexual tension with her sex toys. It was the only way she knew how to control the urges for Ryan besides seducing him.

Fantasy had blocked her ability to speak and work. It had moved slowly into her life and gave her no clarity. She didn't even need the sound effect because the intensity and sensations that arose every time she saw him were estrus. She was in heat to mate.

Sexual desires soon overrode all logic. She gave in and began eating there every day and in the middle of the night, she would make love with him till four in the morning and return to her place. Ryan told her that he understood secretly and her work. It would complicate her life and she would be removed from all of the cases. She drove for an eon and in the awe of thoughts, she pulled over into a hotel for the night.

She doesn't know where she is nor does she care. The place looked safe enough besides she was hungry. She bought some food from the restaurant, checked in, and stayed in her room. She took all of her clothes off and put the robe on.

Memories prelude into her space and since she was on lockdown for the night she permitted them to surface. The more the suppression of her life flowed the faster her emotions will be stabilized and she can return to Ryan. Surprising they were of her and Ryan only. The conversation they had left a warm imprint of true love in her heart. They easily flowed endlessly.

The third time she came in looking for Fiona and Asa, Ryan was sitting on the stool in front and not behind the bar. He was drinking black coffee and watching an old rerun basketball game when she joined him. She didn't know what to expect only that neither of the girls was there. She kept her eyes on the bronzed firmness of his muscular body. His fair fell forward as he looked at her and her breathing was suspended, for a second.

The power of Ryan's arousing hands lifted the last of the liquid in the glass to his sensuous lips making hers parted ready to be sampled.

The scotch straight up had landed in Ryan's stomach, piping down his throat, stirring fear in with love before it took up a quarry in him. Black coffee kept his thoughts together.

He laughed softly and she could see anxiety sweating through him "on the contrary ......I don't think any man has even begun to tap what's inside of you, Olympia. I don't know how to relate to you, Olympia. It's as if you've thrown out the rule book on communication." He said looking at her breathlessly.

"I didn't realize that there was a rule book." She smiled understandingly giving him the answer he sought in her. His cool blue-eyed had turned to a soft light blue and her grin became wider as pink color lit her cheeks into splendor warmth.

"Can you relate to me as a person and forget the gender thing? You know that there's nothing that's written down permanently. There's a bunch of culturally defined rules based on how men and women are supposed to relate; sssh it doesn't work, you make your own and I'll see if I like them."

"No, I don't want to forget your gender. Can you make the rules with me?" Those words did it and she looked at him in wonderment, the shock she had walked out returning of course the next day at the same time.

Ryan saw right through her. She sensed her awareness of him; he was standing close, close enough for her to smell his mild aftershave. She felt her muscles tense in her stomach as she breathed the fragrant of his sexuality. She was aware alright more than she ever bargained for, this was new and exciting!

The third day after they had made love for the first time, she was having her usual meal sitting reading a report of people who were interviewed in Fleischer's murder when he pulled the chair out and set his body upon it. A teasing glint appeared in his soft blue eyes when she looked up puzzled. It took a moment to change space and be with him.

"You know I don't remember much of what happened." He told her in a low sexy whisper.

"Alzheimer's seemed to step in early for you, huh or is it dementia?" She smiled back at him with the same measure of intensity. She knew he was waiting for an answer of whether she would be there tonight. She relieved the tension with a reply of "I'll see what I can do later?" He had grinned wider and pulled his body out of the chair, pushed it under the table, and walked away.

Her eyes had followed him until she realized that everyone in the bar was watching her watching the bar owner walking. The dialogue of memories continued and tears flowed freely. She finished the beer and went for another remembering another time.

"Why are you so argumentive? I bet you'll even argue with God?" Ryan was getting impatient with her when the topic of vacationing together surfaced and she gave him reasons that it was not wise.

"Is there a God? How much are you betting?" Olympia asked him, eating yogurt with peaches.

"There's a God therefore you lose?" He replied secretly smiling as he fixed them a midnight snack of peanut butter and cocoa with rum.

"Is that your way out of losing?"

"You started it. This is silly. Why do I ever bother to ask for more from you?" He signed vexingly.

Why does he want to take her on vacation? He had stood there looking at her and she was looking at him. Time has no space only a current of sensations that drifted between them adding another layer of intensity to their feelings for each other.

Ryan had told her not to measure the chances of their happiness against her mistakes that their relationships meant to trust each other unconditionally.

"I want a relationship with you based on freedom, freedom to choose, and live life. I want to share that with you." He had her that the day he whispered, "I love you." She had lost the number of times he had given her mental pleasure and forgotten how many pulsating waves of freedom he released upon and from her body.

"Tomorrow Ryan, you'll tell me what you're determined not to say." Olympia fell asleep counting the times and woke up determined to go through with confronting him. She curled up in the wide center of the bed and slept on the thought.

#

Meeting with Ryan wasn't easy. It was the hardest thing she had ever done in her life. It was Tuesday and the Twixt Peach was close for the day. She had climbed the stairs earlier and left feeling a panic attack surfing. She walked to her car, sat for a few minutes, and return. She knew he was up in his apartment as she climbed the stairs two at a time.

She knocked twice giving him notice that she's about to enter; after all, he has a gun, therefore surprising him by opening the door when he wasn't expecting her was not a wise idea. The door was locked and she waited for him to open it. It was chilly and the wind was blowing high. She pulled her key out and opened the door. She stepped in and closed the door behind her. She didn't have to look for him he was standing in the path towards the door.

Ryan stared at her in shock. Olympia kept her eyes on the bronzed firmness of his muscular body that hugged the sweatshirt he wore. They could both fringe the gap that stretched between them. No one moved. Alien urges touched the faint flush on his cheekbones. She wanted to move closer, to eat away at the space that separated them and took away the air they needed to breathe.

She smiled, however, her thoughts were disguised and he couldn't read them. His gaze narrowed and his shoulders stiffened. She quivered at his nearness and turned compulsively to look at him. Eyes met and held, blue eyes gazed into blue eyes locking them into each other for a long time.

He had irritated her with his confession of love and that irritation past the point of rational thought. At this moment, in reality, she was searching for someone to share this outrageous irritation of true love. True love had been her enemy; her irritation and how she looked at Ryan and the thought sparked a reflection of her search.

The fear of losing him pushed all thoughts of calm aside and shot to the forefront. Something very strong stood between them; it was tangible. She could reach out with fingertips and touch it.

Ryan was dying to reach over and draw her into his arms, however, he retreated into thoughts and wait, giving her all the time to make the first move. A cold glint came into his eyes of his acknowledging his fears.

Fear kept him quiet. His stomach sinking into his ribs as his thoughts spun into a vortex of uncanny emotions. He wanted to grip the arm of the chair for balance; there was none at least not where he was standing. Mocking glint met icily glittering glaze and she remained stoic. His muscle flexed in his jaw and the fell of suppression lifted the air between them.

Ryan wanted to slam her up against reality instead he gave a weary sigh and kept quiet. He was afraid that anything he voiced would be incorrect; he remained quiet, waiting.

Olympia sensed her awareness of him; he was standing close, close enough for her to smell his mild aftershave. She felt her muscles tense in her stomach as she breathed the fragrant of his sexuality. She was aware alright more than she ever bargained for, this was new and exciting. She took a deep breath and freed him from his thoughts.

She can't explain how it happened and what emotions had been in operation, nonetheless, she drew the assumption that it was the emotion of true love. Her voice was pregnant with feelings and she held his eyes.

"Can we start over? I needed time to think. I need a lot of time to think. I was carrying around a lot of baggage and I had thought I had it all under control until you said you loved me. I fell apart because I love you too and didn't know how to express it. I had to work through the baggage and I'm in the right lane heading in the same direction as you. I still have to work and I don't know how that part of me will fit into you."

"Uh? Oh." It came out in a jury icy tone. Sharpness had entered covering the fear he felt in his heart. Ryan mentally unfolded himself.

Anything else he wanted to say was lost under the weight of what he was feeling for her.

The emotions he always believed himself capable of keeping under control were getting away from him. He didn't know what to do with them except let them out and face the consequence later. "You are starting to sound like a travel brochure." He let out instead of saying how he truly felt. Tiny ribbons of heat uncurling low in her had pulled the truth out.

"I am pregnant." She said watching him.

"How did you know?" A quake of pure love vibrated through him.

"Top secret. Can't tell you my source."

"A satellite? If you can't explain it, it's simply you don't understand it well enough."

"I went to the doctor."

"It wasn't on the agenda." "I know. It's now." Olympia wasn't going to give up until he kicked her out. Ryan wanted to prolong this insanity of this spacious talking, he found a safe spot over her shoulder and laid his eyes there. He was raging with a compulsion to take her this instant. He knew he shouldn't touch her because if he did he would make kissing couples looked innocent by comparison. He wanted to kiss her until they melted into each other as one. He concealed his passion for the moment.

Neither of them seemed to be aware of the moment when passion replaced desires when fear was released and true love took hold. Ryan was ready to receive her love. Olympia was ready to accept his without a doubt. Much power lies within so much yet it took a devastating turn of events to show them a light that can give them lasting fulfillment and enjoyment.

"My dad's gene is a newly acquired one. It would take you years to properly bring it home." His voice surprisingly was soft.

"You're making fun of me?" Hers was still pregnant with deep emotions.

"No, I'm not family material." A rusty-sounding chuckle came out from him.

"Neither am I, Ryan." She ran and stood in front of him, her eyes never leaving his warm ones. Her surprise matched his startling gasped as her hands covered his to comfort him; instead, she received comfort from his warmth that emitted from him.

A roar of laugher from Ryan shimmied up and down her spine when he realized that she was still carrying his seed. It made him felt warmer than any hot summer day warranted. He wanted to embroider "I am going to be a daddy" on his t-shirt.

A little amazed by his suggestion she held his warm gaze and felt herself melting all over again. The love in his eyes she felt it in her heart as it picked up a musical beat in response. Laughter filled the air with the asking for forgiveness. His lips explored her satin fleur scented skin.

"Can I test drive your hot rod?" She boldly asked him after they surfaced for air. "Do you mind sharing that experience with me again?" Worry inched up her spine and gave him a wobbly smile. There was nothing left for him to do; he gathered her, pulling her into the comfort of his embrace. She slid both of her hands through his hair and felt the fine texture between her fingers. This kiss was a deep passionate one that left both trembling with the feeling of true love.

Squealed with crazy urges and sung in rusty-hinge with voices of jaded rock it was the blueprint for a sweet tender seduction. Ryan's tongue pushed and dove into her mouth as his maleness throbbed hard against her pelvis. His torso was lean with muscles as an athlete's.

Ryan pushed her gently away and lowered his eyes to the rounded swell of her breasts going up and down as they surged for breath. Olympia's senses heightened and reached out automatically to his nearness as a lover would in a moment of mating. A throbbing ache in the pit of her stomach kept reminding her with quickened heartbeats and tingling down her spine how much she loved him.

"I love you with all of my heart, Ryan Reyes."

Ryan sucked his breath in as her palms slid over his rigid nipples under his sweater. The tip of her fingers explored the muscular strength of his body as her arms arrived around his neck pulling him closer to her. The touch of her hands moving into his hair sent delightfulness inside of her; her emotions in sweet knots of love. He took her silky strands of hair and clung to her touch as her nails travel to the back of his neck tunneling possessively. She arched her body against him and felt his maleness. He was lost.

Ryan couldn't remember how they became undress except for the ball of his thumb moved softly against her bare shoulder sending shivers up and down his spine as he kissed his way to her nipples then to her lips again.

Olympia turned startled blue eyes on him and his eyes met hers enmeshing her in an intensifying moment of electrifying passion. She dragged her gaze downwards to settle on the masculine curve of his lips and a momentary shiver ran through her as she saw how aroused he was from kissing her. He must have felt her involuntary movement because he smiled in an amused satisfied moment of pure bliss.

"Kill it, Ryland, kill it," Sanari said to Ryland who swam smoothly and expertly to the side and swung his muscular length out of the water upon hearing her cry for help. He was wearing brief navy shorts which cling wetly to his body and left no doubt as to his gender. He stood looking at the snake.

"Kill it, Ryland. Take your gun and shoot it." Sanari was upon the top of the pool table under the umbrella pointing to the object of her fear. The black garden snake no larger than one foot and more afraid of Sanari scooted away with rapid speed.

"What happened to justice?" He asked her upon seeing what she wanted him to shoot.

"It doesn't count for snakes. They're not my friends." Ryland was looking at her loving standing on top of the table.

"Ah, Hell thereeeeee's one behind you!" Sanari pointed down behind his feet. Ryland turned and saw a larger snake maybe the mother or father of the one that ran away in fear of all the noise Sanari was making.

Ryland picked it up and took it over to the grass area where the other one ran to and let it go. He turned and smile at his lady love. Her mouth was opened with her hand in the middle of her bosom, her chakra heart. He loved it.

"Maybe you should get a new friend. This is what you attract to or what is attracted to you." He picked up the conversation where he left it off as if the last few minutes didn't take place. He grinned at her, covering the few short feet between them.

"Do you have any outcasts in your group? You know more of them looking like you." She grinned back at him as he lifted her off the table. Coming aware of his autonomy, he blushed and pulled her into his arms. He kissed her with his wet lips and saw her ran her tongue over her lips; his grin became wider and she thought that it was part of his charm.

"You are losing points you've gained." Sanari not giving in to him for not shooting the snake and ignoring his distracting her with a kiss kept a serious face and upper hand.

"I have points?" Ryland raised an eyebrow. "What points would that be?" He was surprised and very amused, he played along. He loved it when they are in this type of relaxed atmosphere, neither serious. It was good for him to be back to work and out in the open with her.

Olympia Van Amstel came through for him and personally gave him the good news that they caught his partner Donna Baker who was supposed to be dead leaving the country with millions of dollars in an offshore account. She had told Randy about Cooper and he had passed it on to their boss Sam Laketon, who had a plan of action to indict her of the operation.

Ryland had to stay hidden and believe to be dead; she wouldn't be threatened and have to eliminate him. She would eventually feel safe to emerge as the double agent has gone rogue. It was easy with Ryland out of the picture and the only witness dead, Diego's cousin, Jesus.

Donna Baker goes as Delia Fisher was under surveillance as well as Robert Jones. They were lovers and the minute Baker tried to move the balance of money into Canada, she was arrested.

The whole operation started legitimately with Donna and Ryland undercover as a couple until they stumbled on the hideaway for drug money in an old warehouse hidden off the track in an old abandon farmhouse. The farmer was paid off by the drug dealers; he has moved to the Florida Keys with his family. He still owned the land, however, he no longer used the farm.

Donna Baker faked her death in what was a freak accident when she blew up in the car. What Ryland thought he saw was his partner was a dead person from the morgue looking like his partner. Baker was watching her lover Robert Jones, another agent blew the car to bits. By the time he ran to a phone to call their boss Corner Lopez she was gone including the fake crime scene.

Ryland's cell phone was deliberately removed from his belongings at the apartment he and Donna used as undercover and with no phone, he couldn't call in the incident. The payphone was two blocks down the street from where he was and made the call. He was running back to the street when someone opened fire and he had to take cover firing back.

This took a good half an hour and it was another hour before he lifted his structure from hiding and run to the scene of the crime.

As usual, it was in the middle of the night and there was no witness. Not one eyewitness came forward and when he sneaked into the apartment he found a text message "Run for your life or you will be next." Ryland packed his few belongings and ran to the dealer Diego who he had met on a different drug deal. He showed up at the meeting ground in the woods when he was shot and Jesus was killed.

The bureau all knew Donna and Ryland were partners, therefore when Donna saw Ryland she shot at him, missed the first time, killed Jesus, and send the second bullet through him as he ran away from her. He wasn't about to be ambushed; he ran to his sweet angel Sanari, thinking it was his seal's buddy Morgan Fields' father's place. He had visited there one time of course in the middle of the night some fifteen years ago on his way to a Seal assignment with Morgan.

"The ones I give you when you believed me and back me out two days ago from the guy who wanted to date me."

"Oh, I didn't know that we are going on a point system." Thinking more about the poor guy who had spontaneously cornered her at the car wash and detail shop, his grin became laughter. He had left her to go and collect the car while he paid the bill. He returned to see Sanari pinned against the brick wall and the guy harmlessly trying to talk her into having dinner with him.

Another thought bloated up from somewhere and he smiled in surprise. "Oh, I got points in agreeing with you? How much do I have, my sweet love? What can I get with the points?"

"Ah, huh?" She looked at him in surprise and shock at the same time trying to calculate the points. "All right, that's it. You lost the bloody points. You are back to zero?"

"Just like that? How's that?" He leaned into her and kissed her on her neck. She was wearing a strapless blue top with a string that ties both sides to her bikini bottom. Not much left to be exposed. The weather was cool and her nipples stood erect giving him ideas about what he wanted to do with her.

"For calling me sweet love and thinking that you can score with me sexually?"

"Since when can you read my thoughts? That's not fair?" He grinned with a soft laugh and kissed her again on the very spot. He knew from experience that it was a total turn-on for her. He felt her begin to tremble and knew it was him and not the weather.

"Oh, please spare me the details." She pulled on his neck with both hands for a long teasing kiss knowing it told him maybe he might be lucky and maybe not or maybe he had to do better than what he is doing this moment in time. He can't what be teased with a kiss and left guessing. He leaned into her for another kiss and receiving none he smacked her backside and grinned.

She had turned away from him as he was about to kiss her again. She let out an "ouch" and grinned back at him. He doesn't need any more encouragement, he went after her. She saw him move toward her and her brain kicked in fight or flight. She chose to fly and ran further away from him and dive into the pool when she saw him give in to her chase.

Ryland went after her. He caught her as she tried to climb out of the pool and he pulled her to him kissing her breathless. His love reached her and she felt it and sensed the sharing and releasing of his passionate feelings for her. His love for her had finally reached her and she received it.

It was midnight. The moon was full and smiled down upon the lovers.

On the other side of the pool in the far in, Fiona and Blake had just finished sharing a loving kiss. The water kept them warm and the cool air kept them close.

"Hey honey, there's a party down by the clubhouse. You're

invited." She whispered to him in a lazy voice.

"Are you asking me out on a date?" The surprise was the sound of his words. His hand went to his heart indicating how touched he was upon her asking him out.

"Huh? Date? Whatever turns you on?" She said with a twinkle that amazed Blake as much as it confounded him

"Turns me on, is this what this is? What turn me on? Is you, all of you." He closed the few inches between them, leaned in, and kissed her passionately. The second she responded he gently pulled her into him and cupped her face, deepening the kiss. Through the fabric of his short swimwear, his shaft swelled against her, working the exact spot that made her knees collapse and her breath shuddered from her chest in sharp bursts of ecstasy.

He kissed her nose. It's a good thing he's not the jealous type as they sank to the bottom of the pool. Blake pulled Fiona to the top of the pool for air. He shrugged at the thought because she's his weakness. They had flown into Washington to meet his family and when his brother, Devon saw him kissing her he said,

"Branding her?" he had smiled and kissed her passionately again.

"No, I am the one that's branded for life." He had told his brother.

"You better believe it, Devon. I have to. All the girls are after him." Fiona had replied with a flushed cheek at being caught in her lover's embrace. She had leaned in and kissed him on his chest.

Blake had often during their courtship flashed forward to see life with her yet-to-be experience which would determine their future. He liked what he saw and knew that having a great relationship with himself is having a happy connection with his lover and others.

They had discussed marriage and both being divorce agreed that marriage is an endangered institution. He was grateful to her for finding the keys to his imagination and her love was the philosopher's stone that made it possible for transmitting alchemy in his life.

Fiona was his hope fulfilled and exploring life with her was venturing into a new world in which he had sublet some space; where he hoped one day to live presently, however, in the meantime he has a blast in his old age.

In the wooded area, one mile from the retirement community laid Olympia in bed. It has been a tiring day tracking Altner. The court order is in place, however, she doesn't think it's wise to venture into his home and evade his space as yet because her instinct told her that there's more to this than what's visible. She felt or rather her instinct told her there was something fishy about him inheriting the apartment from his uncle.

She felt something that pushed away from her thoughts of doubt and smelled panic and death. She had his history investigated and when Randy forwarded the information she was over the moon with excitement. The information warmed the coldest winter.

She concealed the information from everyone for their protection except Ryland Cooper and Sergeant Blake Belington who are assisting her in surveillance. Trust the instinct her adopted parents always instilled in her; today, she thanked them.

Craig James Altner aka the White Water Killer is his namesake with the same ammo as a serial killer. A couple and two other females are missing for six months. Photographs indicated that Altner is the one dumping the black trash bags in the lake by Devil's creek.

Olympia had enough for one day and one of the rookies from Sergeant Belington's unit is observing him. She had to leave most of the fieldwork to Ryland Cooper and Blake Belington because she was exhausted from the cases. The doctor advised bed rest, plenty of it.

They demanded sleep, she and her twelve-week-old fetus, their twelve-week-old daughter. She wanted a daughter and felt that she was having one, however, there's no evidence that they are having one. They have a doctor's appointment tomorrow. She closed her eyes knowing that Ryan is downstairs working. They had talked about the baby and finishing her cases. They had agreed to share both places until the baby is born.

Ryan is painting the spare room and helping her shop for their coming baby. He also helped her with planning to catch Altner. She never mentioned that she knew he killed Asa Fleischer nor does she want to know why. Knowing who the man he's her instinct told her that he did it for a good reason probably self-defense. Ryan doesn't need to know that she had investigated him or asked questions about this family and life.

"That's your idea of idle chit-chat, asking me about my family history this early in the morning?" He had shot her a sardonic look over his coffee cup, towel in hand heading into the shower. He had moved all the furniture out from the guest room prepping it for painting.

"Well, I want to know what kind of a life you had and why you're beyond handsome and incredibly loving." The teasing note was unexpected yet warm, particularly after the long chill of being away from him. She melted despite herself, nonetheless worry automatically crawled up her spine just in case he was on edge about not having a loving childhood.

"You want me to buy into that?" He asked seriously, too seriously. "And why are you supposed to know."

"Buy, no just wanted to know your family, I have something to tell our daughter." She looked at him square in the eye with her usual wobbly smile.

He understood and told her that he had a sister and two brothers who are all married with a family of their own. His parents are retired in the Keys and he usually goes and visited them about twice a year. He took out an album his mother had put together when he was shipped off to war in Afghanistan and Iraq.

"See that?" Pointing to his young nephew, Jarred, who he held in his arms, and his kid brother, Jarred, the father standing next to him with a Christmas tree in the background.

"Yes." She had replied sarcastically. "I got this thing called vision." Ignoring her sarcasm, he continued, "He would make an excellent Seal."

"Oh Ryan, are you disappointed that we are having a daughter?" Ryan smiled "No." He had long trusted her, therefore arguing with her would be fruitless. He had argued with her that she would be disappointed when the sonogram showed a boy. She was angry with him for not believing and trusting her assumption. As far as he's concerned the jury is still out on the gender of their baby.

"I am allowing myself to be drawn into one of your pointless arguments that you love to thrive on." He heard the anger in her voice and it didn't help to show he was slowly building into a rage inside of him due to her misunderstanding of his intention.

Ryan, however, backed off because he loved her and didn't want to lose her again plus he's still a bit sensitive about her ever finding out about Fleischer. The knot in his stomach tightened as he briefly remembered his agony for that one month he didn't see her.

Olympia had misunderstood his intention of saving her from being disappointed concerning the gender of the fetus, however, as the days drifted by, he learned to trust her because he found out, like him, she thrived from her instinct. He cannot or would not argue with that again. He also learned to take the word fault out of the equation in all conversations a long time ago in his previous relationships.

He was loyal to the women, however, they don't merit his loyalty because they had cheated and blamed him for being in the Navy. They knew that getting into a relationship with him plus his lack of expressing his emotions with them. Emotions, what does that have to do with anything?

Ryan had crept into the room to check to see if she was hungry and smiled with joy as he watched her sleep. He had done this numerous times, sitting in a chair watching her sleep. Things had worked out and he would never sacrifice any of it for anything. He leaned in and kissed her on her mouth.

"I love you, Olympia, and our daughter, too."

49

My eyes are closed and I am thinking of you
My heart is beating because it is calling out to you
I am taking these breaths because I want to be close to you
My heart is nothing without you, a blank sheet of paper
It demands your name so I wrote it
My heart is the blank mirror that I am looking at
It reflexes your beauty to me each time I pass it
I am all alone without your touch
I am thirsty for your kiss
You are in every breath I take, Sanari!

Any opened book is great as long as you can read the language in which it's written. Craig Peter Altner can read and reading from blank pages was his favorite. He does mind the pages with written words; he can read the language to whatever he wanted it to be because he would rewrite them anyway.

"What maggots have taken up lodging in his brains?" He had often asked himself thousands of times only to feel dismayed entering his domain and that he didn't like to feel. Life's not perfect and whenever it is he dismantles its perfection.

Today, was a perfect day so says Craig Peter Altner, and today, he will kill again. He had chosen Fiona because she was perfect and a friend of his lover, Sanari. As long as she was single he let her be she was imperfect. The smile he had summoned on his lips died a slow death a week ago when he saw who collected her.

A man with an outward appearance is not an estimation of his character and he, Craig had plenty. Two stripes against her, one she was dating a black man-of all the men in the world she had to go and fuck a black man.

That's not accepted, a very scary picture: a white girl dating a black man. Last week he saw her with a white man; that t0o is not accepted. Cheating is out of the question; she has to go.

Being scared ticked him off and being ticked off made him angry and wanted to kill. It's a chain reaction that wound itself around his thoughts to simply get through whatever is necessary to come out with what he wanted at the other end. The second thing that made her perfect was she had a partner and people who have a partner were perfect. She had to be imperfect and he's going to make her imperfect.

"Stop poking around inside my head. I don't remember giving any of you maggots permission to read into my thoughts." He yelled at his image in the mirror. He was naked standing looking at himself, a daily occurrence. He didn't trust anyone only the reflection in the mirror. He grappled a cloth and rubbed where Fiona had touched him, however, he couldn't erase the explosion of carnal desire she aroused in him; he couldn't in her, and that hurt.

What Craig Peter Altner didn't remember is that Fiona never touched him, Sanari did a very long time ago.

"She must die just like the others!' He yelled out as if a floodlight just ignited the altar. Being at liberty, the empty room afforded him the echoing of his voice coupled with the voices in his head. "I don't hold people hostage when they do something horrible to me. I kill them, forgive and move on to the next kill. Do you hear me, Fiona?" The high-pitched shriek bulleted right from his brain echoing a hollow into the cement that made the walls solid. The nerve in the infused leg cried protest against the strain of his anguish. "I love Fiona I can't kill her! I wouldn't kill her!" With that said Craig flung his painful body with twisted thoughts onto the bed and fell asleep in agony. Craig Peter Altner had yet again confused Fiona for Sanari and Sanari for Fiona. His perception is corroded to the point that he doesn't know the difference between day and night.

It was midnight when he woke up looking for the knife he went hunting for four days ago. He knew where they would be when he existed at the door of his apartment. It was his day when he saw Fiona and Sanari walking by the lake drinking from mugs. They were laughing; he was in the mood for killing. He decided to follow them and see where it would take him. He came prepared to kill. He was ready.

Craig stood by the tree to the left hiding from their vision. His clothes were black integrating with his hair dyed merging with the blackness of the sky. His structure outlined the bark of a tree, nonetheless assorted with the darkness of the night.

Bushes whose branches were very thin that the length united with the shadowy night. The terra firma was dry and cool on this late February night with no moon. He heard the dog barking in the distance which the two ignored. He knew that wasn't something he would ignore in his field of work. As they came closer to the barking dog, he dipped through the trees where he would go unnoticed and addressed the dog. He was prepared.

Craig waited a minute until the girls turned the corner of the building in front of them. He took out some beef jerky from his pocket. He knew that there were dogs somewhere and whenever he prowled around in the night he offered the jerky to silence them. He smiled triumphantly when he spotted one and held the jerky high for the wind to take it to her.

"Fuck." Talking to the air upon seeing the dog and how fat she was in size. "You are loaded, aren't you boy, mmm girl." Talking to the dog as he came close enough to feed her, "I didn't bring enough to feed a quarry of your broads. The last time I saw you, you were skinny, not fat, and ugly with puppies.

"How much ya carryin' there? Ya see the price you've to pay for a little bit of fun. Yo poor girl. The fucker of a stinking rat didn't stick around when he saw the pound to your waistline nor did you tell him that you were pregnant with his pups? He ran didn't he, old fat girl? Was it that cheesy old bastard down the street? I can take care of him for you?" Craig took out his knife and passed it over his neck indicating to the dog what he can do for her to the sneaky old dog that did her in. The dog opened her eyes wide looking at the last bit of beef jerky that the man held high above his head. The air was sending a rippling smell toward her, driving her crazy.

For the past few weeks, she was always hungry. She opened her mouth and her tongue fell out.

She moaned quietly. "See why I never have sex. Those women would trap you into paying child support. Don't worry old girl you can always sue for puppy support. Find a good lawyer, a woman lawyer, and let her represent you for free. You don't meet trouble halfway; you meet it all the way. To be with a lover means also to be without her." He tossed the last beef jerky to the far side from where he was standing and left the dog trying to run to get it.

How can I kill them both at the same time was the question in the serial killer's thoughts? One for him and one for his uncle; His muscles grew in frustration and at the same time in anticipation as he looked at Fiona and Sanari peeking through the window looking in, with their backs to him, at something that made them giggle.

Craig had the worse luck these last eight weeks and only killed and then raped the young girl who he saw walking toward the woods. He stabbed her and raped her just when she was about to die. The red hair girl no more than thirteen whispered in her last breath, "why" With his hand in her hair he had sprung on her as if he were a mountain lion, ravishing her brutally until his anger subsided for a few moments.

He had freedom. His nose was buried in the bark of a particular tree when he saw her coming into the wooded area from the swamp. His body sparkled as his jewel eyes flickered with the flame of pleasure. This wasn't planned and he loved it. He was embracing a tree trunk naked waiting for something to happen when she sprung out from nowhere passing him.

He left the place vacant and came to her with agog to have sex with him. Her laughter sent a dent in his ego denying him the part that wanted to be loved. He doesn't work well with rejection; he took the knife and moved towards her. Frightened she bent to his will quickly making fearful pleas that he took as a breath of fire for him to release her secret cargo of pain he saw in her eyes.

"Pain, too much pain, you have in you." Her breath left her body with her eyes wide opened looking at her killer. "Am I supposed to know what you mean by that? Nice doesn't do it for me, pain does. And I don't feed into anyone's misery. No thank you."

Lost in the vision of his pain that once terrified him, he raped the dead girl again and again until he lost count. He has bitten into her ear and felt blood; he can leave such perfect trademark of his on them all. He buried her in some pit somewhere. He had to mark the spot on the trunk of a tree where number three of the five bodies are buried then he moved them in trash bags and dumped them in the lake. He couldn't move them because of the FBI agents all over the place.

A man could overly punish himself for so long before desires of killing surged again and he was ready for a kill to justify the anguished he felt. Waiting for life to happen or fate to deliver to him what was rightfully he was not the result he wanted or did he want to make different choices that would speed up the process of emptying his pain by punishing others who are happier.

Craig was so wrapped up in his thoughts that he didn't notice the FBI Special Agent Ryland Cooper following him. Ryland seized the opportunity to call for backup. He made the call when Craig was busy with the dog. He dialed the number of his new partner Special Agent Olympia Van Amstel.

"What, now?" Olympia asked crumply and sleepily.

"Yes, he's on the loose. Sanari and Fiona are tipsy walking around. He's following them." Ryland informed her.

"Can't you keep that woman on a leach? What are they doing up at this ungodly hour? For peace sake, it's ...."

"Two in the morning," Ryland interjected. He let her other remark go because one she's entitled and two she's pregnant. He would never go there with a pregnant female at two in the morning; third, she solved more crimes in a short time than most detectives, including him. She covered Ryan's killing that bitch Asa Fleischer. So what? Knowing Ryan, he had a good reason and Asa needed to leave Planet Earth.

"Ryan, get dress," Olympia ordered the sleepy man lying next to her. "Bring your gun. Do you have a license for it?" She was off the bed, dressing.

"Where are we going?" He wanted to know as he crawled off the bed looking for his clothes.

"To Sussex Place. The girls are in trouble and Altner is after them. We'll take my vehicle. How fast can you drive? It's a mile, you have to get us there in minutes. I'll brief you with the rest."

"Yes, madam."

"Good boy. Let's go." Trust Ryan to be sarcastic in the time of need. She smiled a wary one and pulled her cell phone to call Blake to meet her there with his unit. She didn't mention Fiona. He can find out later when they are face to face.

Fiona and Sanari were mesmerized by what they saw, started to laugh and their laughter became louder. Realizing that they can be found out and thrown in jail for invasion of privacy or something of the sort, they headed for the lake. They took the nearest boat and paddled very slowly across the lake heading for Sanari's place still laughing, more loudly.

Craig's curiosity got the better of him as he wanted to know what the joke was about and did he thinkable. He moved into the very spot that was abandoned by the girls. If it is perfect it would soon be imperfect, he smiled. He looked through the window to see what Sanari and Fiona were viewing and saw naked people in a sexual position.

A woman no less a voyeur was looking at two couples, older couples engaging in sexual acts. One man was in a woman and the other was having oral sex. He was beyond shock and was intrude at the same time that he forgot this plan and kept looking at the orgy. "They have to be on Viagra." He whispered to no one in particular. He had moved his head to the right when a man from the orgy unknown to him hit him on the head with the barrel of his gun.

"That's right you fucking bastard."

Little did Craig Peter Altner knew he was born with a special gift, a gift synesthesia precognition where the sensations that he felt in his body from seeing his uncle in the woods that fateful night was the result of inducement that was applied from another experience with pain.

Being young and inexperienced with processing pain he used his collective pain to describe others' pain; his collective pain evoked the sensations of another due from seeing this uncle inflicted pain upon women; it produced the sound effect by visualization the pain of others as colorful. It was perfect and made him develop a need to kill and kill he did!

50

"911 what's your emergency?" came a tired voice over the orgy man's cell phone.

"I just caught someone peeking at my wife and I having sex in my apartment." He said angrily. They had just gotten started. He has to wait another three hours before his erection goes back to being inflated without sex!

"What? Pardon me, sir!" Shock, laughter came back from the operator.

"You heard me! This is no laughing matter. Send an ambulance cos he's dead or unconscious." He hung up the phone and called his wife to tell her to bring him his sweater and they should get dress, the police are on their way. He was half dress with jeans on. He had seen shadows at the window and hurriedly put his jeans on without underwear; he can feel the zipper is stuck on his pelvic hair.

"Fuck. God damn it." He has to wait until the police showed up because he cannot leave the dead man there. It would look as if he hit and run. His wife appeared with his sweater and told him their friends have left the building. He breathed a sigh of relief.

The flashing of the light from the police car roared as Sergeant Blake Belington drove as fast as he can on the two miles it took to get to Sussex Place. He acknowledged the 911 call and told the operator that he was headed right there. He figured Ryland nailed the serial killer and had called it in. He saw Olympia standing inside the gate. He slowed his vehicle.

"I need a ride. Kill the sound." She ordered him. She had sent Ryan ahead with her car to assist Ryland quite unaware of the 911 call. Blake filled her in and she did the same with him. She rapidly covered the events leading to this moment. He hit the brake when she mentioned Fiona. He could barely breathe and his pulse raced and his eyes widened. She rankled beneath his searching stare. She couldn't tell him what he wanted to know because she doesn't know whether either of the girls was safe.

"Ryland and Ryan are there. Move on. They would need our help." There were two other cars following him as well and they too stopped abruptly. He radioed one of the cars to stay and bring the ambulance in. In less than four minutes they arrived at building ten-fifteen.

Ryan was with a man in handcuffs and a couple. Ryland was nowhere to be seen. Only when two officers stood guard over Craig Peter Altner that Ryan moved over to the opposite side and told them that Ryland had gone to rescue Sanari and Fiona who had stolen a canoe and were on the lake.

Sanari and Fiona were laughing heartily when they heard someone call for Fiona. Abruptly the laughter died and they began paddling faster when they heard the boat engine coming closer to them.

Panic became their laughter then it turned into fear. Thoughts of why they didn't get the boat and leave the canoe ran through them and reality hit when they realized they were laughing and didn't pay much attention as to what they took; now they are paying the price of being caught.

The boat was upon them and Sanari stood up with her paddle to hit whoever we're going to put a foot into their …. the stolen… borrowed canoe. The engine had died and a man appeared, however, before she could move, Fiona stood up and joined her, off-balancing the canoe sending them over the edge.

Coldwater hit their bodies, they surfaced holding on to the rim of the canoe for dear life.

"Sanari, Fiona it's me, Ryland."

"Oh God Ry, honey it's good to hear your voice." Upon realizing that he had to have followed them, her voice picked up a high note of anger. "What were you doing following me? I could've killed you, you old bag of a fool. You got us to dump in the freezing water. You think this is summer? We don't need baths."

"Hold my hand. I will explain later. This is not the time."

"I'll hold your hand," came a trembling voice next to Sanari.

"Traitor." Sanari watched her friend being hulled into the motorboat and before she knew it Ryan had leaned over and pulled her into it too. He ignored them and their shivering state. He started the boat and killed the motor when they reached the broad walk, the very spot they had left a few minutes ago. Blue and yellow lights from the vehicles were flashing, even the ambulance.

People were standing around waiting for them. Spotting Olympia and Ryan, they realized that this is worse than they had suspected.

"What the fuck?" Fell out of Fiona's mouth when she spotted Blake. Sanari turned from giving Ryland more of her thoughts which were not pretty when she heard Fiona. She too said the same thing.

"What the fuck?" Shock registered on both the girls' faces.

Ryan had two blankets a resident who saw the canoe capsized from her balcony had given him who in turn gave them to Blake and Ryland who put them over Fiona's and Sanari's shoulders. He knew that the arbitrator would do about right now for them because they have some explaining to do, Fiona to Blake about the serial killer and Ryland to Sanari as to why he was following them and the serial killer. Better them than him. He smiled and waved as he turned to Olympia who he was only happy to lend his skills to; she can borrow them any time. He has plenty. A smile touched his lips.

Negotiation should be employed not only for the concerns of government issues for diplomatic reasons overall dilemmas also for relationships. As much as opposites attract, negotiation leaves little scars, and in contrast to popular belief, something should be left hidden. He would never explain to anyone why he killed Asa nor would he ever discuss it.

Whether Olympia knew and covered for him he'll never want to know because she never mentioned it, much less discuss it. He would never confess about Asa or about deliberately getting Olympia pregnant. He is not one for much explanation because he has always taken what he wanted or manipulated to get it.

The guilt is gone from the day she showed up and wanted a relationship with him. The past was over and done with and so was his life as a Navy Seal. It happened and now he has moved on with Olympia and her daughter. Yes, it's a girl confirmed by the doctor.

This was the first time Olympia had asked him into her job. She neither knew little about his training nor ever ventured there except tonight. He knew that she trusted him because he didn't ask any questions and he wouldn't either. In the line of her job, she's in charge and whatever she wished to let him know or even not let him know would be splendid with him.

Trust is the key and knowing that neither of them would break it because what they have together is worth more than anything in the world. Ryan felt the distress Blake and Ryland were going through right this moment and he supported him, however, the girls, Fiona, Sanari, and Olympia knew and agreed that to have them, Blake, Ryland, and him in their lives was the best thing ever. The ladies had moved out of their protective environment into theirs without verbally expressing it.

Fiona and Sanari were comfortably wrapped in blankets watching the scene in front of them. The lights from the ambulance and law enforcement cars were spinning into their senses overwhelming them with the effect of danger.

Someone was arrested and they were clueless too furious with their partners for the deception. They knew in their hearts that there was a valid reason, however, it is not working this minute; they felt betrayed.

Blake, Ryland, and Olympia were working the scene of the crime for about twenty minutes before they left to check on them. Blake and Ryland had put the blanket over the girls and made sure that they were comfortable and left Ryan to watch over them. They were too cold and furious at the talking.

Blake and Ryland knew what was coming, however, they also knew true love would pull them through two hot-headed ladies. They can see Blake and Ryland studying their faces for signs of peril. Seeing their love for them shone through, Fiona and Sanari softened their expression and all previous anger disappeared. Blake and Ryland moved in to explain to their partners what took place.

"Ryland, you have the nerve to follow us? How could you?"

Sanari asked him, trying to pretend to be angry. The frown and voice still had a trace of anger.

"Blake, what are you doing here? Isn't this out of your jurisdiction?" Fiona asked. She figured she might as well charm in her piece of verbal expression of what she had felt earlier.

Blake felt Ryland's body stiffen as much as his; he was about to answer when the flow of the chi called. Olympia had acknowledged Ryan with a look of support and nodded to him to take the boys away. She motioned Blake and Ryland to leave.

"I'll take it from here," in her serious FBI no fucking with me voice. Everyone looked at her and silently moved as instructed except for Fiona and Sanari who sat eyes wide looking at her.

Olympia turned to make sure the boys were out of earshot before she voiced her concern to them. "Quite an escapade you two had without me, huh?" The three of them had been friends and hang out often whenever time permitted. "I don't know whether I should be jealous or what? You two have all the fun, while I lay up in bed." Olympia continued to look at them and sat on the grass opposite them. "Craig Altner is the serial killer and ….

"What?" Fiona went into shock. Vivid memories and images popped into her view as she tried to focus on what Olympia was telling them. Sanari's hand came out of the blanket and covered hers.

"Don't worry, Fi there was no evidence of you and him ever being an item. Nothing was in his apartment or you Sanari." Olympia informed the girls in her most comforting voice. She had broken into his place when she didn't have the court order. She wanted to see what was in there and found out about Fiona and Sanari's confusion.

She took photographs and studied them. She found the tree where he buried the last victim and knew that he was after Fiona and/or Sanari. She told her boss at the FBI and asked to assign Cooper as her partner to catch the serial killer. By now, they had assembled the truth of the matter on both of the Altner men. They had evidence plus what forensics would find in the apartment would end his escapades.

Olympia told the girl that he was after both of them and not only Fiona. Ryland knew the truth, however, Blake does now, and with Craig thinking that he had an affair with Fiona, it was best to leave it out.

"Fiona, Blake didn't know that Altner confused you with Sanari and thinks you two had an affair. You two were Altner's next victims. The Gods were working overtime when you both became peeking toms. The man who hit Altner on his head saw someone peeking through the window at him and his wife. He thought it was Altner. I think it was the two of you and then you left and he found Altner. What was going on in there?" Olympia was curious and had to ask.

"Orgy." Sanari and Fiona spontaneously voiced.

"You don't say. I have a feeling that I'm going to miss out on a lot of things." Olympia grinned at them, patting her stomach.

"Oh, we are on vacation for a long very long time," Fiona whispered quietly, frowning.

"Yep, I had enough excitement for a very long time. All I want to do is go home and snuggled next to my lover." Sanari interjected as she looked at the man of her dreams and gave him wide smile. All eyes followed hers and a smile appeared as they saw them standing waiting for them. Smiles were returned in kind.

"Amend." Fiona pushed her weight on her feet and Sanari followed.

"I was there. Snuggled next to my lover, may I remind you two?" Giggles stirred as they assisted Olympia to her feet They walked toward their lovers who met them halfway with open arms.

"Thank you, Livie, we'll make it up to you," Fiona said to their new friend.

"Thank you. We'll take turns and babysit for you both. How's that?" Sanari interjected.

"We'll take you up on that Auntie Fi and Auntie San." Olympia smiled up at Ryan while she spoke. "I've to wrap things up here. Belington took the couple on the right and Cooper took the ones on the felt. Reyes, get me a pen and paper from Officer Rice and see what the neighbors know." Olympia was back to business. The sooner they get the statements the sooner she can go back to bed.

Tomorrow she will deal with Altner's apartment and the lake.

"I'm not someone to reckon with no, are you going to harass me in giving more answers. A thank you is good enough." Olympia replied to the question of what she found out and told the new neighbor that presently occupied Craig's Altner apartment. He signed over the deed to his attorney for him to represent him.

"What did you just say?" Sanari asked her to repeat.

"I don't remember I have a short circuit in my brain." Olympia shot back to both of them. She took a sip of her drink and smiled.

"Oh, alright then. Thank you for all you did for both of us in the last few months. You've been busy since you landed here, I say." Fiona finished and popped a fried in her mouth.

"I lived here for two years, a very quiet and peaceful life. Minding my own business and working quietly. Then the last six months have been nothing but trouble. I have never worked this many cases in one shot in my life as an FBI agent." Olympia signed happily.

"A whole lot of trouble with a little bit of hell," Fiona said to her.

"What?" Olympia asked.

"Ryland said the same and he plus me and Fi here have a renounce respect for you," Sanari added and the choices you made, however, she kept her mouth shut. She figured she knew who killed Asa and let it go.

"Thank you. Can we drop this for good? It has been six months since all of that took place, the time we moved on to a boring life." Olympia moved uncomfortably in her seat.

"Where are Ryan and Ava?" Fiona asked her.

"My wonderful partner is taking care of our daughter. We've moved into my place for good. Ryan gave Melly the opportunity of her life to manage the Twixt Peach. He can be here for us. So, girlfriends how about drinks every night after dinner. It's free."

"Free." Both Fiona and Sanari voiced at the same time.

"Yes, I know the guy who owns it. Well, to put it bluntly, I sleep with The Twixt Peach's owner." Laughter broke out and free drinks were served to them all.

The euphoria of finding and having true love in life is crucial to the existence of the human species. Maintaining true love is essentially easier as everyone in the relationship showed up each day bringing an abundance of integrity. They had all learned to treasure each other because they don't know how long they shall have together. Unknown passion awoke in their hearts and they shaped the passion into the emotion of true love giving birth to a new song.

No one knows just how much bacchanal existed in the retirement community of Sussex place; what is known is that the only facsimile created are by those who are bored, greedy, and have secrets, therefore they have enough influences to determine how their story should end. Unless of course Sanari, Fiona, and Olympia choose to intervene, then there would be a whole lot of hell with a little bit of exoticness.